...On the Sabbath After

Messages of Hope Delivered
on the Sabbath After
September 11, 2001

~A Tribute to the Victims and Their Families~

...On the Sabbath After

Messages of Hope Delivered
on the Sabbath After
September 11, 2001

~A Tribute to the Victims and Their Families~

from
The Ministers' Wives and Ministers' Widows Alliance of
Petersburg, Virginia and Vicinity and a Few Ordinary Americans

The OTSA PROJECT
Brenda A. Spencer, Founder
Dr. Bertie Jeffress Powell, Project Editor

with Special Foreword by
Reverend Benjamin P. Campbell

Brandylane Publishers, Inc.

Richmond, Virginia

Brandylane Publishers, Inc.
1711 East Main Street, Suite 9, Richmond, VA 23223
804.644.3090, Email: *brandy@crosslink.net, www.brandylanepublishers.com*

Additional copies may be ordered directly from the publisher.
Selections in this book have been reprinted with the permission of the authors.
The opinions expressed in this publication are those of individual writers and not necessarily those of the founder, editor or publisher.

At the time of the September 11 tragedy, the prayers included in this book by the following persons were written for use in the aftermath of the disaster, as appropriate: The Archbishops of Canterbury and York; Dr. George Leonard Carey and The Most Reverend and Right Honorable Dr. David Hope, KCVO; The Church of England; and The Right Reverend Claude E. Payne, D. D., Bishop of Texas

Cover Concept and Design:	Bob Saydlowski, Idea Factory
Original Book Cover Idea:	Gracie J. White, Inez G. Scott and Brenda A. Spencer
Book Title:	Brenda A. Spencer and Beth D. Sattes
Publication Artwork:	Courtesy of Council for America's First Freedom,
	The Columbian Block Building, 1301 East Cary Street,
	Suite C, Richmond, Virginia 23219-4117

Royalties, after expenses, will benefit the Comfort Zone Camp 9-11 Fund. Comfort Zone Camp is a bereavement camp for children who have experienced loss of a parent, sibling or primary caregiver. A free copy of the book will be given to the registered families of the 9-11 victims.

On the Sabbath after : messages of hope delivered on the Sabbath after September 11, 2001 : a tribute to the victims and their families / from the Ministers' Wives and the Ministers' Widows Alliance of Petersburg, Virginia and a few ordinary Americans ; the OTSA project, Brenda A. Spencer, founder ; Bertie Jeffress Powell, project editor ; with a special foreword by Benjamin P. Campbell.
    p. cm.
Includes index.
 ISBN 1-883911-51-6
 1. September 11 Terrorist Attacks, 2001--Sermons. 2. Sermons, English--21st century. I. Spencer, Brenda A., 1952- II. Powell, Bertie Jeffress, 1933- III. Minsters' Wives and the Minsters' Widows Alliance of Petersburg, Virginia.
 BT736.15 .05 2002
 252--dc21

2002074772

Share the Spirit

Dear _____,

      I want to share these messages of hope with you because you are very special to me. Together we can keep the flame of hope burning as we remember the victims of September 11, 2001. May you too find comfort in these words.

Presented to_____

      On this _____day of _____, 20__

By _____

On the occasion of_____

_____

_____

                                              May You Be Blessed.

THIS BOOK IS A COLLABORATIVE EFFORT OF

The Ministers' Wives and Ministers' Widows Alliance of Petersburg, Virginia and Vicinity…and a Few Ordinary Americans

The …ON THE SABBATH AFTER Project (OTSA Project) was founded and coordinated by Brenda A. Spencer with special consultative assistance by The Reverend Shady Clark, Jr.
The complete publication was edited by Dr. Bertie Jeffress Powell.

Ad hoc Committee of Ordinary Americans

Robert A. Almond, Centenary United Methodist Church, Richmond, Virginia
Arlene L. Anderson, First Baptist Church (Harrison Street) Petersburg, Virginia;
Co-chairperson, Publicity
B. Friend Briggs, First Baptist Church (Centralia) Richmond, Virginia;
Chairperson, Publication Exploration
Reverend Shady Clark, Jr., Eastminster Presbyterian Church, Richmond, Virginia;
Co-chairperson, Publicity
Louise C. Fothergill, St Paul's Episcopal Church, Petersburg, Virginia; Historian
Lillian B. Freeman, Zion Baptist Church, Petersburg, Virginia
Julian L. Greene, First Baptist Church (Harrison Street) Petersburg, Virginia;
Co-chairperson, Internet Presence
Elva M. Hollins, First Baptist Church (Harrison Street) Petersburg, Virginia
James W. Jay, Congregation Beth Ahabah, Richmond, Virginia
M. Alice Johnson, First Baptist Church (Harrison Street) Petersburg, Virginia
Clyde Johnson, Jr., Grove Baptist Church, Portsmouth, Virginia;
Chairperson, Help Agencies
Natalie Harris Myers, Bethany Baptist Church, Brooklyn, New York
Alva E. Myrick, First Baptist Church (Harrison Street) Petersburg, Virginia;
Co-chairperson, Biographies
JoAnne W. Norman, Laurel Hill United Methodist Church, Henrico, Virginia;
Chairperson, Ways and Means
Barbara A. Perry, First Baptist Church (Harrison Street) Petersburg, Virginia
Sandra M. Poulsen, The Church of Jesus Christ of Latter-day Saints,
Virginia's Greater Richmond and Tri-Cities Congregations, Richmond, Virginia
Bertie Jeffress Powell, Gillfield Baptist Church, Petersburg, Virginia; Project Editor
Susan Rutkoski, Colonial Heights Presbyterian Church, Colonial Heights, Virginia
Beth D. Sattes, First Presbyterian Church, Charleston, West Virginia
Inez G. Scott, Tabernacle Baptist Church, Petersburg, Virginia; President,
Ministers Wives and Widows Alliance of Petersburg, Virginia and Vicinity
Theodore S. Scott, First Baptist Church of Fort Lauderdale, Florida,
Co-chairperson, Internet Presence and Webmaster
Brenda A. Spencer, Oak Hill Baptist Church, Buckingham, Virginia; Project Founder
Monroe D. Spencer, Jr., Oak Hill Baptist Church, Buckingham, Virginia; Photographer

Wanda F. Taliaferro, Zion Baptist Church, Petersburg, Virginia; Co-chairperson, Biographies
June S. Taylor, Mt. Olivet Baptist Church, Petersburg, Virginia
Reverend Adrian P. Varner, St. John Christian Community Church, Petersburg, Virginia; Co-chairperson, Internet Presence and Webmaster
Antrynette S. Walker, Marmora Baptist Church, Sutherland, Virginia
Gracie J. White, Zion Baptist Church, Petersburg, Virginia

FOREWORD

The Faith of September 11

The twin towers fell, the Pentagon was ripped open, and our souls were laid bare. As soon as it happened, in the midst of the torment, tiny seeds of faith began to grow. Nothing could stop those seeds of faith—not vicious hatred, not immeasurable agony, not grief beyond understanding.

The faith grew, and it is growing. Much of the growth of faith is happening secretly, for much of the destruction has happened secretly as well. Entire views of the world are being destroyed. Therefore, we do not even know the depth of the reconstruction that faith will bring. Perhaps you can see the beginnings of it in this volume.

Day after day, in person after person, generation after generation, nation after nation, faith is shaped by the event in which it is formed. Faith is not an abstraction. Its character is taken from the situation in which it is expressed, and the people in whom it is made manifest. It is shaped by contrast to the particular desolation or despair or chaos in which it is born.

We are part of a new and important movement of faith, one whose seed was planted in Manhattan and Arlington even in the moment of destruction, as God spoke quietly with those persons who were dying. This movement of faith will join other streams coming to our world's tortured Twenty-first Century to erode the worldwide power of evil and call community and justice into being.

Even now, in this simple volume of earnest and honest words from ordinary people like you and me, we can see the clear outline of this faith.

It is a faith that God is especially real in the midst of suffering. God is known by all of our writers in this volume as one who stands with us in grief, and leads us forth through desolation into new life.

It is a faith in the incredible beauty of human beings. We see God's power and energy in the courage and compassion, the self-sacrifice and solidarity, of all our brothers and sisters in the human family.

It is a faith which has no illusions about evil. Evil spoke clearly on that tragic day. We recognize its characteristics. It is seen many places. There is an evil lurking in every people, and in every religion, and in every situation in this world. Our writers all know it.

It is a faith which insists that human value is not limited by religion or ethnicity. All of our writers at the beginning of this 21st Century are clear about this. God regards persons of all races and all religions with the same embracing love.

It is a faith which elevates human value above material wealth. Our nation's wealth and power have made us blind to ourselves, to evil, and to cultural developments and economic deprivations in the rest of the world. Our writers are very clear that it is not material wealth which has made our nation great.

The faith of September 11 is a faith which began when we learned how little we knew. Therefore, it is a faith which is certain that the future will differ from the past, that peace cannot be assured by wealth or controlled by violence, and that all nations must share both wealth and wisdom.

This faith begins in humility. But it is a proud faith, based on the startling examples of ordinary people, the self-sacrifice of simple citizens.

What was declared on September 11 is a faith willing to face the future with courage and generosity, with toughness and self-sacrifice. It is the faith of an America willing to engage the toughest challenges, the reaffirmation of things beyond price or status or race or class. This faith is what the world needs from us. The hope of our future is hidden here.

The faith of September 11 is a doorway which will involve us with many nations and many peoples. A great cloud of witnesses longs for the goodness of America to shine forth. Through that doorway, with humility and strength, our sons and daughters will go to serve God in the 21st Century. Bless us, O God, and mature in us the faith described in this volume.

The Rev. Benjamin P. Campbell
Pastoral Director, Richmond Hill
On the six month anniversary of the beginning
of this chapter of faith, March 11, 2002

DEDICATION

What name do we give the *thousands* of family members
who lost *thousands* of their loved ones in the space
of what must have seemed like a *thousand* eternities on September 11?
There is no special name, for they were just *ordinary people* like you and me.
This book is dedicated to those individuals.

ACKNOWLEDGEMENTS

The Ministers' Wives and Ministers' Widows Alliance of Petersburg, Virginia and Vicinity,
Brenda A. Spencer, and the Ad hoc Committee of Ordinary Americans express
sincere appreciation to all contributors to…*ON THE SABBATH AFTER.*
Without you, this publication would not have been possible.
May You Be Blessed.

The Ministers' Wives and Ministers' Widows Alliance of Petersburg, Virginia and Vicinity
expresses sincere appreciation
to Brenda A. Spencer, Founder, The OTSA Project,
for her charitable spirit.

PREFACE

This is unmistakably a time to share with one another as the national tragedy continues to unfold before our very eyes. Although we are now in the re-building phase, minds and hearts are still filled with incredible disbelief, but no matter the form, we have all been equally inspired by the countless efforts to bring despair and hope together. This publication is our attempt.

The organizers of this small project of mercy decided to move quickly so as to be a part of the many efforts to help relieve the suffering, pain, and confusion. Our mission became to capture, bind, and deliver to the victims of this terrible tragedy and to just ordinary people the spiritual medicine that must have been poured out as a mighty blessing all across America and the world as persons of the clergy took to *their* battle stations *on the Sabbath after*. The warmth, the comfort, the encouragement, the wisdom that surely must have been delivered that day no doubt deserve a place in history alongside the tragedy itself. So message-by-message and starting in our own hometowns, we endeavored to revive the spirit of hope so eloquently delivered *on the Sabbath after*.

But something happened along the way. In addition to a collection of heartfelt sermons delivered *on the Sabbath after,* this work has evolved into a moving, interfaith, and geographically diverse eclectic presentation of sentiments from ordinary folk to the victims and their families and to the world. Since the inception of this idea, the term "messages of hope" has taken on a much broader meaning What is most inspirational to those of us who have participated in this labor of love is the realization that we now have in hand a time capsule of sorts—a history of a moment in time—a strong, representative record of what ordinary folk were doing, saying, and most importantly, feeling during the days that immediately followed the tragedy of September 11. Yes, some ordinary folk did preach sermons or deliver powerful words from their holy stations because they had that medium or forum available to them, but others were moved just as deeply to reach out to the victims in the only medium or forum available to them. So they prayed, they sang, they read scriptures, they found and shared words of wisdom and comfort that had always sustained them in times of despair and confusion. The uniqueness of this work does indeed lie in the variety of expressions and in the sources of these expressions. In this book, the man of the cloth stands beside the incarcerated man and beside the man born in Afghanistan who recounts how "…*on the Sabbath after* was a very different world for me." This mosaic is completed by the inclusion of interfaith artwork, placed here as an earnest attempt in these sensitive times to help bridge the gap between cultures, between faiths, races, and between the suffering and the comfort-givers.

Those of us who have toiled over this project, have contributed to it, and now have let go of it know that it has been truly "inspired." With this publication, you hold in your hand the very pieces of the hearts of ordinary folk that bled for the ordinary victims of September 11 and for the world during the early days following the tragedy, but especially *on the Sabbath after*.

Brenda A. Spencer, Founder
The OTSA Project

TABLE OF CONTENTS

LIST OF ILLUSTRATIONS

Council for America's First Freedom, The Annual America's First Freedom Student Competition, Theme: "Religious Freedom—Cornerstone of Democracy"

Council for America's First Freedom [CAFF] is a nonprofit, non-denominational and nonpolitical organization, under the leadership of chair Tommy Baer, president Carol Negus, and executive director Steve Elliott, dedicated to promoting freedom of religion worldwide. Established in 1984 in Richmond, Virginia, the Council educates national and international audiences on the significance of the 1786 adoption of the Virginia Statute for Religious Freedom, the role this seminal document continues to play in our democracy and throughout the world, and celebrates our nation's enduring legacy as the birthplace of religious freedom.

INTRODUCTION

God Bless America

God Bless America
Land that I love…
Stand beside her, and guide her,
through the night with a light from above.
From the mountains, to the prairies,
To the oceans, white with foam,
God bless America,
My home sweet home.

On Monday morning, Americans stood around the proverbial water cooler and still talked of "the event," but more importantly, many shared the spiritual messages that had been delivered by the clergy *on the Sabbath after* the most horrific act ever to touch the United States of America—our home. They drew on each other's strength as they recounted those messages first told in their individual places of worship—places that now stood in their minds, hearts, and souls taller than any building and stronger than any fort. They were ordinary Americans—ordinary folk all over the world—like you and me struggling yet again and hoping to gain some glimmer of insight from the retelling of messages delivered… *on the Sabbath after.*

While it wasn't exactly the water cooler, it really was a gathering of a few colleagues and friends on that Monday morning. We asked each other, "What was the subject of your pastor's message?…and what was yours?…and what was yours?" We even spoke of the messages we had heard over the airways from some of the great orators of our time. Then—suddenly—we realized the magnitude of the collective wisdom that was espoused *on the Sabbath after.*

Faith Sees the Glory

"My Faith Looks Up to Thee"
Faith Sees the Glory
Why Do Bad Things Happen?
Our Changed World
Faith in God

Chapter 1

My Faith Looks Up to Thee

My faith looks up to Thee, thou Lamb of Calvary,
Savior divine! Now hear me while I pray, Take all my
guilt away; O let me from this day Be wholly Thine.

May Thy rich grace impart Strength to my fainting heart;
My zeal inspire; As thou has died for me, O may my
love to Thee Pure, warm, and changeless be, A living fire.

While life's dark maze I tread, And griefs around me spread,
Be Thou my guide; Bid darkness turn to day, Wipe sorrow's
tears away, Nor let me ever stray From Thee aside.

When ends life's transient dream, When death's cold, sullen stream
Shall o'er me roll, Blest Savior, then, in love, Fear and distress remove; O bear me safe above, A ransomed soul.

Amen

Ray Palmer, 1830   *Dr. Lowell Mason, 1792-1872*

FAITH SEES THE GLORY
Scripture: Romans 5:1-5; John 11:1-3, 17-44

Dr. Larry R. Kalajainen, Senior Pastor
The American Church in Paris & The Franco-American Community Center
Paris, France

September 16, 2001 — Ordinary 24

I doubt many of us will forget where we were and what we were doing when the news broke last Tuesday that a major terrorist strike against the United States was under way. Like the attack on Poland on September 1, 1939 that began the Second World War or the attack on Pearl Harbor that brought America into that war, or the assassination of President Kennedy, last Tuesday's attacks were something of a defining moment. It's not clear yet what is being defined, but it feels like something is fundamentally different, doesn't it? That's why most of us will always remember where we were and what we were doing when those attacks took place.

I was sitting with a group of ten other pastors of international congregations and several academic theologians around a large square table at the Ecumenical Institute in Bossey, Switzerland, deep in a very stimulating discussion about the resurrection of Jesus and its implications for ministry in the contemporary church.

Shortly after the attack began, we got the news, and interrupted our seminar to rush next door to watch the events unfold on television. As disaster followed disaster, we knew, despite our shocked minds and spirits, that we were experiencing the reality of the words in the burial service, "In the midst of life, we are in death."

The irony of being engaged in a discussion of the meaning of Jesus' resurrection in the very moment that the abyss of death opened its gaping maw and swallowed thousands of our fellow human beings in one cataclysmic gulp was not lost on us. What demented mind could do this, we wondered. By what twisted logic could someone justify such mass destruction? What cause could produce such horrific rage that it would issue, not in the hot-blooded killing of anger, but in the cold-blooded and calculated destruction of thousands of human beings who were just settling in at their desks for another day at work, checking their emails, getting a cup of coffee, attending a sales meeting or answering phone calls, but certainly not expecting the apocalypse?

I wish I could tell you that a group of pastors and theologians had some profound thoughts and insights that could help explain, help make the unspeakable a little less so, but I'm afraid that wasn't, and isn't, the case. There are no reasons for such horrors—at least none that make any sense to me.

The impact of these attacks lies not simply in the magnitude of the disaster. Certainly there have been natural disasters like major earthquakes that have killed thousands in a moment. We are shocked and we grieve and then we go on, because we know that even though such natural disasters are terrible, they are, after all natural disasters. We all know enough about the planet we live on and the vagaries of wind and the movements of water and the shifting of the earth's crust to know that from time to time such disasters will be visited upon us and, while they are tragedies, they are not personal; they affect us personally, but they aren't the work of a person. They don't manifest personal hatred or rage or the will to destroy human lives for the sake of some perceived grievance or some demonic ideology.

Even if we're sophisticated enough to follow the political rhetoric of terrorists that there are no innocents—that all of us are complicit in systemic structures of social and economic injustice, we already knew that, and some of us even struggle with it. And even if we're honest enough to acknowledge that American foreign policy or economic policy is not always on the side of good or not always benign in its effects, we can't really make ourselves believe that such complicity warrants so ghastly a punishment, and we certainly don't accept it as justification for such barbaric acts.

Our reaction of course, and it is a natural reaction, is to want to strike back, to retaliate, to punish. It would be unnatural if we did not. To defend oneself and one's home against attack is a natural human right. And in that, I'm here to bear witness that pastors are no different from anyone else. As we sat, subdued and in mourning at dinner that evening in Geneva, one of our number, himself a pastor for more than thirty years, said, "At times like these, I need to pray the Psalms of imprecation." Those are the Psalms, like Psalm 10 which we prayed this morning, where the speaker, after asking God the agonizing question, *"Why, O Lord, do you stand afar off? Why do you hide yourself in times of trouble?"* goes on to pray that God will vent his wrath upon the wicked: *"O God, break the arm of the wicked; hunt them down until there are none left."* Or this from Psalm 28: *"Repay the wicked according to the evil of their deeds."* Or this from Psalm 69: *"Pour out your indignation upon them; let your burning anger overtake them. Let them be blotted out of the book of the living."* Oh, yes, such sentiments and even stronger ones are found in many of the Psalms. Why? Because the Psalms are human speech addressed to God. They express everything in human experience, and because they are the prayers, not of individuals, but liturgical prayers of a worshiping community, they invite us to bring our feelings honestly into God's presence. We might as well be honest with God in our prayers, since God already knows our hearts. No point in trying to pretend that we don't feel the need for revenge, for striking back, for retaliation. God knows that we do. And, in fact, as Christians have realized for centuries, the very act of honestly praying our rage is a way of disarming it. Shouting our questions at God, shouting our anger at our foes, giving vent to our grief and our loss in the context of prayer is the way we release those natural destructive emotions, those human furies, those violent impulses in a way that is safe. We invite God to look at those feelings, to see us and know us so that we can be set free from the power of our enemies to determine who and what we will become. We bring our wounds into the sanctuary and give them over to God in prayer, and in that way, we begin to open ourselves to God's healing and transforming work. God cannot comfort a sorrow that we do not acknowledge, cannot disarm a rage we do not confess to feel. That Psalm 10 which we prayed together, does not end with the plea for vengeance, you see, but with a plea that God will care for us and will do justice for the orphan and the oppressed.

Honestly dealing with our need for revenge and praying through our rage at those who have injured us is only a first step, however. Therapeutic it may be, but it is not yet touched by the resurrection to new life. For that, we need both faith and hope. In that wonderful and touching story from John's Gospel that we heard this morning, the two sisters, Mary and Martha, who with their recently deceased brother, Lazarus, were among Jesus' closest friends, express their natural human grief and questions to Jesus. Both of them reproach him: *"Lord, if only you had been here, our brother would not have died."* Doesn't that sound like the question the Psalmist asked and the questions we've been asking God this week? God where were you? How could you have turned your face away when those hijackers drove those planes into those buildings? How could you let such evil loose upon the innocent? If you had been here, God, this wouldn't have happened. Maybe you haven't been asking those questions, but I have. But then, so did Jesus as he hung on the cross. Remember those words that the choir sang so beautifully a moment ago: *"My God, my God, why have you forsaken me?"*

But as I spent some time with this familiar story of Jesus, grieving with his friends Mary and Martha, not only for their own loss, but for his also, for he too loved Lazarus, I began to hear another question, deeper than my own questions, my own outrage, my own grief. Above the clamor of my own demand, "Lord, if you had only been there, these dreadful attacks would not have happened," I began to hear Jesus' question to Mary and Martha, as a question to me also, *"Did I not tell you that if you have faith you will see the glory of God?"*

That, it seems to me, may be the question we've got to hear above the questions of our anger and our loss. As a Christian, I know about the importance of faith. St. Anselm reminded us of that centuries ago, when he said, "I have faith in order to understand." We often get it turned around don't we– thinking that we have to understand, that we have to have the answers to our questions before we can have faith. But St. Anselm was right, and all the other great saints of our tradition got it right: it is faith that leads to understanding. So perhaps this morning we need to hear the voice of the Risen One asking us, *"Did I not tell you that if you have faith, you will see the glory of God?"*

We need to hear that question because our own vision is too near-sighted, we are too deeply and too often entrenched in the immediacy of the tragedy, too shackled by our own unconscious complicity in evil to really understand apart from faith. It is faith which brings understanding, which brings light, which brings us the ability to see the glory of God even in the darkest night of human evil and human loss. St. Paul said, *"Now we see as though in a mirror, dimly, but then face to face. Now we know in part; then we shall understand, even as we have been fully understood."* And I don't think that Paul meant simply that now in our earthly life we only have partial understanding, but that then—someday in heaven, we'll have full understanding. No, for Paul, *"now"* means life without faith, life without the reality of Jesus' resurrection, life lived wholly within the boundaries of our notions of the possible, life on Good Friday with no Easter in sight. *"Then"* is life on the other side of Easter, life that is transformed by trusting in the God who raised Jesus from the dead, life in a world where the decisive battle against the powers of death has already been fought and won, even if those powers haven't yet realized it and are still capable of causing us harm. Faith and faith alone sees that the harm is not ultimate, not the final word.

"Since we have been put right with God through faith (which for Paul always means trust in God, not belief in certain doctrines, but trust of ourselves to God) *we have peace with God..."* Faith gives us a different set of lenses, a different pair of glasses through which to see our sufferings and our losses in a new light. With faith, we see that *"Suffering produces endurance, and endurance produces character, and character produces hope, and hope does not disappoint us, because God's love has been poured into our hearts by the Holy Spirit who has been given to us."* Hope, you see, for Paul, never means hope in the popular sense we often use it, "I hope we'll be able to afford a vacation to Spain this year." "I hope it doesn't rain tomorrow." That's hope as a

wish that may or may not come true. But for Paul, hope is about the *ends*, the goal, that God has for the whole world, hope is about the future of the whole creation, a future in which my destiny and your destiny and the destiny even of our enemies is all bound up—a future whose shape we can begin to grasp in the resurrection of Jesus from the dead. In that future, death cannot and will not have the final word. Life will. To live in light of that future is to live in hope, and hope is something that we grasp by faith—by trust that God has won the victory over death and that that victory will one day be as openly manifest as it is now visible only in fleeting glimpses. Such hope is a reality in which we can live now because *"God's love has been poured into our hearts by the Holy Spirit who has been given to us."* Faith is what turns "now" into "then." Now, we begin to live in the light of God's "then," when we shall see, not in a dim reflection of our imperfect and clouded mirrors, but face to face.

In the end, what else do we have to live by? What's the alternative? The law of the jungle, the law of "eye-for-eye, tooth-for-tooth?" The law of blood feuds, of action and reaction, of strike and retaliation? How many wars will it take to finally convince us that while we may derive a short-term rush of righteous revenge, we will only succeed in planting more deeply than ever the seeds of the next war? There's no resurrection in that. Just acquiescence to the power of death.

We've seen some glimpses of God's glory this week, glimpses of that hoped-for future even before the dust of the shattered World Trade towers had settled. We've seen extraordinary acts of heroism and self-sacrifice on the part of rescue workers. We've seen people reach out to perfect strangers and generously give of themselves to help others in need. We've heard of massive efforts of the churches and synagogues and mosques in New York to put together pastoral care teams to provide grief and trauma counseling. We here have experienced a tremendous outpouring of sympathy and love from our French neighbors and discovered friends we never knew we had. These are all glimpses of the glory that faith can bring. We may even see such a glimpse of resurrection in the voices that are calling for cool heads and concern to act with discretion in the midst of our anger and grief. We've heard of some threats or hate directed toward innocent people of Arab descent or toward Muslim communities in general, but we've also heard voices condemning such misguided and destructive thinking and calling on communities to reach out in reconciliation to build bridges of peace with those in the Muslim world, and they are in the vast majority, who do not rejoice at the destructive actions of a minority of extremists. And we Christians *must, must, must* be among those voices. We cannot allow ourselves to demonize any people or any religion. To do so would be to give the terrorists the victory, for that is what they do, and we would simply become as they are. And where is the hope in that?

Oh, I know that terrorism is a curse and must be dealt with. It can never be tolerated in any civilization. But I also know and believe with all my heart that there has to be a better way than simply retaliating with even more destructive force. There's no hope in that. And if there is a better way, then the only way anyone will know about it is if there is a community of human beings who can model hope in the midst of a world trapped in its own depressing and violent hopelessness. And where else is that community to be found if not among those who have discovered in Jesus Christ the one who is resurrection and life?

WHY DO BAD THINGS HAPPEN?
Scripture: Ecclesiastes 9:11-12

Reverend Rick McDaniel
Glen Allen Community Church
Richmond, Virginia

-Excerpts-
September 16, 2001

What happened this past Tuesday is beyond tragic and it begs the question of why? If God is love then why and why and why? We all want answers today for what has happened to our country, we want to know how to understand this tragedy, we want to know if there are answers. I have answers for you today. I want to give you three reasons why bad things happen.

WE LIVE IN AN EVIL WORLD
Ephesians 2:2 tells us that "He (Devil) rules the world and his spirit has power over everyone who doesn't obey God." Do not be confused, uncertain or perplexed about what you have seen this past Tuesday. It is nothing but the clear, focused, unmitigated handiwork of the Devil. You may ask why can't God stop the Devil, if God is all-powerful? God has given each of us the incredible power of choice, we choose who we will follow. We all have free will; we can do as we will. You don't believe the Devil is real? Then how do you explain evil? Michael Green puts it this way, "Like any general who can persuade the opposition to underestimate him, Satan must be enchanted at the present state of affairs, confident nobody takes him seriously. The more he can do to encourage this doubt of his existence, the better." Evil people chose to do evil acts. That is one reason why bad things happen.

OUR CHARACTER NEEDS TO BE DEVELOPED
I Peter 4:12 tells us "Do not be surprised at the painful trial you are suffering." Sometimes the only way we will listen to God is for Him to get our attention through suffering. God allows temporal suffering to continue so that many will escape eternal suffering. If we will cooperate with it, God can use suffering to shape us into what he wants us to be. God would rather hurt your feelings than hurt your future. Years ago students at St. John's College in Maryland exploded two pounds of gunpowder in a hollow of the "Liberty Tree." The tree appeared destroyed but the prank had the opposite effect. The next year the old tree put out lush new growth; the explosion destroyed the worms that had been gnawing away at it from the inside. God can use trials and pain to accomplish new growth that is necessary for our continued character development.

LIFE IS NOT FAIR
In Luke 13:1-5, Jesus talks about the eighteen people who died when the tower of Siloam fell on them. He asks if they were worse sinners than everyone else, and His answer is no! Underlying Jesus' answer is the assumption that life is not fair. The Jews believed that misfortune was the result of sin. Jesus says everyone is sinful and should repent. We live in a

fallen world where sometimes innocent people suffer. Our fellow Richmonder, the late Arthur Ashe, put it this way, "If I ask 'why me' then I need to ask 'why me' about all the good things that happened in my life." Loss deprives us of control; we never plan on loss. Loss also has little to do with fairness. Our world is unpredictable and unjust. Though we suffer loss we also receive mercy; both are undeserved.

What do you do in a time like this? You understand why bad things happen and you hold on to your faith. We've lost enough already, let's not lose anything more.

OUR CHANGED WORLD

Scripture: Jeremiah 4:11-12, 22-28; Luke 15:1-10; Job 1:1-3, 13-21

Pastor Carol Rogers Thornton
The Mineral and Mount Pleasant United Methodist Churches
Mineral, Virginia

September 16, 2001

At 8:45 AM on Tuesday, Sept. 11, 2001, our world changed. Just as our world changed in December of 1941, things for us I don't believe are ever going to be the same. We have so many questions, and, we have so few answers. I have watched television. I have listened to the radio. I read a prayer service. I have listened to the people in the community. I've heard the children on television. I've talked with other clergy. I have prayed and sought answers, and all that I have been struck by are questions. Why did they do that? How could people be so evil? Who's to blame? Where is God and what are we to do? Questions are hard to answer in times of tragedy. They are sometimes impossible to answer, but if you and I were to take a tour of the Bible, we would find pretty quickly that there is one book in the Bible that stands out with regard to the number of questions that are in it.   That is the Book of Job. There are over 330 questions in 42 chapters. The first book of the Bible, Genesis, by comparison, has only 160 questions, and Matthew, the first book of the New Testament, has only around 180 questions. I find that to be strange because it seems to me every time that Jesus spoke he was asking a question. The book of Psalms with its 150 chapters has only 160 questions. So why does the Book of Job have so many, many more questions? I think there is a simple reason. The Book of Job is a book that tells of a terrible tragedy.

As I read from Job, I heard that Job was a righteous man. He was a good man, and his righteousness made him great. And then suddenly without warning without reason, for no other reason than his being blameless and good—that is to say innocent—his family and his business is wiped out. In the middle of everyday life, two rogue groups from Mesopotamia and Arabia swoop down. They take his livestock and kill his servants, and then his family is lost in a freak accident where the wind came and the four corners of the house fell—the whole house collapsed killing everybody in a pile of rubble. It was swift. It was unwarranted. It was unconscionable.

This nation, this land that we love—that you and I love dearly—has been hit, and, it has been hit hard. And, somehow in many ways the events of this past week seem to me to be strangely echoes of what happened in the story of Job.

Why is there such a similarity between the events of Job and the events of this past week? I think it's because, even though they are separated by 4,000 years, it points up the fact that life—and when *I* say life I mean those things that make life meaningful—has not changed in 4,000 years.

So what do we do? We do what Job did.   Job was silent as he heard the first reports that his business, his livestock, and his servants had been killed. He didn't say or do anything. But when he received the news that his children were gone, he stood up, and he tore his clothing in anguish. He fell on his knees and he mourned, and he said, "Naked came I from my Mother's

Womb, and naked will I return." (Job 1:21) Meaning, in other words, that everything that had meaning in his life was now gone. As he came into this world, Job felt that was the way he would leave it—in a word, barren.

This past week, as the news poured in, we learned that many in this country had experienced terrible losses. Mothers, fathers, daughters, sons, grandparents, aunts, uncles, cousins, and dear life long friends were gone. The daily newscasts showed their faces. It told their stories—sometimes, more than I could bear. I had to turn it off. I had to get away from it. I couldn't take all of that. And yes, we mourn for every family who has experienced any sort of loss. We mourn for those families, for those people. We weep for our nation not because it has been weakened because I do not believe it has been weakened, but we mourn simply for all that has been lost.

Does mourning demoralize us? Does it paralyze us? I don't think so. I think it undergirds our strength, and it reveals our very soul.

So, now, after we have cried about as much as is possible, we start asking questions. *Who is to blame?* I think that is the place where we are now, but the very scary thing about answering this question is realizing that, in this situation, all of the implications are so profound. They seem to point out how small our world is, and how we answer the question "Who is to blame?" really involves the whole world. A journalist said this week that we thought we were impervious to attack because of the qreat barriers known as the Atlantic and Pacific Oceans. He went on to say those barriers now have come down. I'm not sure if they were ever barriers, but they have been breached, and our protection has gone.

Job started out with a hedge of protection. God erected a barrier around Job to keep him safe, but then he took that away by allowing Satan to have his way with Job. This is the Old Testament's way of saying that even the most righteous and best of this earth are not immune to evil. Just because we are good does not mean we are protected from evil, not in this life. The writer of Job understood this, but Job himself could not because he was too caught up in his grief and his loss. Job's friends who came by to help him couldn't comprehend what had happened to him either. His three friends showed up. They said in effect, "Well, only those who have done evil have this problem. The righteous don't have this trouble, the righteous are never destroyed." They thought Job had done something terrible, and this was the way of his suffering; this was the cause of his suffering. "God has lifted the barrier to punish you," they said, but they were wrong.

This week I have heard Christians say this was God's will. I have heard Christians say this happened because prayer was taken out of school or because our abortion laws are too liberal. I think they are wrong. We cannot pin this—we cannot, we dare not—pin this on God. We have to learn what Job eventually learned. The story of Job tells us that as good and great as America is, America—we do not have an exclusive and closed relationship with God. There is a third party in our world, and that third party can intrude into our lives at any moment. Satan and all of his evil did intrude last Tuesday through the hearts and minds of evil people.

There is another question. *Where is God?* Where is God when terrible tragedies befall us? At this question, Job's friends became silent, but Job at this point continues to speak. He wants to know *why he has suffered.* He wants to know why God has allowed this to happen to him, and he finally gets his answer when God visits him out of a storm, and asks him *86 questions*! Can you imagine being asked 86 questions by God almighty. Most of these questions are asked in the last four chapters of the book of Job. Here is God "interrogating" Job, and I want you to listen to some of the questions.

- God asks, "Where were you when I laid the foundations of the earth? Tell me if you know."
- God asks, "Do you have an arm like God? Does your voice thunder like God?"
- "Do you give the horse his strength or clothe his neck with a flowing mane?"

And Job is *silenced* as he realizes he is only a human being, and he cannot possibly comprehend the meaning of the events that have happened to him, and friends, we may never be able to understand or comprehend the events of last week.

Where was God this week? Where was God? I'm going to tell you where God was, and I want you to hear me well. God was in the fireman's suit. God was behind the police officer's badge. He was holding that I.V. bag with a stethoscope around his neck. He was working twenty hour shifts in horrible dangerous conditions. He was manning the heavy equipment and carrying the stretchers. God was the guy with the dogs as they sniffed for survivors. He was in the bucket brigade hauling the rubble down the line with his nai-scarred hands. God is near to the heart of everyone who in the face of tragedy reaches out to a fellow human being and turns to God in repentance. God is with those who in the ashes of these last days turn to him not for answers, friends, but who turn to him because of his promises to us. Well, what are we supposed to do? Just what Job did. We need to mourn and then we need to rebuild. As soon as we have honored those who have died, we need to rebuild.

Who is to blame? You and I and this nation have not done anything to warrant the atrocities that happened on Tuesday. This is the work of evil people. These are people of no religion. There is no religion that I am aware of on the face of this earth that would warrant what happened on Tuesday. These were evil people.

Where is God today? He is here. I see him in your faces. I hear him in your actions. God is here. He lives within us. He lives within us to bring about good for his kingdom and to overcome evil with good. God is here. He will always be here. Don't let anybody ever tell you anything different.

May God bless each one of us, and may God bless America.

(Background information graciously given by Rev. Brett Blair at e.Sermons.com)

FAITH IN GOD

Bertie Jeffress Powell
The Ministers' Wives and Ministers' Widows Alliance of Petersburg and Vicinity
Petersburg, Virginia

September 2001

I am grateful to have been reared in a family that honored God. From my teenage days in the mountains of Pittsburgh, Pennsylvania to my present senior years in Virginia, I have continued an awareness of total dependence on God for fulfilling every joy and sustaining me during every sorrow. It is for this reason that on September 11, 2001, I could find no greater solace than that of leaning on the Lord of my life.

The words of the poem below, which I wrote over twenty years ago, are shared here to encourage those who are "low in spirit."

Faith in God

It's not the smooth life paths that set our faith
Aflame, but smothered hopes that burn the sight
From fumes amassed by times too rough to fight
Away the gloom, too rough to stand the waste
From scattered dreams so torn and out of place;
It's through these paths which show no signs of light
That oft bring hearts to seek their God of might
And lean upon His strength to run their race.

Belief in Him who guides the world around,
Who loves the most and knows the best to give,
Can plant a faith within when it is sought,
Can make this faith expand when it is found,
Can make the deadest hopes begin to live,
In ways unknown to those who trust Him not.

from ENCOUNTER *by Bertie Jeffress Powell, 1977*

Where Was God on September 11?

"Never Alone"
Where Was God on September 11?
A Pastoral Newsletter
The One and Only Jesus: At the Crossroads of Good and Evil
Why Can't I
"Humanity! Humanity! It's Love that Makes Us Great!"

Chapter

2

Never Alone

I've seen the lightning flashing, And
heard the thunder roll, I felt sin's breakers
dashing, Trying to conquer my soul;
I've heard the voice of Jesus,
Telling me still to fight on, He promised never to
leave me alone, Never to leave me alone.

The world's fierce winds are blowing Temptation
sharp and keen, I feel a peace in
knowing My Savior stands between;
He stands to shield me from danger, When
earthly friends are gone, He promised never to
leave me, Never to leave me alone.

Refrain:
No, never alone, No never alone,
He promised never to leave me,
Never to leave me alone.

Amen   English

WHERE WAS GOD ON SEPTEMBER 11?
Scripture: Genesis 22

Rabbi Martin P. Beifield, Jr.
Congregation Beth Ahabah
Richmond, Virginia

-Excerpts-
September 14, 2001

Judaism teaches and specifically refers to this episode in the Torah when it says that God never demands, asks for, nor desires the death of an innocent human being as proof of our love, faith, or obedience to God. Never! Not from us—not from anybody. Not then, on Mt. Moriah—not now at the World Trade Center or the Pentagon. No matter what they thought or believed, and no matter how devoted they were to those beliefs, the terrorists were not acting in accordance with God's will, and they were not acting in a way which was pleasing to God.

I saw plenty of evidence last week of God's presence. If we were looking into the heavens, hoping for a lightening bolt to knock out an airplane, we would have missed the evidence. If we were thinking perhaps that God was in the cockpit delivering some message to us, we would have missed it again. If we thought God was hiding, or was hidden, we would have missed it.

Instead, we needed to do what Job did. Job, a decent, righteous man, lived through terrible personal tragedy and suffering—and for no apparent reason. In some respects, he was a thoroughly modern man. All he wanted was an explanation, figuring that God had good reason. The explanation did not come. Job asked and pleaded, even got angry. Still nothing from God. But Job did find God.

Like Job, we need to look directly into the whirlwind, into the very heart of the maelstrom to find God. God was there last week in the determination and courage of firefighters, police officers, and other rescue personnel who risked and, in some cases, gave their lives trying to save others. God was there in the strong hands of those who guided the hurt and confused down the stairwells into the street. God was there in the presence of mind of those whose clear voices made sense and gave direction. God was there in the compassionate arms of those who comforted the frightened, worried, and grief-stricken. God was there in the quick and skillful hands of doctors and nurses and oderlies and EMTs.

And God remains here with us, by us, in us, as an infinitely strong and eternally present source of hope and comfort as we find our way through the darkness and the smoke into the light.

...On the Sabbath After

A PASTORAL NEWSLETTER

Nancy Ferree-Clark, Pastor
Duke University Chapel
Durham, North Carolina

Dear Friends,

In the aftermath of the terror which our nation experienced on September 11, we find ourselves searching for answers. How could this nightmare be real? Where are the threats of retaliation and revenge leading us? Will we ever feel secure again? For that matter, how do we define security? We have many places where we are turning for guidance, including our elected officials, military leaders, financial analysts, and even media pundits. But I would like to make the bold suggestion that Christians should begin by turning to the church where we can find wisdom and strength in this dark time.

Specifically through the teachings of Jesus we are called to participate in a "ministry of reconciliation" (II Corinthians 5:18). Through Jesus' own words we learn that we are to speak out against evil and that people everywhere will be called to account for their evil actions by God himself. But we also learn through our Lord's life, death, and resurrection that ultimately we are called to reach out in love to one another, even to an enemy, for it is love and not violence or hatred that will have the final word. As members of the church, we affirm that our true security lies in that eternal promise and not in a robust economy or military might.

Having said that, I challenge each of you to consider the ways that we can affirm these beliefs in our own community as we respond to the current crisis. Growing out of fear of the unknown, we have heard numerous reports of attacks against Muslims and people assumed to be Muslim, presumably because they are believed to be militant extremists planning another terrorist attack. As Bruce Robbins pointed out in his United Methodist News Service commentary, making such an assumption is equivalent to believing that every Christian intends to bomb an abortion clinic. We should not fall into the trap of judging another tradition by its worst practitioners while we hold up our saints as typical of Christianity. Sin and evil are present amongst all people and all nations. The individuals who committed the horrific acts of terrorism may call themselves "Muslim" but they do not reflect the teachings of their tradition. As members of one of the three Abrahamic faiths—Islam, Christianity and Judaism—Muslims also worship a God of love. If you have the opportunity to befriend a Muslim or Arab American in your school, neighborhood, or workplace, this is the time to do it. We can become agents of reconciliation by reaching out to those who feel threatened in any way by the tidal wave of anger and fear which has flooded our country since September 11. We can also speak out forcefully against any stereotyping or prejudice against Muslims of which we may be aware.

Clearly we need the Holy Spirit to guide us and our nation's leaders as we ask ourselves the very difficult questions which have arisen from this crisis. How did such hatred of our beloved country ever escalate to this point? What implications does this have for our foreign

15

policy throughout the world? How long will we continue to believe that military power can actually defeat evil? What alternative responses might we as Christians propose that would take into account both the mandates of the gospel and the needs of many oppressed people whom we are about to wage war against? (As Duke ethicist Stanley Hauerwas has suggested, what if we bombed them with bread?) I encourage you to pray fervently for peace, and as you do so each day to keep in mind the Prayer of St. Francis:

> *Lord, make us instruments of your peace. Where there is hatred, let us sow love; where there is injury, pardon; where there is discord, union; where there is doubt, faith; where there is despair, hope; where there is darkness, light; where there is sadness, joy.*
> *Grant that we may not so much seek to be consoled as to console; to be understood as to understand; to be loved as to love. For it is in giving that we receive; it is in pardoning that we are pardoned; and it is in dying that we are born to eternal life. Amen.*

Grace and peace,

THE ONE AND ONLY JESUS:
AT THE CROSSROADS OF GOOD AND EVIL
Scripture: Romans 12:1-2; 9-21

Reverend Martin C. Singley, III
Tellico Village Community Church
Loudon, Tennessee

Fifteenth Sunday After Pentecost, Year C
September 16, 2001

During this time of great national difficulty, we turn to God for comfort, and strength, and guidance. I know that my own inner resources are very low right now, drained by the constant input of tragedy and concern. And on Friday night, when we gathered for our Service of Hope and Remembrance, I could see the intensity of your emotions, too. They were written upon your faces. They made your tears glisten against your cheeks in the soft glow of candle-light.

Life is so much larger than we are, although we sometimes fool ourselves into thinking that we are the general managers of the universe, capable of making life go the way we want it to go. And then something like these terrorist attacks happen, or cancer comes, or a loved one betrays us, or an addiction overwhelms us, or a child makes hurtful decisions, or we come face-to-face with the impossible reality of poverty, or racism, or injustice.

And, all at once, we encounter the vast limitations of our own humanity. And there is nothing we can do, but to cry out for God. Along with the tragic turning of events this past week has come what I believe is a genuine turning to God. And God—the ever faithful One—is with us, and will give us comfort, and strength, and guidance to bring us through.

Our sermon theme during this time—although it was not planned with these events in mind—is *The One And Only Jesus.* And I cannot think of anything more important to preach about given the circumstances that have befallen us.

You know, we Christians can argue until we are blue in the face about who has the truest view of the Bible, who has the right understanding of theology, and who sings the best songs. But sooner or later, life hits us smack in the face—like it did this week—and all those religious things become meaningless in the face of our profuse tears and our deepest fears.

Christianity is not about what you believe about the Bible. In fact, some Christians never had a Bible to believe anything about. Christianity is not about some 19th century theologian's interpretation of what the New Testament says about pre-millennial, mid-tribulational dispensational eschatology. Believe it or not, most of the Christians who ever lived never even heard of such stuff, and those of us who have heard of it certainly cannot even spell it. And Christianity is not about contemporary praise music versus traditional hymns written to the tune of northern European marching music. No, wherever Christians are found, they sing in the genre of their native culture, whatever that might be. The hymns Jesus sang did not sound at all like the ones we sing. The earliest hymns of our faith have the sound of the ancient Middle East. Listen to the chants of Hasidic Jews, or to the calls to prayer sung from the minaret of an Islamic mosque. Then you will have an idea of the kind of music that filled the ears, and thrilled the heart of Jesus!

You see, the greatest danger confronting Christianity in our time is the propensity we have to major in what is minor, and to minor in what is major. We make unimportant things far more important than they have the right or need to be. And meanwhile, the truly important things of faith get lost in the shuffle.

That's why I believe so strongly in this movement of ours that dares to say that we want to be a church whose only label is Christian, and whose only head is Christ. For when you finally cut through all the manmade superficialities and trivialities that fallen and shortsighted human beings have constructed around our faith, you eventually get to Christianity's true heart and soul. *The one and only Jesus.*

If you want to find your way to faith, if you want to find your way through life's difficulties, if you want to find your way to your true purpose and destiny, you have to find your way through all that secondary stuff until you come face to face with *the one and only Jesus.* St. Paul, speaking about this very challenge, told the Corinthians that the whole of the Gospel can be reduced to one key foundation—*Christ and Christ crucified.*

So that's where I want to invite you to come, especially during this time of trial. To Christ. To the cross. To Christ crucified. For it is there—in the man who went to the cross for us, and in what took place there—that we find the key to abundant and triumphant living.

I heard once about a little boy who came home from Sunday School all excited. He was excited about the songs. He was excited about the classroom experience. He was excited about the other students. And he was especially excited because his Sunday School teacher was none other than Jesus' *grandmother!* The boy's mother looked at him a little curiously, and asked him how he knew his Sunday School teacher was Jesus' grandmother. He said, "Because all she does is show us pictures and talk about him!"

Now, I've seen many of you do the same thing about your grandkids. And Sandy and I intend to do the same next April—show *you* pictures, and tell you all about *OUR GRANDKID.*

And in a similar way, one of the most important things you can do as a Christian, and we can do together as a church, is to hold up before our own eyes and the eyes of all, pictures and stories of the Lord. And the most important picture of all is the image of Christ …crucified.

Now on this particular Sunday, as we continue to reel from the terror of the past week, and the violent onslaught of evil against all that is right and good, the cross is an appropriate, and important gathering place.

You see, the cross of Christ means so much more than is captured in the simple idea that Christ died for us. What does that really *mean*? How does that really *apply* to our lives? What does that have to do with the frightening world in which we find ourselves living just five days after the horrors of September 11th, 2001?

I want you to come deeper today—past the Sunday School jingles—beyond the trite little idea that all the cross means is that we'll go to heaven someday when we die.

Come back to Good Friday with me, and notice what's *really* going on. A cross is being raised at life's most important intersection—at the very crossroads of good and evil.

You see, it is here, at the cross, that the power of evil attempted its most vicious attack against good in the history of the world. The most beautiful man who ever lived—a man who knew no language other than love, no touch other than healing, no embrace other than one that includes everyone and excludes no one—a man who was so good that he is described as the only man who ever lived without sinning—this most beautiful man who ever lived was overtaken by the forces of evil. He was betrayed. He was arrested. He was falsely accused. He was unjustly convicted. He was beaten. He was tortured. He was spat upon. And when they had inflicted upon him every evil thing they could imagine, they made him carry his own cross to a hill, and there they put him to death through crucifixion.

Oh, the cross is more than pretty jewelry that we wear around the neck. It is more than elegant decoration that we display in sanctuaries. No, the cross is the symbol we wear, the symbol we hold up to remind ourselves and the world of the monumental battle between good and evil that was waged through Christ crucified.

And for a moment, it appeared that evil had won. Where was God on Good Friday? For that matter, where was God last Tuesday? Where was God when evil touched your life last month, or when tragedy swept upon your family last year? And where is God today as we face these evil times?

When William Sloane Coffin was pastor of the Riverside Church in New York, his 24-year old son Alexander was killed in an automobile accident in which the car plummeted into a river, and Alexander was unable to get out.

Ten days later, Bill Coffin preached a sermon at Riverside in which he addressed the question of God's whereabouts in times of tragedy. He thanked the members of his congregation for their love and countless expressions of support. Then he told them this:

"When a person dies, there are many things that can be said, and there is at least one thing that should never be said. The night after Alex died I was sitting in the living room of my sister's house outside of Boston, when the front door opened and in came a nice-looking, middle-aged woman, carrying about eighteen quiches. When she saw me, she shook her head, then headed for the kitchen, saying sadly over her shoulder, 'I just don't understand the will of God.' Instantly I was up and in hot pursuit, swarming all over her. 'I'll say you don't, lady!' I said. For some reason, nothing so infuriates me as the incapacity of seemingly intelligent people to get it through their heads that God doesn't go around this world with his fingers on triggers, with his fists around knives, his hands on steering wheels."

Then Bill Coffin went on to say that the one thing that should never be said when someone dies is that it is the will of God. Never do we know enough to say that. Then Bill Coffin continued:

"My own consolation lies in knowing that it was NOT the will of God that Alex die; that when the waves closed over the sinking car, God's heart was the first of all our hearts to break."
Where is God when evil comes?

God is WITH US in love! God is weeping with us, agonizing with us, pacing the floor with us, tossing and turning with us at night! Whenever a human being suffers a broken heart, God's heart breaks first of all.

Where is God when evil comes? He is with us in love.

And what is God doing? God is at work.

We see it so clearly in Christ crucified. Tears and agony and commiseration are not enough for this God of ours. The crucifixion of goodness cannot be allowed to stand! Evil must not win the day! And so there at the crossroads of good and evil where Christ is crucified, God engages the powers of evil in the greatest struggle of all time.

And, on the third day, Easter comes!

What does it mean that Jesus died and rose for *us*? It means that God included all humanity—even you and me—in his victory over evil at the cross. Knowing Christ—and Christ crucified—is knowing that whatever evil you are facing today, God is on your side, fighting for you, and as Luther powerfully assured the people of his day, God *will win* the battle!

So how shall we then live?

First of all, we must live as people who are not afraid to discern and confront the powers of evil wherever they are found. Someone on the television this week said something along the line of, *"Who are we to say that the religious belief that called these terrorists to do what they did is wrong?"*

Well, if we are not able to recognize the difference between good and evil, we are in serious trouble. I don't care what fancy name you give to whatever motivates people to kill innocent men, women and children—call it Jihad, call it the Crusades, call it the Final Solution, call it White Supremacy or something nice-sounding like Separate But Equal—it is, at its heart, nothing less than the religion of evil. And Christian people are called to discern it, and to oppose it, and to stick up for those who are its victims.

In the same way, there are many people of Middle Eastern descent living among us—many of them followers of Islam—who will be stereotyped, and ostracized, and persecuted by our own neighbors. And we must stand in the way of it.

To be a Christian is to dedicate your life to confronting evil *wherever* it is found, and standing up is good and right. This is the message of Christ crucified.

Second, we must live as people who bring people to God, and point the way to God's love, when they are going through difficult times. We need to take those six little words that we and others have spoken in the midst of our own and other's tragedies—*"It is the will of God"*—and throw them away never to be used again in the face of human tears. Instead, we must be people who reassure others that God is steadfastly against the evils that have drifted into their lives—that God is *with* them—that God is on their side—that the first heart to break over their loss, their tragedy, their difficult burden, was the heart of God. Our message is that God is light, and in him is no darkness at all. And when we bring that message to others, we make available to them powerful spiritual resources that will help guide them through the darkness. This is the message of Christ crucified.

And finally—although we could go on and on with this—the message of Christ crucified is that God promises that *good* will ultimately overcome all evil things. And that gives us marching orders to be people who practice doing good.

You know, in the 21st chapter of Revelation, we are shown the future vision of a new heaven and a new earth. And then we see a new Jerusalem coming down out of heaven from God. I like to imagine that when we see the Holy City that day, when evil is fully conquered, and only good prevails—when the kingdom comes—we will look up at its mighty walls and notice that the stones of the wall have names on them. And your name will be on some of them. And my name, too.

And we will say to the Lord in that moment, *"Lord, how is it that MY name is inscribed on the stones of the walls of the kingdom of God?"*

And the Lord will say, *"Do you see that stone there? That is the time you spoke a word of comfort to your grieving friend. And that stone there? That's the day you fed my hungry children at the Knox Area Rescue Ministry. And there are the stones you brought the day you forgave the person you hated, and the day you befriended a lonely neighbor, and the day you stood with black neighbors and sang 'We shall overcome!' There's the stone from when you made a casserole and brought it to a shut-in, and there's another for the help you gave a stranger, and there are stones all over the wall from when you prayed for others, and for strength to make a difference in the world!"*

And on that day, we will fully understand the message of the cross—the message of Christ crucified: *the Kingdom of God is being built not out of massive boulders too large for us to handle, but out of all the small stones human beings bring forth through acts of kindness, and generosity and good.* This is the message of Christ crucified!

So come today, and gather around the one and only Jesus—Christ crucified. For here, standing at our own crossroads of good and evil, we find strength and hope and guidance. God loves us! And God is at work! Don't be afraid! Come and join God in overcoming evil with good!

"WHY CAN'T I"
Otho Neil Smith
WLSA Radio, Louisa, Virginia

September 2001

In offering love, sympathy, and condolences to the family members and friends of those who lost their lives in that terrible tragedy that occurred on Tuesday, September 11, 2001, this song is dedicated to them.

Why Can't I

You left me to roam this earth alone
Now in the twilight I see your face.
You were part of my life and home, sweetheart
No one else can take your place

We live and love, fade, and die
like the leaves in spring and autumn do.
In autumn when the brown leaves fall
I recall fond memories of you.

In spring when the leaves turn green and flowers bloom I think of your love so true.
Now you have gone to heavens home, and, I will always remember you.

I will walk life's road without you
till we meet again in the sky,

where leaves and flowers never fade
and loved ones never die
You were meant for me don't you see, sweetheart
No one else will ever do.
When we had to part I said from the start
why can't I have you, oh, why can't I have you.

HUMANITY! HUMANITY!
IT'S LOVE THAT MAKES US GREAT!
(Tune: "America the Beautiful" by Ward)

words by
Pansy J. Jackson
Petersburg, Virginia
Copyright 1997

O, People of the Planet Earth,
Wherever you reside;
Whatever race, whatever creed,
Whatever is your pride:
Humanity, Humanity, it's LOVE that makes us great.
Strife vanishes;
LOVE banishes
All prejudice and hate.

O, People who have been oppressed
More than you could withstand,
Simply because of race or speech,
Or need for someone's hands
Humanity, Humanity, we forge a brotherhood
When we put LOVE
High, high above
What's not for common good.

O, Children all around the world,
Much suff'ring you endure
From wars, diseases, famines long;
For these there's just one cure:
Humanity, Humanity, it's LOVE that brings us peace.
When we extend
Our hearts to men,
Then all the wars will cease.

O, People of the Planet Earth,
Cherish your hopes, your dreams.
Let LOVE become your guiding light,
There's healing in its beams.
Humanity, Humanity, our God LOVES everyone
Whose blood is red,
Whose soul is fed,
By His Beloved Son.

Rebirth of a Nation

"God Bless Our Native Land"
Rebirth of a Nation
Making Light of the Important
Search and Rescue Mission
When the Sky Falls In
In Whom I Trust
The Year of Hope

Chapter

3

God Bless Our Native Land

God bless our native land; Firm may she ever stand,
Thro' storm and night; When the wild tempests rave, Ruler of
winds and wave, Do Thou our country save By Thy great might.

For her our prayers shall rise To God, above the skies;
On Him we wait; Thou who art ever nigh, Guardian with
watchful eye, To Thee aloud we cry, God save the state.

Doxology:
To God, the Father, Son, And Sprit, Three in One,
All praise be giv'n! Crown Him in ev'ry song; To Him your
hearts belong; Let all His praise prolong, On earth, in heav'.

Amen

REBIRTH OF A NATION

Compilation of Messages Submitted by
Sandra M. Poulsen
Director of Public Affairs, Central Virginia
The Church of Jesus Christ of Latter-day Saints
Virginia's Greater Richmond and Tri-Cities Congregations
Richmond, Virginia

September 2001

Bishop Edgardo Marquez—a congregational leader for The Church of Jesus Christ of Latter-day Saints, Chesterfield County, Virginia—stood in horror on the sidewalks of New York City, as he witnessed the Twin Towers ablaze, then crumbling to the earth. A native of Argentina, a young Edgardo had moved to the United States in the early 1980s in pursuit of a homeland that would offer more freedom—more peace. His place of employment had once been within the renowned towers. Amidst his tearful memories of September 11th, he continues to share his conviction of America's strength and "God's love for this elect nation and its people".

On Friday, September 14th, Latter-day Saints met in memorial services throughout the nation. On Sunday, the events of September 11th continued to dominate the messages, the hymns and the conversations in the hallways. Carol Gill, president of the Relief Society (Church women's organization) in Powhatan, Virginia, was one of many Sunday speakers represented within the congregations of The Church of Jesus Christ of Latter-day Saints in the Petersburg and Greater Richmond vicinity. In her remarks she noted, *"We are sobered by the network and resources of a faceless enemy with no home address...A generation of adults, as well as children, has never experienced a crisis like this."* But her message proceeded to bring purpose, amidst the sorrow and disbelief, as she continued: *"What does a crisis provide that is otherwise absent from our daily routine? A sense of purpose—a sense of purpose that galvanizes our strength and our energies into a laser-like focus."* Sister Gill referred to the horrific and heroic events of September 11th and the days following as events combining "to help us reframe the world."

Many Sunday speakers throughout the Latter-day Saint congregations referenced quotes from Church president, Gordon B. Hinckley. In addition to counsel and hope shared during a Friday, September 14th Church satellite memorial service, President Hinckley's words had been heard during an interview on *Larry King Live* that same evening.

Larry King asked: *"Couldn't He (God) have prevented this?"*

President Hinckley responded: *"...I believe He's all-powerful, yes. But I have confidence, over-whelming confidence in the fact that He, who sees life in its true and eternal sense, will provide for those who suffer...God loves us. He loves his children and He will provide for us. I have no doubt of that."*

Members of The Church of Jesus Christ of Latter-day Saints believe that God "will not suffer you to be tempted above that ye are able". [I Corinthians 10:13] Speakers and conversations frequently referenced this belief, offering reassurance that the terror and losses of September 11th would not be beyond our abilities to cope and move forward. President Frank

Ramsey, president of the Richmond Virginia Chesterfield Stake (diocese) noted: *"Even when we have faith in Jesus Christ and His atonement, it is not a protection against the sorrows of this life. But it gives us the knowledge and strength to cope with the trials and tribulations we all must face. The Apostle Peter understood this as he wrote: 'Beloved, think it not strange concerning the fiery trail which is to try you, as though some strange thing happened unto you: But rejoice, inasmuch as ye are partakers of Christ's sufferings; that, when this glory shall be revealed, ye may be glad also with exceeding joy.'"* [1 Peter 4:12-13]

True to those beliefs, the families of those who had died and who had been injured in the attacks were serving as a foundation of strength and dignity for the entire nation. Americans were gaining deepened insight into how to be better parents and sons and daughters and neighbors and citizens—and were putting that heightened insight into action. It was evident that the lives taken that day would be justly avenged, but the lives taken and given that day would also be catalysts, inspiring and enabling the rebirth of a nation.

President Hinckley went on to further testify: *"I have no doubt, none whatever, of the fact that life is eternal, that we are immortal beings and that when we step over the threshold from this life to the next, it will be…a pleasant and uplifting and wonderful experience…. Life is not only that phase that we call mortality…there is beyond this life another, which is as real, as certain as is the life that we now live. And those who have gone beyond will continue and will, in fact, make preparations for their loved ones who will follow. I have no doubt of this…I bring you a message of peace and hope and comfort—that comfort which comes not from man, but from God Himself, who is the father of us all…."*

To you, the families of those who gave their lives, to you, the families who have given us so much insight and strength from your example amidst your struggle, we offer our testimony of eternal life and our testimony of the eternal love that our Heavenly Father has for you and those loved ones, who have moved on to the next glorious phase of their eternity. We thank you; we thank those who sacrificed their lives, wittingly or not, for their important role in the "rebirth of our nation."

MAKING LIGHT OF THE IMPORTANT
Scripture: Matthew 22:1-3

Reverend Grady W. Powell, Pastor Emeritus
Gillfield Baptist Church
Petersburg, Virginia

-Excerpts-
Delivered at Fourth Baptist Church, Richmond, Virginia
September 16, 2001

Today, we who live in the United States and even in the world have a heavy burden. Thousands of lives have been suddenly snuffed from us in a senseless tragedy. My sermon was prepared before this sorrowful event, yet it is an example of making light of the most important quality for living—and that is love. The press reported that there were those who, upon hearing about the terror, rejoiced and danced in the street. How can this be, I thought. It is because there are too many people who make light of love—the important.

The chosen text is the story of a certain king who did everything for the marriage of his son. He invited persons to share in the joyous occasion, but they "…made light of it…and would not come."

As I mused over this, I wondered why the guests refused to attend. Was it because they did not like the King? The truth is no matter how sacred an event or the stature of a person, there are those who possess such hate that they will embarrass anyone and spoil any event. Too often this happens in our everyday surroundings. Perhaps this same motivation was the underlining cause of the destruction of the World Trade Center and the Pentagon. We mourn and sometimes cry, asking, WHERE IS THE KING? How could this happen when the King rules over all? And yet we know well that God gives us the freedom to love or hate.

Second, the parable moves to a satisfying conclusion. The King had a back-up plan. The servants, the story said, went out into the highways and gathered together other persons who were delighted to come to the wedding feast. It is here that we remember—there will always be those who respond to goodness and love. Examples of such genuine caring can be seen among us at this very moment. We observe it in this church, among family and friends, in New York and Washington, and in a myriad of other places. All of us can rest assured that whenever wickedness sows its seeds of destruction, God's love within us can provide the healing balm.

Finally, I am persuaded that our King has not abandoned His world. The sun still arose on Wednesday, September 12th, the air still had oxygen, and God is still God. In the final analysis, love will conquer hate and truth will be on the throne. It is this faith in the God of love that will carry us through.

SEARCH AND RESCUE MISSION
Scripture: Luke 15: 1-10

Reverend Nancy Ross-Zimmerman
Northminster Presbyterian Church
Cincinnati, Ohio

-Excerpts-
September 16, 2001

Ironically, one of the lectionary passages for this particular Sunday was Luke 15: 1-10; the story of the Lost Sheep/Lost Coin. I chose my text and title one month before 9-11, and had intended to speak of God's rejoicing when the lost are found. However, the "Search and Rescue Mission" I described after September 11 took on a much different picture: of surreal shadowy creatures moving in and out of smoke and debris, searching desperately on "The Pile" for survivors. Back in August, I had read this text and envisioned a shepherd, moving along rocky cliffs in the dark, searching for a lost sheep—the bleating noises in the distance encouraging him to keep moving, to keep searching…much like the cellular phone calls placed by victims hidden in the rubble that encouraged their would-be-rescuers to keep at it. I had also imagined a lost woman frantically searching her home for a small coin. Lighting her precious oil lamp and sweeping every corner—desperate, but determined to find the coin.

There are many differences and similarities in these two search and rescue stories. One is news, told in print as well as pictures. One is from the Bible, told only in words. One is told because it is news and the other to teach a lesson: God is both the shepherd and the poor woman and God searches relentlessly because we MATTER to God. We are precious to God and God does share our pain. When tragedy strikes we often feel betrayed, abandoned by God. Feeling the absence of God is the reality of grief. But, when folks scoff and ask, "Where was God on 9-11?", I encouraged folks to answer, "God was right there, grieving and weeping with us…but, more than that, God will continue to be with us, to dry our tears, to create life out of death, hope out of despair, forgiveness out of sin, and wholeness again from shattered lives.

WHEN THE SKY FALLS IN
Scripture: Book of Job

Pastor Gary Hohnberger
New Hope Ministries
Beaver Dam, Wisconsin
September 16, 2001

HE IS BLESSED BEYOND EVERYBODY ELSE IN THE WORLD (Job 1:1-3 NLT)

There was a man named Job who lived in the land of Uz. He was blameless, a man of complete integrity. He feared God and stayed away from evil. {2} He had seven sons and three daughters. {3} He owned seven thousand sheep, three thousand camels, five hundred teams of oxen, and five hundred female donkeys, and he employed many servants. He was, in fact, the richest person in that entire area.

HIS CHARACTER IS ATTACKED (Job 1:6-12 NLT)

One day the angels came to present themselves before the LORD, and Satan the Accuser came with them. {7} "Where have you come from?" the LORD asked Satan. And Satan answered the LORD, "I have been going back and forth across the earth, watching everything that's going on." {8} Then the LORD asked Satan, "Have you noticed my servant Job? He is the finest man in all the earth—a man of complete integrity. He fears God and will have nothing to do with evil." {9} Satan replied to the LORD, "Yes, Job fears God, but not without good reason! {10} You have always protected him and his home and his property from harm. You have made him prosperous in everything he does. Look how rich he is! {11} But take away everything he has, and he will surely curse you to your face!" {12} "All right, you may test him," the LORD said to Satan. "Do whatever you want with everything he possesses, but don't harm him physically." So Satan left the Lord's presence.

THE SKY FALLS IN—UNEXPECTED DISASTER (Job 1:13-21 NLT)

One day when Job's sons and daughters were dining at the oldest brother's house, {14} a messenger arrived at Job's home with this news: "Your oxen were plowing, with the donkeys feeding beside them, {15} when the Sabeans raided us. They stole all the animals and killed all the farmhands. I am the only one who escaped to tell you." {16} While he was still speaking, another messenger arrived with this news: "The fire of God has fallen from heaven and burned up your sheep and all the shepherds! I am the only one who escaped to tell you." {17} While he was still speaking, a third messenger arrived with this news: "Three bands of Chaldean raiders have stolen your camels and killed your servants. I am the only one who escaped to tell you." {18} While he was still speaking, another messenger arrived with this news: "Your sons and daughters were feasting in their oldest brother's home. {19} Suddenly, a powerful wind swept in from the desert and hit the house on all sides. The house collapsed, and all your children are dead. I am the only one who escaped to tell you." {20} Job stood up and tore his robe in grief. Then he shaved his head and fell to the ground before God. {21} He said, "I came naked from my mother's womb, and I will be stripped of everything when I die. The LORD gave me everything I had, and the LORD has taken it away. Praise the name of the LORD!"

IN WHOM I TRUST
Scripture: Psalm 91 (Jerusalem Translation)

Message by Tracy Muffett Mills
Pittsburgh Theological Seminary
(HM37 – Dr. Teresa Lockhart Stricklen, Assistant Professor of Homiletics)

September 12, 2001

…I had such a good sermon. All whipped up and ready to go. It came from out of the Book of Acts and it had these great images and tie-ins and it made perfect sense. Even if it did liken the Kingdom of Heaven to a big pot of homemade potato soup. It was a potato soup kind of sermon. Cozy, warm, went down easy, felt good. And it would've worked, it really would've worked.

…Until Tuesday morning. Until I came out of my 8:30 class, wandered into the Shak for a midmorning candy bar, noticed the crowd around that little black-and-white TV down there, and wandered over to see what was going on. Until I saw and heard the terrible news that we all know by chilling rote, by now. Four planes hijacked. One crashed practically in our backyard. Three beaten into deadly arrows that flew in the daytime—one into the Pentagon, two into the World Trade Towers. A thousand fallen in DC, ten thousand in New York City. The scourge wreaked its havoc in broad daylight, the plague stalked in the dark, and my nice little sermon from the Book of Acts just wasn't going to cut it. Because you can't throw a little bowl of potato soup on the fires of hell itself.

And we are, indeed, a people who've seen the fires of hell itself. Our dearest idols have been brought to flaming ruin. Our wealth, our strength, our legendary world leadership have not protected us. Our precautions, our contingency plans, our disaster drills have not saved us. Our mighty nation has been kicked to its knees, and by whom? a scruffy handful of nameless, faceless desperadoes, outside our law and beyond the pale of all human decency. And now, so soon after the terrible events, all we can feel is a numbing mix of shock, denial, outrage and despair, and we ask ourselves and one another: How could this be? How could this have happened? How could God have *let* this happen?

These are big questions. And they are valid. We don't do ourselves or our people any good by brushing our feelings or our questions under the rug in the name of 'protecting' God or our faith. If it helps, these feelings, these questions, these Whys? and Where Were Yous?…they put us in good company. They put us in company with the People who give us the Psalms. For they, like us, were a people who knew all too well what it was to be kicked to their knees. They knew how it felt to have their dearest idols brought to flaming ruin. They knew how it felt to have their city, their nation, their sense of well-being crippled by scruffy desperadoes—outside the Law and beyond all human decency. And certainly, they knew how it felt to have their most fervent prayers go unanswered, how it felt to ask why, and more specifically, Why, God? The Hebrew people knew all about the terrors of night, and the arrow that flies in the daytime, and the plague that stalks in the dark, and the scourge that wreaks havoc in broad daylight. These things all happened to them: disease, drought, famine, starvation, war, siege, occupation, terrorism, slaughter of innocents, it all happened to them. Them! Israel! God's chosen people, the people who had *been* a superpower under David and Solomon! The people with the shining Temple on the top of the mountain! They, even they, were not spared the arrow that flies by day, the scourge that wreaks havoc. The Israel that gave us the Psalms was an Israel that could, all too certainly, feel our pain in these terrible days.

With that in mind, we can understand why they left us Psalms like 22 and 79 and 137, those psalms of heart-rending lament and blistering complaint. We can tune in to those kinds of psalms: Where were you, God? Why'd you let this happen? And *When* are you going to wreak a little vengeance on our behalf? But what we have here, from this same people who knew all those terrors and questions and doubts, is Psalm 91. Not a psalm of complaint, but a psalm of confidence. Not a psalm in denial that bad things happen, but a psalm in assurance that the faithful shall overcome. The same God that let the drought happen and the famine happen and the plague happen, the same God that seemingly turned His back and abandoned his people to the desperadoes, this same God—says Psalm 91—is the very God who will rescue, cover, shelter His people.

How can this be? We can do our homework, we can read this psalm as it probably was meant at first, as something of an opening and closing hymn for public worship, we can expect it, under those circumstances, to be a little optimistic. But can even that account for what seems to us right now to be bald-faced lies? "You yourselves will remain unscathed,"—tell that to the people in New York City. "No disaster can overtake you,"—tell that to the people in the Pentagon. "Look and see how the wicked are repaid"—tell that to the people whose Moms and Dads, sons and daughters, sisters, brothers, husbands, wives...won't be coming home anymore. On the surface, the promises of Psalm 91 sound like the same old potato soup: Be good, love God, and everything will be all right. That kind of soup leads to two possible conclusions: that either everyone who died yesterday deserved their fate, or the Bible doesn't know what it's talking about. Neither of these conclusions is especially good!

Nor are they especially faithful. Because the only faithful response to this kind of paradox in scripture is to Go Deeper. To rethink what 'safety' and 'deliverance' and 'life' and 'protection' might mean, not in the language of Hebrew or English, but in the language of God Eternal. Maybe the Psalmist anticipates Jesus' promise—that "life" is something more than just that physical thing that keeps our heart beating and our neurons firing. Maybe Psalm 91 anticipates the day when Jesus would tell his followers not to fear those who could destroy the body, but rather to fear that which could throw both body and soul into hell. Maybe Psalm 91 challenges us to look for the real deadly arrows behind those hijacked planes—the arrows of human hatred and injustice, the powers and principalities very much alive and at work in this world. And maybe "life," to the psalmist, is not just our mortal, earthly existence from start to finish; maybe "life" is the God-given ability to face the arrows of hatred without letting them pierce and consume us, without letting the monsters make monsters of us as well.

For already, this danger exists and it is very near to us all. Already the airwaves and the Internet are full of calls for blood. Bomb something, anything. Wipe entire nations off the map. Teach the jerks a lesson they'll never forget. Find suspects and execute them without trial. Innocent along with the guilty? Too bad, so sad. Already people, even people in our own churches, regress to calling people "towelheads" and worse—shoving them off at arms' length, setting up enemy camps of Us and Them. These are not bad people who are making these terrible suggestions; these are ordinary folks, the you and me of our society, speaking out of our raw emotion. And make no mistake, I'm not saying that we should just sit back and let our enemies get away with this. For we are called as Christians to stand against the forces of conscious evil, wherever it inbreaks upon the world. It wouldn't be faithful of us, as Christians, to do otherwise. What I am saying is we have to be careful about the fine line between serving as God's instruments of righteousness in this world, and trying to make God serve as *our* instrument of what we *think* is righteousness. For we hear the blood of our brothers and sisters, crying out from the flames and the rubble. We read the rest of the Psalm 91, and we want it. We want to tread on the lion and the snake right now, we want to trample those savage lions and those dragons. Vengeance may be the Lord's but we want to be the Lord's instrument, thankyouverymuch. We don't want to be warned about not struggling with monsters lest we become monsters ourselves. We don't want to be warned that the deadly arrows and the stalking pestilence might be coming from our own hearts as surely as from the morning skies.

And that is *exactly* why we need such a warning. Psalm 91 reminds us that we are not the first People to suffer injustice or tragedy. It reminds us that we are not all by ourselves, that we do not live *or* die without meaning. Psalm 91 reminds us that we belong to something and Someone bigger, that our "life" is not limited to the sum of our blood and bones and brain cells. It reminds us to focus *first* on God, that we may be delivered from making twisted idols of our misfortunes or our enemies. Most of all, it reminds us that we are not the first people to find out that our mortal strength and our mortal wealth, impressive though they may be, are still Not Enough. Like Israel, we have got to learn that there are forces greater than ourselves. We learned half of that equation all too well yesterday morning: we cannot deliver ourselves from evil by the force of our might alone. Now it is time to learn the other half: that we cannot preserve, protect, or rebuild ourselves by the force of our might alone. We certainly didn't need what happened yesterday; nobody ever needs that sort of thing. But it happened, and now we *do* need our God, and our faith in that God, and our best efforts at building right relationship first *with* God. Only then will we be able to deal rightly with the scourge that wreaks havoc.

There are those, even within our own churches and families, who might try to tell us that this kind of faith is like a little bowl of potato soup right now: may feel good going down, but really isn't good for much against a disaster of this magnitude. I say, Not So. Faith is *not* a little bowl of potato soup thrown at the fires of hell; it is hundreds of strangers coming together to make soup and sandwiches for the rescue workers. Faith is *not* shedding blood for blood; it is block-long lines to give blood for those who need it. And most of all, faith is *not* a little umbrella of worn-out platitudes and cliches that we hold up as the Towers come crashing down on top of us. What faith is, is 200 firefighters running straight into their own deaths, knowing all about structural dangers and fully aware that this is exactly what they might well be doing— but doing it anyway, because they had "a job to do." Because they heard the call of need upon their hearts and they responded out of who they are. *That* is what faith is. It is being who we are and Whose we are, every step of the way, unto whatever end awaits us. Faith does not call us to run away and live; it calls us to come and serve the Christ, yes, even die with Him, if that is what must be. It does not call us to safety, but rather into the thick of danger. It does not call us to avoid our troubles at all costs; rather, it calls us to be faithful through them. Faith calls us to do these things out of a realization that there is so much more to life than just our here-and-now existence, that there is so much more that can be lost than one's physical existence, that there is so much more to be gained than mere physical comfort and safety.

Faith demands a lot of us, especially in times like these. But it has a right to demand it, because it is the Lord who calls us to that faith: the Lord, who rescues all who seek and cling, the Lord who protects, who answers us, the Lord who is with us in time of trouble, The Lord who brings us eternal safety and eternal life, the Lord, who lived dangerously, suffered terribly, and died horribly…*and yet overcame.* The Lord who lives that promise, *Is* that promise, makes that promise. That is the Lord of whom the Psalmist speaks. That is the Lord who calls us to faith, even now, especially now. And that, though the cities crumble and the planes fall from the skies, is a Lord who will deliver us all, step by step, right here in it with us, through the fire, through the valley of the shadow, to that place and that time when All, yes, All, Will Be Well. Amen.

The author is now Pastor Tracy Muffett Mills, First Christian Church (Disciples of Christ), Greensburg, PA.

THE YEAR OF HOPE!

Amer A. AL-Zubaiah
Al-Kufa Newsletter
(Dr. Hanif D. Sherali, Honorable Editor)
Kufa Center of Islamic Knowledge (KCIK)
Roanoke, Virginia

The hearts of men should be filled with love and kindness toward their fellow humans. They should seek the harmony of differing cultures and faiths, and make every effort to help ease the suffering of others.

Those who sincerely want to be guided aright should keep the company of the righteous ones, and should also keep themselves aloof from the misled, misguided, and wicked impostors, and feel repulsion for their wicked ways and evil thoughts. Moreover, conflicts that obstruct a global community must be eliminated.

The oppressors who exercise power over the powerless are no more than a handful. Those who lead and have authority of administration over humanity, should be among the best ones, who are courageous, friendly, brotherly, forgiving, and just toward fellow humans, so that mankind can achieve and implement peace with justice, and security and comfort for all.

O' Lord, bring the people of the world closer to each other,
as individuals and families, communities and nations, and promote goodness
from them that would benefit humanity, and let the world be a safe place to live.
O' Lord, grant to all guidance and let piety prevail over the evil.
We wish all blessings and happiness in this coming year and always, Ameen.

Lost and Found

Chapter 4

"Guide Me, O Thou Great Jehovah"
Lost and Found
A Wind Too Strong
Are You Prepared for the Journey?
A Service of Remembrance with the American Community
in the United Kingdom
Held by Our Faith

Guide Me, O Thou Great Jehovah

Guide me, O Thou great Jehovah, Pilgrim thro' this barren land;
I am weak, but Thou art mighty; Hold me with Thy pow'rful hand;
Bread of heaven, Feed me till I want no more,
Bread of heaven, Feed me till I want no more.

Open now the crystal fountain, Whence the healing waters flow;
Let the fiery, cloudy pillar, Lead me all my journey through;
Strong Deliv'rer, Be Thou still my strength and shield,
Strong Deliv'rer, Be Thou still my strength and shield.

When I tread the verge of Jordan, bid my anxious fears subside;
Bear me thro' the swelling current; land me safe on Canaan's side;
Songs of praises I will ever give to Thee,
Songs of praises I will ever give to Thee.

Amen

William Williams   *Dr. T. Hastings*

LOST AND FOUND
Scripture: Luke 15:1-10

Amy Schacht
Laurel Presbyterian Church
Laurel, Maryland

September 16, 2001

We are lost, as lost as that sheep that wandered away, as lost as that precious coin covered in dust. We are lost. Though we've been told other countries around the world have had to live with this terrifying reality for decades, we rack our memories trying to come up with something as devastating as this. And when we hear that people from around the world—people who are citizens of countries like Australia, Japan, Germany, China are among the missing, we realize, we are lost, but so is everyone else. So what happens then?

The network television executives have placed a large amount of money on the assumption that watching real people who are really lost would be entertaining tv, and a new sub-genre of reality television was born. The hope is that these shows would be entertaining enough that the executives could sell advertising and thus make money, hopefully, lots of money. Then someone came up with a brilliant idea to up the stakes. If it was entertaining to watch strangers duke it out in reality tv—strangers thrown together on an island, in the outback, in a house—how much more entertaining it would be to eavesdrop and watch people who were related to one another or who cared about each other hash it out under high stress circumstances. If it was fun to watch strangers back stab and yell at each other, how much better it would be to watch husbands and wives, fiancées, fraternity brothers, sisters, brothers, parents and children, fight under the stress of being lost in front of our eyes. We could gleefully laugh as the struggles and stressors of their relationships broke those relationships apart, all from the privacy of our living rooms.

So much for what tv executives know about human nature. So much for what tv executives know about how God made us. Put us under extreme stress, and perhaps you won't find back-biting and yelling to be characteristic of how we treat one another, stranger or loved one. Perhaps, how God made us comes to the surface once everything else is stripped away.

A clinical psychologist, who specializes in depression and anxiety, was on one of the bridges going into Manhattan when the first, then second airplane flew into the World Trade Towers. He was interviewed on the radio, not just because of what he witnessed, but because he spends his professional life analyzing and listening and observing human behavior. In the interview he described how the cars just all stopped, and even when the news on the car radios made it clear what was going on, and warned people not to be on the bridges that were such obvious targets, there was no going anywhere.

The last question the interviewer asked him was if he was willing to share what was going on inside him, what he was feeling even as he watched the drama and tragedy unfold right before his eyes. He talked about how everyone had gotten out of their cars, and everyone was facing the same direction, but the longer everyone watched, with radios blaring in the background, the closer they were drawn together. It's not that anyone guided the crowd stuck on the bridge to come together. It's not that someone suggested they hold hands and pray. Some folk were praying, others were quietly singing, some were weeping. But it was as if some magnetic force drew them closer and closer together, until everyone was standing very close to everyone else—much closer than the average American would normally be comfortable standing next to strangers. The psychologist commented that it was as though that primal need for human contact and connection with other humans, that primal need that guides from the time of our birth, was uncovered. Witnessing that tragedy stripped away all else, until there was nothing left but the need to be together. And I would say, of course, for this is how we are made. It's in our genes, in our hearts, in our souls. It is humanity as God intended it to be, even as we witness the worst humans can do to one another.

My mother, who teaches boys in a maximum security prison for juvenile criminals, told me about one fifteen year old's response to what was unfolding before him on television. He said to her, "Ms. Schacht, I haven't prayed for a long time—A really, really long time. But Tuesday night, I just had to get down on my knees, and I prayed Ms. Schacht. I prayed. I couldn't help it. I didn't know what else to do, but get on my knees. So I did." This criminal, who hadn't given anyone but himself a thought for years, in spite of only being fifteen, thought about someone else that night, and what they were going through, and he was connected with them and with his Maker.

And how we were made to be is right there, for God made us to be a people who understand this horror represents a terrible terrible distortion of Islam, the same distortion Timothy McVeigh had of patriotism; a people who will work twenty-four hours around the clock in dust up to their knees, choking their lungs, even if all they can do is bring out the bodies of the dead that someone loved, that someone was hoping would come home that night; a people who will listen patiently over and over and over again to the stories of loss, and devastation, and broken-hearts in an effort to help people know they are not alone, even as it threatens to break their hearts; a people who found sanctuary in their churches and prayed and sang; a people who lined the police security line with flowers and notes and cheered the rescue efforts; a people who fought the hijackers in an effort to save people on the ground. This is how we were meant to be.

Yes, this is a time of great stress, more stress than any people should ever have to bear, and it is a time of looking for God. This is a time when gentleness and compassion with one another is the rule and standard of the day, for who knows how that other person was touched by this tragedy.

Yes, we are lost. People, thousands of people, are literally lost, missing, or dead. Millions of Americans are lost, wondering how this could have happened, what part did our attitude in the world play, how do we go on from here. We are lost. People from around the world lost lovers, children, spouses, parents, and people from around the world lost the sense that it wouldn't, couldn't happen to them. We are lost. Mothers and daughters, and fathers and sons throughout Afganistan suspect they are lost and will lose in the end. World leaders are feeling their way through, wondering how to proceed, knowing they must proceed. And the terrorists themselves are lost, and in their lostness, turned to evil that spilled out and contaminated us all.

And yet, though we are lost, we are also being found. Just as the firefighter was pulled out of the wreckage, just as the wife found her husband's name on the hospital list receiving treatment after days of being missing, we are being found. God seeks out the lost, for every lost coin and every lost sheep is precious to their Maker. Even as we are lost, how God intended us to be together in this world is being uncovered, a witness to being found. We are lost, we have lost, but we are being found, and we have found: We have found what it can mean to be fully human, huddling together in the comfort of one another, for God calls us close. We have found that God is in our midst, to hear our rage, our cries, our confusion, our relief, our thanksgiving, our questions. Our God will not rest until every one of us is found, and thank God, we know, our Maker will not let us go, though the way be dark, Christ will be our light. Thanks be to God.

...On the Sabbath After

A WIND TOO STRONG
Scripture: Jeremiah 4:11-12

Richard Groves
Wake Forest Baptist Church
(Chapel on Campus of Wake Forest University, Winston-Salem, NC)

-Excerpts-
September 16, 2001

"At that time it will be said to this people and to Jerusalem: A hot wind comes from me out of the bare heights in the desert toward my poor people, not to winnow or cleanse—a wind too strong for that. Now it is I who speak in judgement against them."

Thusly did God speak through the prophet Jeremiah in the last days of the nation of Judah. A wind will come out of the desert upon my poor people, Yahweh said. Not an evening breeze that cools the skin after the heat of the day; but a blistering sand storm, roaring in from the desert when the afternoon sun is at its peak. You will not be able to get away from it, you will not be able to defend yourself against it, you will not be able to make it stop. A wind too strong—it will wreak havoc on your individual lives and on your life as a people. It will break your hearts. It will break your spirits.

Before Jeremiah's long ministry was over, a hot wind did indeed blow in from the desert—from Babylon—leaving Jerusalem a smoldering ruin; its walls pulled down, its magnificent temple burned to the ground, its people cursing their enemies in their hymns, and its exiled singers wondering, "How can we sing the songs of Zion in a strange land?" (Psalm 137:3).

At 8:48 a.m. Tuesday, September 11, a wind too strong roared out of the skies and crashed into the twin towers of the World Trade Center and the Pentagon, taking thousands of lives, destroying the sense of safety that made us feel secure in the world, revealing a vulnerability we didn't know we had, unmasking an inherent weakness, and initiating us into the worldwide community of victims of political violence.

We watched in stunned disbelief as scenes of horror unfolded before our eyes. Some of us watched in company with others, finding a sense of community as members of temporary congregations that clustered around television sets in public places. Others watched in seclusion. Wherever we watched we wept. On the streets, on campus, we struck up conversations with people we didn't know, assuming a commonality that we would not have suspected on any other day. We gathered here in Wait Chapel or down the hall in Davis Chapel or on the quad, and in places of worship across the country, to affirm our faith, to pray, to read scriptures, turning almost instinctively to the Old Testament, to psalms of assurance and national lament. We shared the freshly broken body and newly spilled blood of our Lord.

The week wore on, and our grief morphed into national pride and the flying of flags, expressions of anger and outrage. The reality was sinking in. And we were trying to sort out what is an appropriate response for us to make, as a nation, as individual Americans, and as individual Christians.

It is true that Jeremiah said that the wind that swept Judah off the map was from God and that it was a wind of judgment. The idea that judgment comes through the forces of history is certainly biblical enough, but history is messy, and discerning the will of God in history requires divine inspiration. In the muddled moment no one I know claims to have such direct and clear access to the mind of the Almighty.

We should remind ourselves of the terrible tragedy that took place in Samaria during Jesus' lifetime (Luke 13); Pontius Pilate sent his troops into a place of worship and slaughtered those worshipping there. Later, Jesus asked rhetorically if the worshippers had been killed, if they had been singled out by God, because they were sinners. He answered clearly, No. He refused to speculate further on what the transcendent meaning of the event might be, saying only that such horrors should cause us to examine our own lives and to repent, and that we should use even tragedy to bring glory to God. That, it seems to me, is exactly what most Americans—whatever their religious persuasion—are doing.

There is a response that is not worthy of the name Christian, though we have heard it from Christians. Thursday morning I received a call from a total stranger, a woman who was clearly distraught. Earlier she had gone to the street to talk with a Muslim woman who walked past her house every day, taking her daughter to school. She knew the woman was Muslim by the traditional clothing she wore. Her intention was to assure the woman that good and decent Americans do not hold her and her daughter responsible for what happened in New York and Washington. When my caller approached the woman on the sidewalk, she could not help but notice that she was wearing Western style clothes, complete with a baseball cap. Trying to blend in. She even denied that she was from the Near East, which she clearly was. She said she was Italian.

But that isn't all. I was the third Baptist pastor my caller had phoned in an effort to find a minister who would support her in her concern. The first two had said the same thing to her: "Don't you know that Muslims worship a different God than we worship? Don't you know that they are persecuting Christians in Afghanistan?" My caller told them both, "You're the reason I don't go to church," and hung up on them. When I told her that I had just called the home of Imam Khalid Griggs, she burst into tears and thanked me.

Across the country Muslim leaders and organizations are making public statements, affirming their love for America, reminding their fellow Americans that Islam does not condone such atrocities. There is something sad about that. Sad that they think it is necessary to distance themselves from cold-blooded murderers. Sadder still that it may be necessary.

Much that has been said in recent days is not worthy of the name Christian. But much that has been said is worthy of the name, for it flows out of the words of Jesus as preserved in the Gospels and from the depths of his Spirit who lives among his people. That which is worthy of the name is about peace and justice without vengeance, it's about forgiveness and reconciliation, a new world and a new humanity. Here are some samples.

"Now, as never before, it is time for Christians to attest a higher ethic that opens our eyes to the sacredness of all human life. I see this only dimly, not with the clear vision of saintly souls who have lost loved ones and, even now, pray for their enemies." (John Oliver, coordinator of the Orthodox Peace Fellowship)

"We call upon our people to pray and work for peace. We must never raise the sword. Our Lord commanded Peter and all of us to put back our swords and to take up our cross."

(Dennis Lotz, general secretary, Baptist World Alliance)

"The biblical injunction to 'love our enemies' is often deemed unrealistic. (What is) unrealistic (is) to think we can successfully seal off an entire country to terrorist attacks. Indeed our most realistic hope for safety comes from working to make sure that everyone in the world community is treated fairly, and being just as willing to give our lives in loving the enemy as the terrorists were willing to give their lives to kill the enemy." (Christian Peacemaker Teams, a program of Quaker, Mennonite, and Brethren churches)

"The terrorists have offered us a stark view of the world they would create, where the remedy to every human grievance and injustice is a resort to the random and cowardly violence of revenge—even against the most innocent. We can deny them their victory by refusing to submit to a world created in their image. We assert the vision of community, tolerance, compassion, justice, and the sacredness of human life, which lies at the heart of all our religious traditions." (Jim Wallis, Sojourners; Rev. Wesley Granberg-Michaelson, Reformed Church of America; Rabbi David Saperstein, Religious Action Center of Reform Judaism; Dr. Bob Edgar, National Council National Council of Churches; Dr. Ron Sider, Evangelicals for Social Action)

"For Christians to fail to forgive is to hedge on Jesus." (Ken Sehested, Baptist Peace Fellowship of North America)

"Vengeance and retaliation cannot be the answer to this situation. These persons should be brought to justice through legal means and the accepted standards of international law, not by the law of the jungle and collective punishment. Justice and peace are realized through just and peaceful means, for means and ends are interrelated." (Fellowship of Reconciliation)

And this, a prayer from the Eastern Orthodox tradition, sent to me last week by a church member: *We beseech Thee, O Lord, to grant our enemies true peace and forgiveness of sins; and do not allow them to leave this life without true faith and sincere conversion. And help us repay evil with goodness…* If you think that is an impossible prayer to pray, especially under these circumstances, I remind you that on his cross the Lord whom you and I serve prayed this prayer for his murderers: *Father, forgive them, for they know not what they do.*

The terrorists who were responsible for untold suffering last Tuesday morning knew nothing of our Lord's final prayer, or if they knew it they had no respect for it. We know it, and we profess that it reveals the very heart and will of God. It is incumbent on us, then, to allow our lives, hearts, souls, and our spirits, to be shaped by that prayer, and by the spirit and the mind of our Lord Jesus Christ.

ARE YOU PREPARED FOR THE JOURNEY?
Scripture: St. Matthew 24:36-44, 25:13, and 28:19-20; Romans 6:23

Rev. Dr. Whitfield Scott
First Rock Baptist Church
Prospect, Virginia

-Excerpts-
September 16, 2001

We praise God for this great opportunity to share with you a divine message the Lord sent through His messenger to His people on the Sunday after the great tragedy against this Nation, September 11, 2001.

This is a message of comfort, confirmation, warning, and fulfillment of prophecy. The message is directed to the hearts and souls of everyone because of the sudden death of those who were at Ground Zero and died an instant death. Our hearts and prayers go out to those who mourn and weep because they cannot understand how a tragedy of this sort could happen so swiftly in a country so powerful.

The main focus includes some vivid facts before us at the time. As usual, these everyday folk left their homes or dwellings that morning. They departed at their usual times and expected to return after they had completed their work obligations. No doubt, none expected to be separated from their loved ones so quickly as they gathered to work and began their daily routines. Everything seemed normal. The environment and the view from their particular vantage points overlooking the beautiful city were the same. As far as they were concerned, all systems were on go. They were enjoying the freedoms that came with this great country, bearing in mind that Freedom is an Eternal seed given by God.

They were set for the day; however, the tragic scene unfolded as sin began to play its role against humanity, but the Word of God hovered over that place also.

"Be ye also ready for ye know not the day nor the hour the Son of Man Cometh."(Matthew 24:42-44). "For the wages of sin is death, but the Gift of God is eternal Life" (Romans 6:23). "Lo, I am with you Always, even to the end of the World" (Matthew 28:19 -20).

Now the great question of being prepared came into focus for those who died and for those of us left behind because our day of departure is also at hand at this very moment. The message becomes personal with the question: Are you prepared for the journey? This comes with strong spiritual emphasis, as though we can see and feel the hand of the Lord pressing upon our very souls as the question is asked.

We need a savior to be with us all the time—one who can keep us from falling and hold us up at those times in earthly life when the circumstances are beyond our control. This Savior must be able to instantly pick us up and transfer our spirit to the eternal state so that we can live in peace with Him forever. We need this kind of Savior everyday and moment of our lives. It has to be an eternally trusted relationship with Jesus our Lord.

Additionally, the event was seen by the world which suggests how the second coming of the Lord will be, and how many will be unprepared when the time comes. It is a verification of how we take life for granted each day without concern for eternity. God has given us a great country and framed it by His Word, yet we have drifted away from Him. Finally, look at yourself. Are you prepared for the journey? It's coming soon, and you need a Savior.

A SERVICE OF REMEMBRANCE
WITH THE AMERICAN COMMUNITY
IN THE UNITED KINGDOM, ST. PAUL'S CATHEDRAL

a sermon by
THE ARCHBISHOP OF CANTERBURY
Dr George Leonard Carey, the 103rd Archbishop of Canterbury

Anglican Communion News Service

14 September 2001

We have gathered today, not only inside this great Cathedral but outside as well, to share in America's grief and to mourn the loss of so many lives.

Like millions of others I watched in horror, as the towers of the World Trade Centre disappeared under a cloud of dust and smoke. A modern icon of America had been reduced to rubble. A senseless evil had been perpetrated against America and against the free world.

In the aftermath of such shocking events, various emotions arise within us. We may feel despair at man's inhumanity to man. We may feel helpless that we can do so little for those who have suffered so much, among them hundreds of British people; they and their families are very much in our thoughts and prayers at this time. We may feel anger against those who planned and carried out such evil, despicable deeds. We may want to see revenge. We may just feel numb.

But my first word today—echoed I know by every faith leader present and by us all—is a simple message to the people of America through the American ambassador: a message of love and solidarity; a message also of hope. What you have gone through in these last few days is beyond our imagination. As we gather with Her Majesty the Queen, Government and other political leaders, our hearts go out to you; you are all firmly in our prayers. We hope you know that we are with you in your hour of need.

And next let me affirm that true faith is never overcome by disasters of this kind. There is something unconquerable about the faith we share. With St. Paul we trust that 'neither death, nor life, nor angels, nor principalities, nor powers…nor any other creature shall be able to separate us from the love of God in Jesus Christ our Lord.'

And even in the darkest hour, such faith in God gives birth to hope. So into the trauma of the people of America let us declare the hopeful words of the prophet Isaiah, first spoken at a time of disaster and despair in the life of his own people:

They shall build up the ancient ruins,

They shall raise up the former devastations,

They shall repair the ruined cities…

I am hopeful for the people of America: hopeful that as ruins are rebuilt, so also a shaken people will be restored.

For, as the twin towers of the World Trade Centre disappeared amid the smoke and carnage, across a short stretch of water another, older, American icon was not submerged. The September morning sun continued to shine on the Statue of Liberty, her torch raised like a beacon; a beacon of hope, and to millions around the world, a symbol of all that is best about America. Liberty has always been at the heart of the American vision. That liberty must be defended. It is the awesome responsibility of the leaders of America to decide how to respond to this evil inflicted upon their people, this assault on their freedom and security. The leaders of America need our prayers. May God give them wisdom to use their great power in such ways that further evil aggression is indeed deterred, and the security and well-being of all is advanced in our interdependent world.

For the flower of democracy to flourish it must grow in the soil of justice. Yes, those responsible for such barbaric acts must be held to account. But we must be guided by higher goals than mere revenge. As we battle with evil, our goal must be a world where such violence is a thing of the past.

The ideal of liberty at the core of America's greatness—the liberty symbolised by that statue emerging unscathed from the pall of devastation—was founded on a noble community of values in which we are proud to share. Values like tolerance and compassion, justice and mercy. Values at the heart of the Christian faith and also of other faiths. Let us keep them before us now—like a torch, like a beacon—even as we mourn and grieve. For if we are steadfast we know that, by the grace of God, no darkness, no evil can ever extinguish that beacon of hope.

HELD BY OUR FAITH

Reverend Lynn Thomas Strauss
River Road Unitarian Church
Bethesda, Maryland

September 16, 2001

Why is it that suffering brings us together? In this week of tragic loss and shared mourning, we see one another differently. Each day since Tuesday, when we leave home and when we return, we kiss our loved ones and connect with our friends with a new kind of gratitude. A gratitude for one more day of safety, gratitude for one more day of life. We feel that gratitude this morning as we look at one another's faces, as we breathe together in this sacred space.

Perhaps suffering brings us together because it reminds us of our very human frailty and of our deep need of one another. Perhaps it's because we are all wounded. We realize we have always understood one another's deepest sorrow. In the aftermath, we are all exhausted, irritable, afraid. Each day we awake to a new dimension of reaction to the crisis. Each day we feel a little more lost.

Rabbi Arthur Blecher spoke to the Beth Chai congregation here in this sanctuary on Friday night he spoke of how all of us are imperfect, how all of us are broken, and he said, it is too soon to talk of healing. I, too, think we must stay with our wounds, not rush to find the right words, the right solution, the right response to the events of this week.

Healing takes time and it takes forms that we cannot now imagine.

Some have said, that this tragedy will bring all of us to more spiritual living. That it will bring more of us to God and to faith perhaps it will.

I must tell you that in the midst of my sorrow and fear, I have felt well-served by our UU faith this week. I hope you have also.

As I read article after article in which writers seemed sure of cause and effect, as I listened to radio call in shows, I found comfort in our acknowledgement of doubt and mystery. Questions of the causes and purposes of evil are no more answerable for me today than they were last Sunday. In the face of the senseless murder of thousands, we struggle to understand and accept the unacceptable. We hold to no easy answers. For most of us, no thoughts of heaven relieve our grieving.

As I spoke to my teenage son about the future, I found comfort in our humanist tradition—a tradition that grounds good and evil in this world, a tradition that affirms the human spirit…its resiliency, its compassionate light.

As we gathered here in a vigil on Thursday night, speaking out of our hearts with very different points of view, I found comfort in our ethic of reason, that encourages each one of us to struggle for our own understanding and to rely on our own experience and speak our own truth. And our ethic of tolerance that teaches us to listen to one another and to honor the tension of our disagreements.

As I read and heard so many calls to war and retaliation, I found comfort in our social justice tradition that calls each one of us to be witness for peace and for justice. A tradition that calls us to action for the common good. We are already working along with the Social Justice chair of Beth Chai to strategize action in support of the Arab-American and American Muslim communities in our area. If you wish to be an ally to witness for peace at the Mosque door or the Arab business establishment, let me know.

As I thought about the terrorists following an ideology unto death, I found comfort in our commitment to democratic process, which teaches that we should all take responsibility for decision making and never blindly follow any leader.

As I searched for words that mattered, I found comfort in our Judeo-Christian heritage, that gives us scripture and guidance from other suffering peoples and from prophets who challenged both God in heaven and the political status quo.

When I heard about hatred being directed at Arab and Muslim Americans, I found comfort in our affirmation of other religious traditions. At a meeting on Wednesday morning at the Montgomery County School Board headquarters I was able, because of my knowledge and commitment to religious diversity, to speak clearly and with practical suggestions in support of our Muslim brothers and sisters who are feeling so much fear of reprisal. I encourage each of you to be a voice of reasoned compassion, to correct whenever possible misperceptions about our Muslim brothers and sisters. Let people know that the Quran does not condone killing, that no religion advocates murder.

As I woke up in the night listening for planes and feeling alone, I have taken comfort in our belief that love is the spirit of life, that love is the face of the holy, that a divine love lives in and among us…a love that is universal and all embracing…a love that holds us to be our best selves to create and sustain reverence for life. In the final words spoken by those who used their cell phones in their final moments of life their message to their families was a message to us all…I love you, I love you was all that needed to be said.

My faith has been tested this week and I have found it strong.

I have been held this week by my faith and by this faith community. All of the words we speak in our weekly celebration of life have taken on new and deeper meaning. All of the rituals of prayer, and mindfulness, of kindness and simplicity…all these have become my strength.

I encourage you to be gentle with yourself and others. To speak softly and with kindness. To walk out of doors…to listen to beautiful music. To talk out your feelings…to seek help when you need it. To see the sacred light in each person you encounter. I encourage you to show gratitude for each precious day.

I am moved by the power of this faith we share. May it be a light guiding each of us in the difficult weeks ahead. I pray for you…that your faith will be to you a blessing…that you will be held, comforted and strengthened by Unitarian Universalism and all that it stands for. That you will return to this religious community to be held by love and the spirit of life to be held as the form of our healing, and the healing of the world, is slowly revealed.

So May it Be/Amen/Blessed Be/ Shalom/ Salam

The Lonely City

"Come Ye Disconsolate"
The Lonely City
Prayers
Struggling for the Words
Growing A Soul, Changing A World
Silence: Silver and Gold (A Time to Keep Silent)

Chapter 5

Come Ye Disconsolate

Come ye disconsolate, wher e're ye lanquish;
Come to the mercy seat, fervently kneel;
Here bring your wounded hearts, here tell your anquish.
Earth has no sorrow that Heav'n cannot heal.

Joy of the desolate, light of the straying,
Hope of the penitent, fadeless and pure;
Here speaks the Comforter, tenderly saying,
Earth has no sorrow that Heav'n cannot heal.

Here see the Bread of Life; see waters flowing
Forth from the throne of God, pure from above;
Come to the feast of love; come, ever knowing
Earth has no sorrow that Heav'n cannot heal.

Amen

Verse 1 and 2. Thomas Moore, 1816; Verse 3, Thomas Hastings, 1830
S. Webbe, 1740 – 1816

THE LONELY CITY
Scripture: Psalm 13; Lamentations 1:1-2a; John 14:27

Jack McKinney
Pullen Memorial Baptist Church
Raleigh, North Carolina

September 16, 2001

He looked back as he fled the scene. Smoke billowed into the air. The destruction was catastrophic. The landmark of the city was in ruins and his world would never be the same. All around him were others fleeing for their lives: women dragging their children and men who bore the wounds of having been too close when the final blow came. The stream of people moving away from the center of the city flowed like raging river. There was little time to gather possessions. There was no use stopping to ask for assistance. Everyone else was headed in the same path. And as he turned back for one more glimpse at what was once the most familiar skyline in his world, he said: "How lonely sits the city that once was full of people! How like a widow she has become, she that was great among the nations! She weeps bitterly in the night, with tears on her cheeks."

Tradition says that the prophet Jeremiah spoke these words, found at the beginning of the book of Lamentations, as he fled Jerusalem with his fellow citizens while the city was destroyed by the Babylonians. As he looks back he laments that this fortress of a city, once believed impenetrable because of its location, and God's favor, was going up in flames. The temple in Jerusalem, the most spectacular and powerful symbol of God's presence for Jeremiah and his people, was devastated. And as he moves away from the scene, looking back over his shoulder, Jeremiah is struck by the emptiness of this once vibrant place. "How lonely sits the city that was once full of people!"

Watching scenes from lower Manhattan this week in the wake of the suicide attacks on the Twin Towers brought this scripture to mind. We saw people fleeing the site. We saw the devastation on their faces. And we saw one of the most recognizable landmarks in this country, located in one of the most thriving districts in the world, suddenly vanish. The area is now a ghost town except for the emergency workers heroically searching the rubble for any sign of life. "How lonely sits the city that was once full of people! She weeps bitterly in the night, with tears on her cheeks."

We have wept this week, and we continue to weep, not only for those lost in New York City, but also for those who died in Washington D.C. and Pennsylvania. A cloud of grief has settled on us and it is right that we weep for our dead, and pray for their families. But part of the grief we feel is not just for those strangers we are watching on television; we are also weeping for ourselves. The emptiness of the city is a symbol for the emptiness in our souls. We have lost something more than people and buildings this week. We have lost part of our security, part of our freedom, and much of our joy. Our world changed on Tuesday, and we, too, weep bitterly in the night with tears on our cheeks.

But in the midst of our national grief, as is often the case when tragedy strikes us, some things have become clear. We suddenly have recognized what is important and what is trivial.

So much felt trivial this week. Small concerns and irritants seemed pointless even to consider. We knew there were far more substantial things on which to focus. This hit me profoundly on Friday night when I went to the airport to pick up my mother. Because of the new guidelines no one was allowed to go to the gates to welcome their loved ones. So we all waited in a fairly confined area, watching the escalator as people descended from on high. And time after time when someone stepped off of the escalator there was a person there to clutch them and hold on to them. These were not your typical airport hugs and kisses. Some people clung to each other for thirty seconds, not giving a thought to the crowd watching them. We all understood. We all knew what was important.

But there were other things that became clear for me this week. The goodness of God and God's creation were manifested in countless heroic deeds and loving gestures in the face of these awful events. I heard from many of you who are concerned about our Muslim friends in Raleigh. I saw many of you gather for the prayer vigils and services we held this week to mourn and hope and pray. I felt the intensity of your commitments as you expressed what you would be doing to make this world a better place in light of Tuesday's unspeakable attacks. The nature of God's world is not revealed when something horrible happens. No, the nature of God's world is revealed in the just and loving reactions to that horror.

Another clear revelation that came to me this week is the fact that we are truly not alone. We have heard from our sister church in Matanzas, Cuba. They send their love and prayers today as they grieve with us. I had a lovely note from a friend who is the pastor of the South Ybarra Baptist Church in Melbourne, Australia. He wanted us at Pullen to know that his church would be praying specifically for us on this Sunday. We have worshiped this week with our sisters and brothers from Temple Beth Or; we are planning to be a part of an interfaith service that will include Muslims and other faith traditions, and it is all a powerful reminder that we are in this together. Our grief has no boundaries, and our mutual concern and love have no boundaries, either.

Sadly, some painful truths became clear this week as well. We were reminded that there is a dark side to religious faith, a violent side, and its power to persuade people to do and say odious things is truly frightening. The people who committed these atrocities appear to have done so in the name of God and as an act of religious martyrdom. But let us remember, if indeed the perpetrators of these crimes were fundamentalist Muslims they no more represent the truth of Islam than the Ku Klux Klan represents the truth of Christianity. Every faith has adherents who believe their grip on the truth allows them to impose their hatred and bile on others.

Another thing that became painfully clear this week is the reality that our words matter. In recent years we have heard much rhetoric about America being a Christian nation. While this is historically inaccurate, and constitutionally absurd, many people in the church have perpetuated this annoying error in the name of civil religion. Now, what seemed like an irritant has the potential to divide us in a serious manner. Already Arab Americans and Muslims are becoming targets of violent words and deeds, and we are hearing declarations that people of Middle Eastern descent and Muslim heritage should leave this Christian country. Memories of Japanese internment camps during World War II should cause us to shudder at these things and vow to resist attempts to violate the rights of our fellow Americans.

But there is more rhetoric floating through the air that has grave potential. We have already declared war on an unidentified enemy and may be laying the groundwork for a battle with serious religious undertones. Christian America, as so many insist we are, appears to be gearing up for war with the Muslim world. Have we learned nothing in the thousand years since the Crusades? I fear the recklessness of our words, spoken from the anger of our grief, may push us to even more reckless actions. What we do in the coming months will sow the seeds of violence or peace for years to come. Let us pray that we can tone down our rhetoric and step back from the heat of the moment. Let us hope that our President and the congress will act with prudence and justice.

But more than anything else this week it became clear to me that we are citizens of two realms. We are citizens of this great country, but we are also citizens of God's realm, the Peaceable Kingdom. And while we would like to believe that the goals, and values, and purposes of these two realms always coincide, of course they do not. There are moments when we have to decide whose values we will embrace. Will it be the vengeance and retaliation of military might, or will it be the way of the peasant carpenter who said, "Love your enemies and pray for those who persecute you." These are hard choices, and I do not wish to minimize the complexity of our current situation, but the values and goals are not the same. Our dual citizenship puts us in a difficult place. I pray we have the wisdom and love to choose well.

The sight was one of incredible horror. For those who watched it was indescribable. How could others, so cruel, believing to be acting zealously for their God, perform such a heinous crime? The death of the innocent, for them, was explained away as an expression of their religious faith. According to them, their enemy had to die. Those who grieve ask, 'If this could happen to the innocent, what is to prevent it from happening to us?' The crowd stood back, stunned, filled with all kinds of emotion. A darkness covered the land. Some feared for their very lives. Others cried, uncontrollably, hysterically. Friends and relatives held each other, caught between helplessness and grief. But to make matters worse, there were those who laughed, mocked, the senseless death of the innocent that caused so many others to despair. The natural human response is anger, hatred, the vow for revenge. The divine response, however, of the innocent hanging from the cross was, 'God, forgive them, for they know not what they do.'"
(Adapted from Stephen Portner, Lightstreet United Methodist Church)

PRAYERS

The Right Reverend Claude E. Payne, D. D.
Bishop of Texas
Episcopal Diocese of Texas

*(Bishop Claude E. Payne has written this prayer for use in the aftermath of the
September 11, 2001 disaster as appropriate.)*

Almighty God, eternal source of comfort for all victimized, source of strength for all bereaved and source of hope for all who grieve, we turn to you in this time of anxiety and stress, knowing you are our hope and strength, a very present help in trouble. Help us, we pray, in the midst of our uncertainties and fears, and in the tradition of the faithful through the centuries, to use this time of horror to recover from ravages of the demonic which we face.

Enable us to utilize our strengths and our resources, our accumulated wisdom and experience, together with the promise and power we have from you our God. Keep before us our calling as people of faith, that in times of crises we are challenged to exercise our spiritual resources to restore confidence and support those who have been devastated, as well as to address the sense of loss with those in our immediate midst and in ourselves as well.

So hallow this time, we pray, that as we move through this period of depression, we may be restored, even as we pray that those lives who have been taken may be even now raised in your nearer and fuller presence. Remembering that weeping may spend the night, but joy comes in the morning, may we renew our strength in you and in the power you give to enable the triumph of good over evil, love over hate, and light over darkness. This we pray in the name of the one who endured the same brutality in another age, only to rise again to a higher glory, your Son, Jesus Christ our Lord.   Amen

STRUGGLING FOR THE WORDS
Scripture: Romans 12:9 – 13:10

The Rev. James C. Peck, Jr., Minister
First Congregational Church, United Church of Christ
Austin, Minnesota

-Excerpts-
September 16, 2001

We should take Paul's words to the early Christians in Rome seriously, difficult as they are to hear and to follow. I am reminding us of these difficult teachings because we will move out of shock and outrage into a more troubling time both emotionally and intellectually.

We will debate our policies with regard to immigration, internal security, and foreign relations. These debates may become heated, but they need not become hateful. We will cease to be Americans if we turn on each other. And we will cease to be Christians if we stop loving our neighbor. "Do not repay anyone evil for evil, but take thought for what is noble in the sight of all," writes Paul.

This past week was not a week only for words, but also for images. Perhaps we should call them seens—that's s-e-e-n-s—things we have seen but still cannot really believe happened.

These are "seens" we will never forget. We will never forget the hurtful, painful moments and events. If we dwell on *them*, if we pick at these images like the wound they are, we may slow our own healing. Scars do need to form, my friends, for us to move ahead.

I offer you two images that may help you.

The first is an editorial cartoon in Wednesday's St. Paul paper. It shows the Statue of Liberty kneeling on her pedestal, her torch across her lap, a hand covering her face as she trembles, sobs, and mourns.

In my mind, I drew two more cartoons. On Monday morning, she stands up again, wipes her eyes, and brushes off the dust and ash.

On Tuesday morning, she thrusts the torch back into the sky, its bright beams of freedom piercing the evil still lurking in our world.

And remember that there *is* a force in the universe that overcomes death with life. It is the God of Abraham and Sarah, of Hagar and Ishmael, the God of our Savior Jesus Christ, and our God. The cross is the symbol for Christians of God's conquering power.

Dwell on it, and allow its transforming beams of grace to defeat the evil that would creep into our hearts. Amen.

GROWING A SOUL, CHANGING THE WORLD

Rev. Diane Teichert
First Parish Unitarian Universalist-Canton, Massachusetts
Canton, Massachusetts

September 16, 2001

At times such as these, we need one another. At times such as these, we are drawn to be together. At times such as these, we need religion—for the roots of the word "religion" merely mean "to bind together."

But, *what* kind of religion is it that we need?

Usually my sermons in September are designed to be somehow introductory, for the benefit of newcomers after our summer's hiatus. So it was for today. The short sermon description that appeared in our monthly newsletter for today's service said, "Unitarian Universalism offers a vision of love and justice that is both personal and public—good news the world needs to hear. Please bring your friends and neighbors who you think would like to know who we are and what we believe."

Today, as I looked out at the fuller than usual pews at the start of the service before our young people and their teachers left, I saw that some of you *did* bring your friends and neighbors, and that other newcomers are here today as well, plus many regulars and numerous some-time-attenders. Somehow, I *doubt* you were drawn here by my teaser in the newsletter!

At times such as these, we need each other. At times such as these, we need to be reminded of, and be deeply and personally bound together by, our Unitarian Universalist good news of love and justice. We need to shine its light on our personal, and our public, responses to the events on Tuesday and since.

We need our religion now, some of us—many of us—just to get by. These past days haven't been easy. There have been times of intense emotion of incredible range and even times of disassociation with the whole event as if we had no feelings at all. It's been a crazed emotional roller coaster; we've been dazed by repeated frightening images and constant commentary. There's been sorrow, fear, anger, helplessness, solidarity, outrage, compassion, worry, desire for revenge, regret, vulnerability, energy, despondency, and probably more.

For some of you and thousands of others, there is terrible grief for loved ones and acquaintances who are known to have perished, or, what may be even worse, are feared to have perished. The anguish of the unknown has been so hard for so many. For the thousands of witnesses and survivors, there is more than terrible grief for the co-workers who they left behind—there is also terror in their awful memories of falling and crushed bodies, flying debris, and collapsing buildings.

For some of us here and thousands of others, there is tremendous relief that the ones we know who work in Lower Manhattan or at the Pentagon are safe, and that the friend or relative who was supposed to take that fateful flight or routinely show up for work that morning didn't.

In some deep and profound sense, though, both the terrible grief and that tremendous relief seem to resonate inside us on the same chord. And, so, we are bound together, deeply connected to each other by this tragedy whether it is grief or relief that we feel.

Even those of us who have no personal connection through grief or relief, feel such sorrow for the victims and their friends and families. This public mourning may reverberate with your own past sorrows—loved ones who have died, painful endings, depressions—so that the depth of your sorrow may take you by surprise. It's as though this public mourning we experience today is amply magnified by the unrelated previous personal sorrows we've known.

But, most of us have known grief and sorrow before, and we can bear it now. With a little help from those who love us, we are learning again this week that love is stronger than death and outlives it. Love lasts. It outlives grief, sorrow and even death.

More difficult than grief and sorrow are the feelings of fearful new vulnerability and unfamiliar outrage that many Americans have been feeling. How do we go on with daily life, how do we help our children go on, when we fear for our personal safety and theirs? What do we peaceful people do with our anger and outrage?

First, I believe we must accept these difficult feelings as facts. What we feel is real, and suppressing feelings does not banish them. It helps to use words—in prayer and meditation, or with adult friends or family, or your minister (who was this past week, as always, deeply honored by your trust). Please, don't suffer alone.

Second, feelings of fear and anger need not command our will. Our feelings may give energy to our actions, but let reason set their direction.

Our new-found fear should energize us—as a nation and as individuals—to take reasonable and ever-improving protective actions in our airports and elsewhere, but beyond that let us choose hope over fear. Let us choose to trust in the good hearts of most people rather than be immobilized by fear of the few. Let not our fear diminish our capacity for love. Let us be sure to especially love as ourselves our Muslim and Arab neighbors, or anyone who could be confused with them. Can we even open our hearts to the Palestinians who danced in the streets when they heard the terrible news of our dead and injured? How did we come to be so hated?

Likewise, our new-found anger should energize us—as a nation and as individuals—to take action toward justice. I believe the events of the past week call for two kinds of justice, a two-sided sword of justice: both retribution and re-distribution.

On the one hand, I believe our country should seek retribution, taking reasonable and decisive action against what appears to be a network of terrorists both here and abroad determined to undermine our security as a means to their larger aims. This side of the sword, I believe, is about targeted strikes, arrests and trials of individuals based on intelligent information; it is not about imminent military attacks against entire communities or countries. Done well, it will be a long process, making slow progress. It will require the services of our best minds and sacrifices from Americans financially and in our personal freedoms and conveniences. Done poorly, it will be a quick flash, producing even more hate in response, and possibly nuclear chaos.

And, on the other hand, I believe we must seek another kind of justice: a re-distribution of the goods and benefits of civilization that Americans have enjoyed far in excess to what we really need, to the great detriment of impoverished people in the Middle East and elsewhere who lack even the minimum food, shelter, health and education. This side of the sword, I believe, is about democratic and economic empowerment, not foreign aid and loans to corrupt governments. Done well, it will be a long process, making slow progress. It will require the services of our best minds and sacrifices from Americans accustomed to material gain and abundance. Done poorly, it will be a quick fix, producing even more corruption in response, and increased terrorism.

These are the ways in which reason directs my fear and anger as I come up out of the shock and sorrow of the past week: Reasonable self-protection as individuals and as a nation. Love of our neighbors. Retributive justice for those who supported the attacks and/or plan others. More equitable re-distribution of the world's resources.

I acknowledge that reason may be directing *your* fear and anger in other directions. In our Unitarian Universalist tradition, this is a free pulpit and yours is a free pew; we may from time to time not see eye to eye. But, given that we share the same religious tradition, I feel confidant that *reason* has been your guide. Reason is, after all, one of the three hallmarks (along with freedom and tolerance) of the Unitarian side of our religious tradition, going as far back as the early Roman church when our predecessors applied reason to the doctrine of the Trinity and rejected it.

Not only do I feel confident that your views have been guided by reason, but I also know that your reason and mine are drawn to the same set of ideals. These ideals are expressed in various ways in our tradition—in the covenant of this congregation that we recite each week, in its Mission Statement printed on the back of your order of worship, and in the Covenant adopted in 1985 by the Unitarian Universalist Association of congregations of which First Parish is a member.

The latter is printed in the front of our hymnal. If you would please open your hymnal to Hymn #1 and then flip one page back toward the title page, on the left side, you will see in large capital letters "We the member congregations…covenant to affirm and promote…" and immediately below are the seven statements that comprise what we call the Principles and Purposes of that Covenant, our current best effort at expressing our ideals. I thought we might benefit from reading them aloud together.

"The inherent worth and dignity of every person;
Justice, equity, and compassion in human relations;
Acceptance of one another and encouragement to
spiritual growth in our congregations.
A free and responsible search for truth and meaning;
The right of conscience and the use of the democratic process
within our congregations and in society at large;
The goal of world community with peace, liberty, and justice for all;
Respect for the interdependent web of all existence of which we are a part."

"Inherent worth and dignity of every person…Justice, equity, and compassion in human relations…" *Every* person? What is *justice*, for whom? In our present anger, in the complexity of the global world disorder, how can we even know what these words mean, never mind promote them?

Our challenge in the coming days and weeks will be to understand, hold onto and promote our religious ideals in the face of fear and anger, danger and chaos. Meeting this challenge is spiritual work, and it is best done—not alone—but in community, together, here, with others who share our ideals.

As the late A. Powell Davies, activist minister of All Souls Unitarian Church in Washington DC once said, "life is just a chance to grow a soul." At times of crisis, the chance to grow a soul looms larger, and the necessity to do so is all the greater. Life is just a chance to grow a soul—and, for that, we need one another together.

On Friday morning, I was on my way to Canton when I heard on the radio about President Bush's request that Americans go to a house of worship for prayer on their lunch hour. "Duh," I realized, "then the houses of worship better get ready."

I painted two big signs for out front by the sidewalk proclaiming "Open at Noon." I cleaned up after the tenants the night before, straightened the pew cushions, set out memorial candles for people to light, put a plant on the altar table, lit the chalice, and I opened the sanctuary doors wide. People trickled in, sat in the silence, maybe lit a candle, and eventually left—maybe fifteen all tolled by 1:30.

I remember one young woman, a stranger to me, who sat longer than the others. I spoke with her as she got up to leave. I asked her if someone she knew had died on Tuesday or was still missing. She said, "No, I just feel so sad for all those people and their families. It's so terrible." Her eyes welled up, and she wiped away the tears. She went on to say, "We've had it too good here, compared to the rest of the world." "Yes," I responded, "and we've been smug in our false sense of security." She nodded. And quickly added, "Not that I don't feel like dropping a bomb on somebody." She paused. I waited. "Sitting over there,' she concluded, nodding toward her pew, "I realized I really have to work on it. Or the anger I feel will win out."

If we didn't know it before, we surely know it now: we all have spiritual work to do, of one kind or another. Our religion provides the support community for that work, and the ideals that might guide it.

The events of the past week have shown us the worst—we hope it's the worst—of what humans can do. But, they've also shown how the worst can bring out the best in compassion and self-giving. We can't forget the horror of this week, but we must remember the good. And, we must do what humans can do when bound together—grow our souls and make the world a more just, and safer, place for all. Amen.

SILENCE: SILVER AND GOLD
A Time To Keep Silent
Scripture: Ecclesiastes 3:7

Reverend. Dr. Curtis W. Harris
Union Baptist Church
Hopewell, Virginia

-Excerpts-
September 16, 2001

There is a common proverb which says, "Speech is silver and silence is golden." There is a silence that means cowardice; there is a silence that means stability; and there is a speech that is more precious than gold:

I.   There is the silence of emotional fullness. It is a physiological fact that great emotions choke the utterance. For example, in one of Jesus' parables (Matthew 22:12) , the king reprimands a guest who had come improperly dressed. "And he said unto him. Friend, how cometh thou in hither not having a wedding garment? And he was speechless."

When we discovered that terrorists had attacked our Nation's Pentagon, the World Trade Center in New York, and a plane in Pennsylvania, we were all shocked, speechless, and silent.

II.   There is a silence of righteous resignation. It is said that Aaron held his peace. Also, the Psalmist said, "I was dumb, I opened not my mouth; because thou didst it." (Psalm 39:9)

III.   Then there is the silence of sincere respect. This was the silence Christ displayed before his judges. Anyone who stands and listens to the language of ignorance, bigotry, and personal insults addressed to him in an offensive spirit and offers no reply, exerts a far greater power upon the minds of his assailants.

The Unseen Enemy Strikes

"Give to the Winds Thy Fears"
T.U.E.S (The Unseen Enemy Strikes)
Prayer Answered
September 11, 2001
United We Stand
On the Sabbath After: A Different World for Me

Chapter 6

Give to the Winds Thy Fears

Give to the winds thy fears; Hope, and be undismayed;
God hears thy sighs and counts thy tears; God shall lift up thy head.

Thro' waves, and clouds, and storms, He gently clears thy way;
Wait thou His time; so shall this night Soon end in joyous day.

What tho' thou rulest not! Yet heav'n, and earth, and hell
Proclaim, God sitteth on the throne, and rulest all things well.

Far, far above thy thought His counsel shall appear,
When fully he the work has wrought, That caused thy needless fear.

Amen

Paul Gerhardt, 1653   *John Wesley, 1739*

T.U.E.S. (THE UNSEEN ENEMY STRIKES)
Scripture: Ephesians 6:12

James S. Perkins, Pastor
Oak Hill Baptist Church
Buckingham, Virginia
and
Chief Cornerstone Baptist Church
Dillwyn, Virginia

September 16, 2001

Tuesday morning, September 11, 2001 at approximately 9:00 a.m., another day had begun in these United States. America, the most powerful nation with her military might; America, the wealthiest nation with her economical and industrial might; America, alive and well! Without warning, The Unseen Enemy Strikes.

T - The Ruler of darkness (Ephesians.6:12); the prince of the power of the air (Ephesians 2:2); the god of this age (2 Corinthians 4:4); the king of death (Hebrew 2:14); the prince of this world (John 12:31); the deceiver (Revelations. 20:10); the wicked one (Matthew 13:34), bringing death to thousands of defenseless people and destruction, fear, and injury to many others.

U - Unseen, they are invisible, they have the ability to control humans (Judges 9:23); they possess intelligence (2 Corinthians 2:11; 11:3); they possess memory (Matthew 4:6); they possess desire (Luke 22:31); they possess wrath (Revelations 12:12); they possess great organizational ability (Revelations 12:12); they have their sacrifices (1 Corinthians 10:20); they blind men to the truth (2 Corinthians 4:4).

E - Enemy — Who is the enemy? Will the real enemy please stand up? The humans who carried out the plan of death and destruction on **T.U.E.S.**, September 11, are all dead. They were human sacrifices for evil. Who is the real enemy? Is it Bin Laden and the Taliban army? No, I don't think so! Bin Laden and his followers are just humans used by the Real Enemy! The real enemy is unseen and invisible. The real enemy is Satan and his demons (1 Peter 5:8); Apollyon-destroyer (Revelations 9:11); Belial—vileness—ruthlessness (2 Corinthians 6:15); Leviathan—one who dwells in the sea of humanity.

S - Strikes - What is his mission? To lie, steal and kill. He steals the word of God from the human heart. (Matthew 13:19) and replaces it with a lie, for he is a liar and the father of it (John. 8:44; Genesis 3:4-5). He blinds men to the truth (2 Corinthians 4:4); he resists the prayers of God's servants (Daniel 10:12-13); he hinders the works of God's servants (1 Thesolonians 2:18); he instigates false doctrine (1 Timothy 3:1-4).

Yes, my Christian friends, the enemy has been made visible through the tragic events of September 11. Please be mindful that we of the "household of faith" fight not against flesh and blood. The war that we are engaged in is spiritual. Our Commander-in-Chief is Jesus Christ, the righteous. He said, "The thief does not come except to steal and to kill and to destroy. I am come that they may have life and that they might have it more abundantly." (John. 10:10) I say to you, "Put on the whole armor of God that you might be able to stand against the wiles (tricks) of the enemy—the (devil). (Ephesians 6:11)

Church, it is praying time! "I will call upon the Lord who is worthy to be praised: so shall I be saved from mine enemies. The sorrows of death compassed me, and the floods of ungodly men made me afraid. The sorrows of hell surround me; the snares of death confronted me. In my distress I called upon the Lord, and cried out to my God. He heard my voice from his temple, and my cry came before Him, even to His ears." (Psalm 18: 3-6) Like the Psalmist, let us pray to the Father.

> *Father, in the name of Jesus, we give thanks for the United States and its government. We hold up in prayer before you the men and women who are in positions of authority. We pray for the President, the Senators and Representatives, the Judges of our land, the Policemen and Firemen, as well as the Governors and Mayors and for all those who are in authority over us in any way. We pray that the Spirit of the Lord rest upon them. Father, our troops have been sent into battle. We petition you, Lord according to Psalm 91, for the safety of our military personnel. We look beyond human instruments of conflict and address the forces and authorities and rulers of darkness and powers in the spiritual world. We petition heaven to turn our troops into real peacekeeping forces by pouring out the glory of God through our men and women. Lord, use them as instruments of righteousness to defeat the plans of the devil. In the name of Jesus Christ we pray. Amen*

PRAYER ANSWERED

M. Alice Johnson
Ministers' Wives and Ministers' Widows Alliance of Petersburg and Vicinity
Petersburg, Virginia

I asked for strength that I might achieve;
He made me weak that I might obey.
I asked for health that I might do greater things;
I was given grace that I might do better things.
I asked for riches that I might be happy;
I was given poverty that I might be wise.
I asked for power that I might have the praise of men;
I was given weakness that I might feel the need of God.
I asked for all things that I might enjoy life;
I was given life that I might enjoy all things.
I received nothing that I asked for, all that I hoped for,
My prayer was answered.

Author Unknown

SEPTEMBER 11, 2001
Scripture: Luke 13:34

The Reverend Majorie H. Holm, Chaplain
Deerfield Community Chapel, Deerfield Correctional Center
Capron, Virginia

September 16, 2001

*"O Jerusalem, Jerusalem, the city that kills the prophets and stones those who
are sent to it! How often have I desired to gather your children together
as a hen gathers her brood under her wings, and you were not willing!"*

We think that the city to focus on this week is New York City, where five thousand people were slaughtered, cremated in towers of melting steel, crushed by beams and boulders and stabbed by flying glass daggers. We think that the city to focus on is Washington D. C., where 200 people died in the Pentagon, and perhaps thousands more were targets of failed attempts. We think that the city to focus on is Baghdad—the only government that did not condemn the acts of the terrorists this week—Baghdad where Saddam Hussein disclaimed any responsibility for the terrorism, but congratulated the terrorists for their successful mission. We think the city to focus on is Kabul, Afghanistan, where the Talibahn government simultaneously condemns terrorism with their lips but harbors known terrorists by their actions. But neither Tripoli, nor Tehran, nor even Kabul is the source of terrorism—*"O' Jerusalem, Jerusalem, the city that kills the prophets and stones those who are sent to it. How often have I desired to gather your children together as a hen gathers her brood under her wings, and you were not willing!"* The source of terrorism is Jerusalem. The holy city of Judaism, the holy city of Christianity, the holy city of Islam is, as Jesus knew, also an unholy city of Satan. For from Jerusalem, the same Satan who tempted Jesus from pinnacle of the temple two thousand years ago is enticing people to unspeakable sin in the name of religion. Whether they claim to be Jewish, Muslim, or Christian, the same religious fundamentalist extremists who killed Jesus two thousand years ago— the same people who believe in their demented Satanically deranged minds that God would allow anybody to kill his own children in his name—slaughtered millions of people in the concentration camps of Germany fifty years ago and slaughtered the thousands in New York City and Washington D. C. five days ago.

The enemy is not Islam or the Muslims. The enemy is not Judaism or the Jews. The enemy is evil itself—the enemy's tools are the ones he has always used successfully: intolerance, hatred and fear. The *enemy* is the anti-Semitism of Kristalnacht. The *enemy* is the anti-Muslim sentiment that threw bricks through the windows of the Islamic Center at Old Dominion University last week and issued bomb threats against the mosques.

The *enemy* is the racism that caused Klan members to terrorize Afro-Americans. The *enemy* is the sexism that denied women their rightful places of leadership in the world. The *enemy* is the homophobia that tells gay and lesbian people that they are somehow less than fully human and undeserving of God's love. The *enemy* is the evil hate that caused Ted Kasinzski and Timothy McVeigh to build bombs of terror. The *enemy* has plucked out all eyes for eyes, and teeth for teeth, limbs for limbs and lives for lives throughout the long and arduous history of the Middle East. And the *enemy* gorges itself upon the human race—sucking life out of both the terrorists and the people they terrorize. Even though evil's spiritual tentacles reach throughout the world, its spiritual headquarters is in the same place as the spiritual headquarters of the three great religions of the world—Christianity, Judaism and Islam—Jerusalem. For you see, evil masquerades always as good. Evil always dresses up in the religious clothing of Judaism, Islam and Christianity and pretends that somehow God has endorsed hatred and murder.

"O Jerusalem, Jerusalem, the city that kills the prophets and stones those who are
sent to it! How often have I desired to gather your children together as a
hen gathers her brood under her wings, and you were not willing!"

But the enemy has picked on the wrong people this time. As devastating as the attacks were on us, the enemy is being annihilated by the loving kindness of our responses. As terrorized as people were watching the planes shatter buildings, the enemy is even more horror stricken by every cell phone call from the crashing airplanes and collapsing of the Twin Towers where the last words on dying peoples lips was not hate, but how much they loved each other. As much as evil rejoiced at the taking of innocent blood, it is agonizing in fear for every pint of blood that has been donated to the Red Cross throughout our world. As much as Satan celebrated every tumbling brick and cascading sheets of glass, he agonizes over every bucket of rubble cleared away by careful and loving hands. As much as the evil one plotted to bring cacophony (disharmony) to the world, he screamed in pain to hear the first time in history the British Army Band playing the *Star Spangled Banner* at the changing of the guard at Buckingham Palace; or when the stock markets in Europe paused for a moment of silence and stopped all world trading, or when bells rang in every church across the country at twelve noon on Friday, or when nearly the entire world is brought to bended knee in sorrow and grief for people they did not even know. As much as Satan wanted to bring political disunity, he is in torment as NATO has declared this attack to be an attack on each and every member nation.

The point is this: if we want revenge for this incredible act, let us take revenge in doing good—knowing that every good deed done, every comforting word spoken, every merciful tear shed, and every generous thought is beating down Satan under our feet.

For the Evil One has not triumphed. The Evil One has not destroyed over *5,000* lives in this action—the Lord of life has had them firmly in his embrace all the time. The righteous souls, both dead and alive, are still in the hand of God and no torment will ever touch them again. At the National Cathedral prayer service in Washington D. C., Billy Graham said, "The people who perished in this disaster are with God, and it is so wonderful, they don't want to come back." They cannot be hurt by the Jerusalem that crucified our Lord, they cannot be harmed by the Jerusalem that stoned the prophets, they cannot be injured by the Jerusalem that plants car bombs, they cannot be rendered homeless by the Jerusalem that bulldozes down Palestinian homes, they cannot be destroyed by the Jerusalem where tower and temple fall to dust, they cannot be killed by the Jerusalem that launches religious wars—for they are no longer subjects in the Old Jerusalem. They are in the New Jerusalem.

Make no mistake, Our Lord Jesus Christ by his death and resurrection has already conquered the Evil One. Satan is mortally wounded. What we are seeing in this world is the Evil

One's dying agony—a last desperate effort. Regardless of what we do as a military response at home and on foreign shores—and we must do whatever is necessary to assure that this will not happen again in our lifetimes. *We must take that action as a matter of prevention, not vengeance.* For vengeance belongs to God. "Vengeance is mine; I will repay," says the Lord. But it is our solemn task to prevent terrorist activities from happening to the United States or any other nation in the world ever again.

Meanwhile we can hasten the death of the Evil One, we can help God beat down Satan under our feet by doing good. And let me assure you that by doing that, by combating intolerance with friendship, and hatred with love, we will cause Satan great agony and hasten his demise. Simply by being the good and great and decent and kind and loving people we are in this nation, we can show the world how absolutely wrong and evil our attackers really are.

I heard Nathan Baxter, the Dean of the Washington Cathedral, interviewed on television Friday morning. He said, "The one thing we must not do is to become the enemy whom we deplore." That is the one thing we must never do, no matter how much we grieve, hurt and feel anger.

Wiping evil from the earth is not something even the superpower of the United States can do. But, be of good cheer, because it is God's good pleasure to do for us what we cannot do for ourselves. Satan's doom is sure and certain in God's good time—when we all will enter the New Jerusalem.

Amen.

UNITED WE STAND

Words & Music by
Dr. Martha H. Sobaje, Minister of Music & Education
Phillips Memorial Baptist Church
Cranston, Rhode Island

© Martha H. Sobaje 2001

Verse 1
America, a people diverse,
America, for better or worse,
America, a land that we love,
We will protect her with help from above.

Chorus
United we stand, each woman and man.
With God as our leader, we say "I can!"
With love in our hearts and peace on our lips,
United we stand, throughout this great land!

Verse 2
America, a people so blessed,
America, from the East to the West,
America, the land of the free,
America, where we want to be.

Chorus
United we stand, each woman and man.
With God as our leader, we say "I can!"
With love in our hearts and peace on our lips,
United we stand, throughout this great land!

Permission to photocopy is granted by the composer.

ON THE SABBATH AFTER: A DIFFERENT WORLD FOR ME

Bashir Ahmed
Baltimore, Maryland, USA
(born in Afghanistan)

September 2001

On the Sabbath after, it was a different world for me. I became filled with a feeling of despair. I longed to be with my family: my wife, my six year old daughter, my three year old son and especially my newborn daughter, whom I've never met. You see, even though I'm a U.S. citizen, I was born in Afghanistan.

Now on the Sabbath after, I'm filled with despair because I know war is inevitable. My native country has witnessed war for many years now. But this Sabbath it feels like we are on the brink of a new terror.

Not all is despair however. I'm comforted by the fact that a couple of years ago my small-young family moved to Pakistan. Pakistan, though relatively close to the battlefield, is not a direct target for retaliation. I am comforted by that, for now my family is out of harm's way.

I am still a worried husband and father. Politics prevent me from bringing my family here, even though I am a U.S. citizen. They have granted my wife permission but not my kids. Now you tell me if that makes any sense. Am I to just leave a couple of toddlers, one with heart failure problems, to roam a war-torn country by themselves?

Other individuals might be filled with rage. I, however, believe in Almighty-God. I find comfort in him. A deep calm fills me, for I believe that He has my family protected under his wings, and He looks after them day and night.

Most importantly, I find comfort and give thanks that my family is alive, well, and has food and shelter. The victims of this terror and their families are the ones we need to pray for most right now.

Sacred Silence

"Blessed Quietness"
Sacred Silence
The Face of Evil
The Sin of Not Seeing
The Wrath of God

Chapter

7

Blessed Quietness

Joys are flowing like a river
Since the Comforter has come;
He abides with us forever,
Makes the trusting heart His home.

Bringing life and health and gladness
All around, this heav'nly Guest
Banished unbelief and sadness,
Chang'd our weariness to rest.

Like the rain that falls from heaven,
Like the sunlight from the sky,
So the Holy Ghost is given,
Coming on us from on high.

See, a fruitful field is growing,
Blessed fruit of righteousness;
And the streams of life are flowing
In the lonely wilderness.

What a wonderful salvation,
Where we always see His face!
What a perfect habitation,
What a quiet resting place!

CHORUS
Blessed quietness, holy quietness—
What assurance in my soul!
On the stormy sea He speaks peace to me—
How the billows cease to roll!

Manie P. Ferguson
W. S. Marshall
Adapted by James M. Kirk

SACRED SILENCE

Pastor Frank Hall
Unitarian Church in Westport
Westport, Connecticut

September 16, 2001

THE SILENCE OF GRIEF

The events of this past week are, as they say, "Of Biblical proportions." Many stories that are a collection of legends and myths, mixed with history, come to mind.

One that came to my mind is the story of Job. You know the story. Or do you?

God and Satan devise a plan to test poor, innocent Job. God was bragging about him and rubbing Job's goodness into Satan's face. So Satan said, "Let's put him to the test," and God agreed. Satan heaped enormous, overwhelming suffering on Job.

The story says that Job's three closest friends heard about the great tragedies which Job had suffered and they came to him. As they approached, they didn't recognize him, at first. Then they realized that this big mess was their old friend Job. The poem says, "They raised their voices and wept; and they rent their robes and sprinkled dust upon their heads…"

Then, the poignant poem says, they stayed with him for a week: "They sat with him…seven days and seven nights, and no one spoke a word, for they saw that his suffering was very great."

What an amazing thing to do: to sit together for an entire week without uttering a word. This is the source of the Jewish custom of sitting shiva; the word "shiva" is from the Hebrew word for "seven."

Now that's a sacred silence. When they finally broke their silence a friend says: "If one ventures a word with you, will you be offended? Yet who can keep from speaking?"

We were reminded of the story of Job this week. Oh that we could take a lesson and sit shiva for a week, or even a day or two…to mourn, and to express our humility as well as our overwhelming sense of grief.

Job's friends finally spoke, and Job was, indeed, offended. They told him that God was a just God, so he got what he deserved. They told him that God was a merciful God, so he deserved even worse punishment.

These theological assertions were not pleasing to Job! This terrible theology which Hebrew poets put in the mouths of Job's friends thousands of years ago, turns God into a monster. Yes, Job was offended, and so am I, and so are you. Job told his friends that his suffering was bad enough, but they made it worse.

WHERE WERE YOU…on the morning of September 11?

On Tuesday morning I heard from our church sexton, Bobby, that a plane had hit one of the towers at the World Trade Center. "What a terrible accident," I thought.

Then I got on my motorcycle and drove to a regularly scheduled clergy meeting in Mt. Kisco, not knowing that the plane that hit the North tower was not an accident. I had no radio on the bike.

After arriving at the meeting we listened in shock to an eye-witness account of things unfolding and learned about the attack on the Pentagon as well as the World Trade Center and knew, then, that America was under attack...an attack more horrendous and far-reaching than Pearl Harbor.

I came back to my office, to re-write my newsletter, my Dear Friends letter.

Then I telephoned the First Selectman's office and suggested a town-wide service of 'hope and healing.'

I was invited to a meeting of town officials at the Emergency Operations Center at the main firehouse in Westport.

The Police Chief, Fire Chief, First Selectwoman and various department heads briefed the clergy and one another. The atmosphere in the room was serious and somber, of course, but the Police and Fire Chiefs and the First Selectwoman provided a model of calm and a sense that they were in control.

They were making plans and formulating strategies for the terrible tasks that would unfold.

There was a sense that trustworthy people were in charge. There was a sense that we were safe, now, here in Westport.

As the meeting was coming to a close, the First Selectwoman asked me to organize the service I had suggested for the following night. Then she asked me to lead that group in prayer.

A SACRED SILENCE

I almost said, "Please ask someone else." During the meeting I had been watching the television monitor—no sound was needed. It was the first visuals I had seen, and I was stunned. I felt dazed, as if I had been hit over the head and rendered senseless, unable to think straight, much less to put coherent sentences together. I felt like I didn't have adequate words.

The room was packed with community leaders so we had to form concentric circles, holding hands for a time of prayer, and I wondered what words would come to me from that deep place, or if I would be able to tap into it. I said, to cover the uncomfortable silence, "We begin in silence." I don't know what else I said. I did not invoke a deity—I did not ask God to alter the universe for us, since such a request suggests that God had a hand in the disaster happening to begin with!

I asked that our leaders, those in this room and elsewhere, find the inner strength and wisdom to face the awesome assignments each of us, and each of them, faced.

I used Emerson's phrase: 'There is a deep power in which we exist...' This is the broadest way I know of to call upon those inner resources that we need to know is available to us.

The truth is, I felt inadequate to the task I'd been assigned in that moment—to offer an adequate prayer for this diverse group, most of whom expected me, as a clergyperson, to talk to God on their behalf...something like that.

Truth be told, I wasn't feeling the presence of any kind of god at that moment, and I've had a hard time with feeling the presence of the kind of god I hear other so-called religious people talking about.

That day I was consciously aware of feeling a very real and deep distance from any such thing as a god who is involved in this tragedy—a god who is involved in the day-to-day affairs of this world, to say nothing of the god invoked by religious fanatics—the Taliban, or Osama bin Laden.

In the hours and days since planes were turned into bombs and aimed at the Twin Towers and the Pentagon, I have listened to and read thousands of words, spoken by well-meaning religious and political leaders, written by colleagues, some who went on and on and on.

During most of my life I've felt like I have something to say and I appreciate the chance to say it. Even before my careers in teaching and ministry…as early as elementary school I remember wanting to be called on, wanting to be able to give the answers or give my opinion or idea.

Seldom have I felt such a loss for words. Seldom have I felt such a need for silence…a sacred silence that comes from respect and humility. Marianne Moore said, "The deepest feeling always shows itself in silence; not in silence but restraint."

Sometimes we experience a silence that is profound, a sacred silence…a respectful silence…a holy, devotional silence.

"Go placidly amid the noise and haste and remember what peace there may be in silence…nurture strength of spirit to shield you in sudden misfortune, but do not distress yourself with imaginings. Many fears are born of fatigue and loneliness…in the noisy confusion of life keep peace with your soul."

"…AND A TIME TO SPEAK"

But silence isn't always sacred.

Some silence is a form of shunning. When we've had a falling out with someone we say that 'we're not speaking.' Some silence is cowardly, as when we fail to speak up in the face of blatant racism, anti-Semitism, homophobia or xenophobia.

Not everyone who has been waving a flag this week is a patriotic American who wants to preserve the 'freedom and justice for all'—words they recite mindlessly when they pledge their allegiance to that flag. Some silence is not sacred.

No matter what happens in the days and weeks ahead, we must be ready and willing to speak up, to defend the Muslim and Arab-Americans who are living out their allegiance to this nation.

"For everything there is a season…a time to keep silent and a time to speak…a time to speak up!"

Fanatics attacked America on Tuesday in New York and Washington, and equally deranged fanatics attacked Arab-Americans in Bridgeport and San Francisco.

Some of the meanest, most dangerous madmen who ever walked this earth have been motivated by what they say is a sacred cause. Some of the most foul and obscene deeds have been committed in the name of religion. Some people drape themselves with a flag and commit atrocities, and patriotism is blemished the same way religion gets blemished by insensitive remarks.

As we respect the variety of faiths in which our brothers and sisters find comfort, may we also have the courage to speak against the prejudices which pave the road to violence.

We need one another, not simply to agree with ideas and opinions, not simply to have people willing to listen so we can get something off our chest, but to help us to 'know ourselves more moderately.'

We need one another, now, so that we can mourn and be comforted. We need one another, now, because this is a time of trouble; we need one another, now, to recall us to our best selves; we need one another, now, so that we can endure and continue the great task which remains before us:

To preserve this great nation, conceived in liberty and dedicated to the proposition that all are created equal. It is once again being 'tested.' It can endure. And with the help of that 'deep power in which we exist,' the best part of our human nature, which some call God…with help from that deep, inner source, it will endure!

Amen.

THE FACE OF EVIL

The Rev. Dr. Francis H. Wade
St. Alban's Episcopal Church
Washington, DC

September 16, 2001

Last Tuesday we decided to have a service of prayers for our nation here at St. Alban's. In preparing for that service I became aware of something that I had never realized before. Our Prayer Book with all of its prayers, eucharists and services fashioned over the centuries did not have anything that was an adequate response to an experience of evil on the scale of Tuesday's attacks. The first prayer ever written in English included the lines: "From the fury of the Norsemen, Good Lord deliver us." Fury means madness. During the plague years there were prayers about evil in the form of illness. But over recent years we quit praying about madness, tragedy and terror on this scale and allowed ourselves to think only of individual badness and community injustice.

It was not only the *Book of Common Prayer* that was little help. As near as I can tell none of our institutions or conditioned responses were ready for this expression of evil. People rushed to give blood, but there were too few survivors to use it. We dispatched an aircraft carrier to the waters off New York, a grand sight to be sure, but it might as well have been trying to protect us from the West Nile Virus for all the good it could do. Somehow our prosperity, self image, sentimental theology, priorities and I don't know what else have conspired to allow us to forget about the reality of evil. On September 11 we were reminded of it. I would like to talk with you about the evil that attacked our cities and continues to attack our souls.

Evil is a reality in life. It is a force whose origins and reasons we do not and cannot know. When the writer of Genesis told the story of the Fall of Humanity, the snake representing evil is just there in the garden. It has no explanation or portfolio; it is just there, like it is today, a reality and a force. Evil is that which seeks to destroy what God is calling into being. For humans it usually lives among our instincts alongside and sometimes mixed with love, hope, happiness, sentiment, courage, compassion and the other capacities that animate human life. Evil is not just a presence among us, it is also a force in life. We know it is a force if only because it requires effort to resist. Think of the last time you wrestled with temptation and recall that it took genuine effort. That is because evil is a force against which we can and must press. If dealing with addiction is part of your story, you know what a willful, crafty and persistent force evil is. The Genesis writer described the snake as "more subtle than any other creature." If you have ever experienced rage, you know how it can shed its subtlety and burst forth as epithet and a capacity to hurt others that we did not know was in us.

This past week has shown two of the ways that evil can affect human beings. It isolates the mind and kills the heart. When our minds are isolated from some of God's other children, we become very dangerous. An isolated mind disregards the essential value of others. Isolated minds allow others to become faceless, uniqueless, discounted and expendable. That sort of isolated thinking is the root of all prejudice. It is what allowed the hijackers to try to kill anyone in the buildings no matter who they might be. It allows some of us to hold all Muslims or Arabs accountable for the attacks, which makes as much sense as blaming all who know how to fly jets or those who own box cutters. But to a mind isolated by evil the association is easy. When evil kills the heart it takes away love, compassion, understanding, forgiveness and gentleness. It is only dead hearts that can act in cold calculation to distort the purposes of God. The hijackers spent years preparing for Tuesday; their hearts were dead before they started. The Middle East is filled with the rhetoric of dead hearts where people foolishly seek the absence of their neighbor rather than community with them. The hatred we let flourish in us is a heart-killer and we are as susceptible to it as those whose work we saw on Tuesday.

In the baptismal service there is a set of promises that usually go by with little notice. It is the call to renounce and resist evil. The candidates are asked "Do you renounce Satan and all the spiritual forces of wickedness that rebel against God?" "I renounce them" is the reply. "Do you renounce the evil powers of this world which corrupt and destroy the creatures of God?" "I renounce them," they reply. "Do you renounce all sinful desires which draw you from the love of God?" "I renounce them," say the candidates. You may notice that the words have a medieval sound to them. That is because we have avoided the reality of evil for so long we have not developed modern words to describe it. We must rely on our ancestors who knew this truth more completely than we do.

Renouncing evil at this point is going to be a difficult balancing act. Our nation is gearing up for war. War is sometimes right and sometimes necessary but it is never good. Think about that distinction for a moment. When the children of the one God are reduced to killing each other for whatever cause or necessity, it is not a good thing. It is not God's plan for earth or for the human family. We may need to do what war requires but as soon as we can we need to get back on the path that leads to where we all want to be. War itself will not take us there.

Resisting evil is also difficult, for evil can be as seductive as it is ugly. We could see the monstrous ugliness of evil in the pain caused on Tuesday. Yet there is something in us that cannot wait to do the same to someone else. That is evil and we have to resist it. If we do not resist its seductions, evil will lead us off the hard path that Jesus beckons us to follow and set us on the impossible path that spirals easily into cycles of revenge. We must begin now to resist evil—even as we prepare for the necessities of war, even as we begin to bury our dead—and to work for the better day when we can reconcile with those who hate us and break bread with those who have hurt us. That is a harder job for the heart than the task our eyes have finding the terrorists. It is a harder job for the soul than the work of grieving. But it is work that needs to be done if we are to renounce and resist evil.

C. S. Lewis once said that the two worst mistakes one can make about evil is to not take it seriously enough or to take it too seriously. For years we have done the former. We do not make much progress if we now jump to the latter and take it too seriously. Evil is a force that seeks to destroy us—but we are still here. It has not accomplished its goal. If evil had ultimate power, we would be long gone and far worse off. The fact is that hate has never erased our instinct for love. This week we all saw community rise to new heights from chaos. Harmony remains our desire even in the worst clamor of discord. On Tuesday we may have lost our innocence but we did not lose our principles. Tall buildings have been brought low but the moral high ground is still open. What is right and good remains before us, unscathed and ready for brave hearts to claim it. We have seen evil around us and in us and it has not triumphed. While our distractions are powerful, we can still keep our eyes on the Lord Jesus and follow where he leads.

Evil cannot completely thwart God's plan anymore than darkness can extinguish a candle. The smoke of evil may be thick, but it no more threatens the Truth of God than a cloud threatens a star. Evil is a powerful force but it is not the final word. The final word belongs to God.

Turn if you will to page 302 in the *Book of Common Prayer.* Stand and affirm once again.

Do you renounce Satan and all the spiritual forces of wickedness that rebel against God?
    I renounce them.
Do you renounce the evil powers of this world which corrupt and destroy the creatures of God?
    I renounce them.
Do you renounce all sinful desires which draw you from the love of God?
    I renounce them.
Do you turn to Jesus Christ and accept him as your savior?
    I do.
Do you put your whole trust in his grace and love?
    I do.
Do you promise to follow and obey him as your Lord?
    I do.

That is the path to take in the face of evil. May God give us the courage and the will to follow it.   Amen.

THE SIN OF NOT SEEING
Scripture: Amos 6: 1-7; Luke 16:19-31

The Rev. Francis H. Wade
St. Alban's Parish
Washington, DC

The Seventeenth Sunday after Pentecost
September 30, 2001

In today's lessons there is the unveiling of a sin that I will bet most of us did not know we were accountable for. I am sure that you are thinking what good news that is right now. With all of the trouble in the world, what we all need is a new sin to worry about. I know the timing is a bit off, but it is here before us and we do well to acknowledge it. The sin revealed in the lessons is connected to some of the soul searching we are doing as a nation as well as to some of the visioning we are doing as a church. Even with all of that, this sin always seems to surprise people, as it did in Amos' day and in Jesus' time. In those days people were quietly doing their own thing and then suddenly held accountable for something they did not know was their responsibility. The sin is that of not seeing. Hold that phrase in your mind for a while. It does not make a lot of sense right now, but I think it will in a few minutes. Consider with me the sin of not seeing.

In the Gospel for today, Jesus tells a familiar parable. When I was learning this story, the rich man was called Dives. He is not so named in the Bible, but that is the Latin word for rich, and so it came to be his name. The story is about Dives and a poor man named Lazarus. This is not the Lazarus who was raised from the dead. That was a real person and this one is fictional. In the story, Lazarus lives in misery at Dives' gate. Dives comes and goes, lives his life in a presumably decent manner, but he never really notices Lazarus. He never connects with him. At death, their roles are reversed. Dives is held accountable for not seeing Lazarus, for not responding to him, because God expected him to see and to relate to the poor man at his gate. Several centuries earlier, the prophet Amos made the same point. He told of wealthy people lolling about on ivory beds, enjoying the good things of life, but they were not "grieved over the ruin of Joseph." For Amos, "Joseph" is a metaphor for the common people. The point is that God required the wealthy to be sensitive to those with whom they shared the land. In each case, it is not the wealth that is the problem. It is the blindness that wealth often brings with it. This blindness comes from the disconnect that privilege makes easy and that a preoccupation with security makes necessary. It is the same point that Jesus made in a more famous saying when he told his followers that he was sick and they did not visit him, naked and they did not clothe him. They rightly wondered, "When did we ever see you that way?" And Jesus told them that what they do or do not do for the least of his brothers and sisters is being done to him. If we do not see them, if we do not see Christ in them, then we have a serious blindness and that blindness has consequences.

The reality of the teaching of these texts is beginning to dawn on our land. Pundits across the nation are announcing with alarm that America is no longer an island separated from the world's issues or its lunatics. Now we know that these things are real and we are connected to them. But before September 11 we did not see them. They were not a blip on our screen, not a quiver to our conscience. We did not bother to distinguish between the legitimate aspirations of people in pain and the madness of people in power. Like Dives in the parable or Amos' couch potatoes we were just doing our thing. We were not hurting anybody; sometimes we were actually doing really good things. But we failed to see the essential connectedness of life and people. And that failure is sinful because God expects us to make those connections. In an entirely different application of the same truth, we at St. Alban's have been slowly coming to the realization that we have been missing something very basic about being faithful. The way we have been looking at serving our God and being a community of God's people has had some blindness in it and it needs to be corrected. There are opportunities we have not seen, open doors we haven't noticed, roles we've not tested. They've been here and we haven't seen them. How do you correct such blindness? How could Dives have done differently? What options did Amos' people have? How does a nation or a church go about seeing what it has not seen before? The answer is simple even if the process is not. The answer is wonder. Not the kind that we think of as in "wonderful." Not anything like awe. It is not the wonder that poets write about. It is a much more basic and practical kind of wonder—the wonder of detectives. It is to question.

To wonder is to know that the situation is different without knowing how and realizing that we must figure something else out. Sometimes that wonder comes upon us naturally—a baby is born, cholesterol shoots up, a recession looms, a decision is made. All of these things let us know in no uncertain terms that we are going to be living differently and we just have to figure out how. The beginning of a healthy response to those questions is wondering at the difference the difference makes. Sometimes the need to wonder bursts upon us violently as it did September 11th. Our world is exactly the same as it was before that date, but our perception of it has changed dramatically. What we must do now as a nation is wonder about how things are different. Sometimes the call to wonder comes gently, ploddingly, through prayer and conversation. God is calling this church to new understandings of service and community. What we are doing now as a congregation is wondering about how things are different. These are confusing times full of bad ideas, and intriguing ones and we're not sure which is which. These are uncomfortable times because we know something will change but we don't know what. We can anticipate the loss without having a clear picture of what is gained. Our nation is doing that sort of wondering now. The airwaves, emails and editorials are full of that wondering. And it is the right thing to do. The church is doing that in different ways. In each case we are trying to repent of the sin of not seeing. Dives never took that step. Amos' wealthy people didn't either. We must.

There is another step beyond wondering. It is called transformation. It means actually being different. It is seeing things in a new light coupled with doing things in a new way. An English mathematician named G. H. Hardy once said, "For any serious purpose, intelligence is a very minor gift." The truth of Hardy's insight is endorsed by the harsh fact that we often have funerals in this place for people who had the wit and intelligence to know that their life styles needed to change, but they lacked the determination to change them. Hardy's insight means that it is not enough for us as a nation or as a church to have the intelligence to know how things have changed. We require the courage, confidence, boldness and risk-taking to find new ways of living into that change, new ways of being American, of being Christian, being human, being good, being faithful, being loving.

The consequences of remaining blind or pretending not to see is what the lessons for today are about. In the parable, Dives, decent sort that he is, pleads to have someone go and make the situation clearer for his brothers. The answer he gets is, "No. They have all the information they need. They can figure it out from that." I think that Jesus is saying the same to us. We must wonder about what we already know. We already have all the information we need. That wondering must lead us to transformation. Our perception of reality in the church has changed slowly and prayerfully. Our perception of reality in the world has changed dramatically and violently. As Christians and as citizens, we must wonder what it means and then be transformed to live in this newness. That is a big job. Amen.

THE WRATH OF GOD
Scripture: Amos 8:4-12

The Rev. Dr. Francis H. Wade
St. Alban's Episcopal Church
Washington, DC

September 23, 2001

In the 1960s The Second Vatican Council was convened in Rome. One of the minor results of that important meeting was that a new lectionary was developed from several old ones. A lectionary is the listing of Bible readings to be used on any given Sunday or special occasions. The Biblical and liturgical scholars deep in the bowels of a Vatican library did such a good job that other churches took their work and used it as the basis for their lectionaries. The Episcopal Church was one of those. That is how it came to be on the second Sunday after The United States was attacked and all are wondering how and why and what for, we find ourselves reading the words of the Prophet Amos:

> *"Hear this, you who trample on the needy and bring ruin to the poor…I will turn your feasts into lamentation; I will bring sackcloth on all loins…I will make it like the mourning for an only son and the end of it like a bitter day."*

This is an image of an angry God smiting people hip and thigh for the sins of greed and pre-occupation with money. And here are we, the richest people the world has ever known, mourning as for an only child and wincing in a bitter day. It is no wonder that some persons are ready to interpret September 11 as another divine tantrum by an emotionally unstable God. I do not believe it. I believe that we have some serious correcting to do in regard to our priorities and our common life. But I do not believe in the God of Wrath who is so easily recruited into one cause or another. I believe that God is deeply involved in our individual and common life. But I do not believe that the interventions of God leave a trail of dead Americans or Afghans in their wake. I would like to talk with you this morning about God's presence and action in days like these.

After the dramatic services at St. Alban's and the Cathedral on Friday the 14th, I took a breath outside the church on Wisconsin Avenue and there was quite a scene. There were swarms of people leaving the cathedral service, getting onto buses to return to what must be awesome responsibilities. And there was a man in the midst of them holding up a sign which said, "This happened because you turned your back on Jesus." That theme has also been picked up by others. There is something in all of us that gravitates to such simple solutions, even if they are appalling and obviously flawed. People who feel strongly about something like to think that God is slapping others around in support of that cause. It is not just simplistic signwavers or quick-fix religious leaders. Any one of us who has faced tragedy, illness or loss and wondered what we did to make God mad at us is operating out of the same assumptions. The assumption is that God is loving and forgiving, but decidedly unstable when he gets close to the biblical seventy times seven on the forgiveness scale. That was Amos' world view and that of his fellow prophets and storytellers. In Amos' age, people believed that God was the source of all that happened. All of it—good or bad. If your crops grew well, it was because God did it; if they failed, God did that. If you won a war, it was because God gave it to you; if you lost, it was because God took it away. Issues of children, prosperity, adversity, illness, cure, all were determined by an act of God. The responsibility of people in this worldview is to choose a powerful god and stay on the good side of him. This is an admittedly brief description of the theology of our ancestors, but it is not unfair and it is still current among us. We know that life and human responsibility are far more complex than that, but the simplicity of such an understanding has great appeal in times of confusion. I would hold up for you a view that is not reducible to placards or bumper stickers, but hopefully more valuable in these confusing and painful times.

The approach has to do with the reasons we call ourselves Christians. We are the followers of Jesus Christ. We call ourselves that because we believe that Jesus embodies and most clearly represents the nature of God. When we want to know what God is like, when we want to know where God is coming from, we look to Jesus and that's how we figure it out. What we know of Jesus is how we sort through the images and dictates of the Old Testament. It's also how we sort through our own instincts and the pressures of cultural norms. We use what we know of Jesus to tell us what is likely to be of God and what is not. That is why we call ourselves Christians. Looking through the lens of Jesus, one does not see a rampaging and vengeful God. What we see is a God of beckoning hand, not balled fist. We find in Jesus, not a stealthy killer, but a still, small voice. We find a God who intervenes to heal, not to hurt; a God whose response to evil is a cross, not a crusade. The closest God's warriors-in-waiting can come to violent wrath in Jesus is the cleansing of the temple, but it was an act to stop an evil, not avenge it. Five days later, Jesus died for the sins of the moneychangers.

What is going on is that we have enormous power to hurt and to heal. That was given to us by God. God is continually beckoning and guiding us in the use of that power. That's what is going on with us as individuals, as households, as a church, as a nation and as a community of nations. Sometimes we do not hear the voice of God and the consequences are great. Sometimes we hear, but do not follow and the consequences are great. Sometimes we hear and we follow and the results are awesome. In spite of our hurt and anger, the purposes and the ways of God have not changed. Sometimes we want them to. The poet Thomas Carlisle wrote these lines: "O God, I hate your enemies with a perfect hatred/Why can't you do the same?" But God's ways have not changed. We are neither God's hammer nor God's anvil for retribution. But we are still God's children for reconciliation. Osama bin Laden was not the instrument of God's anger and neither are we. The God we see in Jesus is continually calling us together—all of us—no matter how painful the distance between us.

So if God is not turning feasts into lamentation and making days bitter, do we throw out Amos and his message? I think not. We need to listen closely to what he says, for he does speak the Word of the Lord. I have to admit that I cannot hear the message very clearly right now. I am much too caught up in the lamentation and the bitterness of these days. All I can do is file it by title and hope that we can come back to it some day soon. When I file it by title, the title looks something like this: On Thursday night, the president said that people hate us because of our freedom. No doubt that is true. But I think that people also hate us because we are rich. Of all of the things that Jesus talked about while revealing to us the mind of God, the single most mentioned topic was the spiritual danger of wealth. We are the richest people the world has ever known. As a consequence, we live in the greatest spiritual danger that has ever been experienced. It's not about having money or not having it. It's what we do to get it, the lengths we go to keep it, the principles we serve with it, the meaning it has for us. I am not ready right now for a serious look at those things. I am too angry, hurt, confused and tired. But I know that the long struggle we have undertaken needs to include some serious wondering about those things.

For now it is enough to know that God revealed through Jesus Christ is not the God of vengeance, but of reconciliation. We need not fear the balled fist of God, but we must not avoid the still, small voice of God. Amen.

Not by Might

"A Mighty Fortress Is Our God"
Not By Might
Psalm 121
There's Still Hope
The Beginning of All things New
The Many Forms Grief Will Take
in Response to this American Tragedy

Chapter

8

A Mighty Fortress Is Our God

A mighty fortress is our God, A bulwark never failing:
Our Helper He, amid the flood Of mortal ills prevailing.
For still our ancient foe Doth seek to work us woe; His craft and pow'r are
great, And armed with cruel hate, On earth is not his equal.

Did we in our own strength confide, Our striving would be losing,
Were not the right man on our side, The man of God's own choosing.
Dost ask who that may be? Christ Jesus, it is He; Lord Sabaoth is His
name, From age to age the same, And he must win the battle.

And tho' this world, with devils filled, Should threaten to undo us,
We will not fear, for God hath willed His truth to triumph through us.
The prince of darkness grim,—We tremble not for him; His rage we can en-
dure, For lo! His doom is sure,—One little word shall fell him!

That word above all earthly pow'rs—No thanks to them—abideth;
The Spirit and the gifts are ours Thro' Him who with us sideth.
Let goods and kindred go, This mortal life also: the body they may
kill: God's truth abideth still, His kingdom is forever.

Amen

Martin Luther, 1521   Martin Luther, 1483-1546   Tr. F. H. Hedge, 1853

NOT BY MIGHT
Scripture: Luke 15: 1-10; Zechariah 4: 6

Rev. Robert L. Brashear , Sr. Pastor
West-Park Presbyterian Church
New York, New York

September 15, 2001

"Not by might, nor by power, but by my Spirit says the Lord God of Hosts"
Zechariah 4: 6

These words stood for over 100 years over the door of West-Park Church, carved in stone. They fell off; letter by letter as the wind and rain wore them away. I believe we need them now, more than ever.

It's so hard to know what to say. It's too early for comfort, though words of comfort must be said. It's too early for analysis, political or theological, although for those who do that, like me, it's a way of maintaining sanity. It's too early to give up anger. Or grief, or fear, whatever we are feeling. Only if we allow ourselves to know and own those feelings can we ever move beyond them. And it's way too early to forgive. Even when we understand that *forgiveness* is giving up all hope of a different past. (As my friend and colleague, Alistair Drummond says, quoting an unnamed source.)

But some things I can, and must, say. First of all, *God didn't do it*. We cannot assign to God responsibility for what happened. Neither can we invoke God's name in the sure and certain coming military response to what has happened. At my clergy study group meeting last Wednesday—one moment of grace in this strange time—I called before going to see if the meeting was still on. No one answered the phone. So I went anyway. And the room was filled.

The Lutheran Pastor from up the street said that the Baptist Pastor from nearby had come into her open sanctuary, just looking for someone to talk to. There were several firefighters in his congregation who were lost. "God is not surprised," he said. She had told him that while she understood how he felt, she had to disagree. No way could this be God's will.

My Catholic priest friend said that God is *always* surprised by the depth of evil that God's creatures are capable of in the *good* creation that God created. It is ultimately we human beings who are responsible.

This leads me to say that just as we cannot blame God, neither can we distance ourselves by saying that it is just demonic. Perhaps you were moved as I was when the names of the hi-jackers were first released. They were human names. Some even Holy names. And it means nothing that that they are Arabic or Muslim. They could just as easily been American names, like the white Americans who bombed the Black church in Birmingham 1963. Or the American boys who hung Matthew Shepherd on a fence in Wyoming. Or the Protestants in Belfast two weeks ago who threw stones and shot at little Catholic schoolgirls. It's not a *Muslim* thing, it's a *human* thing.

The seeds of the same hatred live inside of *us*. And when I read the words of preachers condemning the ACLU, feminists, abortionists, gay men and lesbians; I understand the depth of hate .We share the same DNA. We are people who are salt and light, but also we are people with the capacity for prejudice and hatred. And that hatred unchecked can lead to great destruction, great tragedy.

Today, we have not read most of our lectionary lessons. They just weren't appropriate. But I have kept the Gospel lesson, the story of the lost sheep, the lost coin. There is so much a sense here of the desperate search for the lost, the least. Even as we are gathered here this morning, heroic workers are continuing to dig in the ever diminishing hope that some might be found alive.

So the question is before us, What is lost?

We have all lost so much, but within that general loss are particularities. This doesn't place any loss as greater or lesser than any other; you can't do that. But there are experiences that are *particular*.

I've realized during this week that the financial community in this city is like a small town, about the size of the town I grew up with. A community within our community. And this loss has been particularly heavy for financial community. I remember the face of my neighbor as she had returned from going to work a little late on Tuesday. "The place I work doesn't exist anymore," she said. And a couple of days later, I saw her, shaken. Dozens upon dozens upon dozens of friends, acquaintances, colleagues, just plain *gone*. I have heard this story over and over again.

But in the final analysis, when the digging is over, the face of the lost will include security guards, delivery people, messengers, service workers, people who worked in restaurants, passersby…they will look like us…many nations, many classes, cultures, faiths….

What is lost? There is no such thing as security. Security is an illusion. Terrorism is the weapon of the desperate, the humiliated. You don't have to have read Franz Fanon's *The Wretched of the Earth* to realize that as long as there are desperate and humiliated people on this earth, none of us is ultimately secure. The vast majority of people of all faiths and cultures will always live within our common humanity, but there will always be those driven (or broken) by discrimination and hatred who will strike out, strike back, in ever more spectacular ways. This operation was maybe five years in the planning. We must take care not to sew the seeds now of further desperation, humiliation that may take years to fester and explode.

"Not by might, nor by power…"

Back to normal…

On Thursday, I was sitting at the Avenue restaurant, outside, with a friend, an intern from the United Nations. It was a beautiful, sunny day. I was having my usual lunch of Granny Smith apple and chicken salad along with avocado salad, just like normal. I was drinking iced tea, just like normal. People were rollerblading, driving cars, taking taxis, walking, just like normal. And yet all had changed.

In that conversation, I began to realize something. Yes, I have experienced this as an American. There is a painful hole blown into our collective soul. Even more, I have experienced this as a NewYorker. But I guess I know now more than ever what it means to live in the world, a part of the *world*…

Some of our parents may have experienced Dresden or London during World War II. In our own day there is Beirut, Jerusalem, Gaza City, Sarajevo….We know what it's like to live in Chechnya or Kosovo or Sudan. For much of the world that is what life is like. The bomb goes off, the pieces of life are shattered and scattered. Then we pick them up and move on. That's what we do, like Berthold Brecht's *Mother Courage* pushing her cart across war ravaged Europe.

Still, there are signs of hope. The firefighters, the rescue workers, volunteer, risking and giving life. And smaller heroes. Like last Wednesday, the Park was filled with families picnicking, playing with one another. There was one man, wearing a goofy hat with a propeller, organizing crazy games for the children of the two families. I thought, *you are a hero.*

And the teachers, the unsung heroes. Many suffering losses of their own, going to work on Wednesday to reassure their children, give them some semblance of normal, of safe, of secure….

Maybe the point Jesus was trying to make is that God never stops searching for us….and if we keep on living, we're easier to find.

"Not by might, nor by power…"

Finally, there is so much we can't control. So much out of our control. What did you go to bed worrying about Monday night? What person have you decided never to speak to again? What made you say you'd never set foot *there* again? Twenty-four hours later, how did those same concerns look? How do we take care of one another? That is the question. For God's sake, for Christ's sake, we must be kinder to one another. Look at the person beside you. If you're near someone you love, look at them. *Touch* them. If you're here by yourself, bring to mind the face, the name of someone you love, who cares for you. If there's someone here you're angry at, look at *them*. What divides us is *so tiny*. When you're ready to walk out, close the door, leave, go one level deeper. Seek the Spirit of God that flows within the other, call it forth. Call it forth from yourself. In this most fragile of lives, let us be kind.

"Not by might, nor by power, but by my Spirit says the Lord God of Hosts" Zechariah 4: 6
Amen.

Selected quotes found on Columbus Avenue

"All that is done in this world is done by hope." —Martin Luther

"What lies behind us and what lies in front of us is tiny compared to what lies inside of us." —Ralph W. Emerson

"Our flag may be red, white and blue but our country is a rainbow. Red and yellow, black, brown and white, we are all precious in God's sight." —Jesse Jackson

"It's not getting knocked down that counts, it's getting back up…" —Vince Lombardi

'We know that God plays dice. Just sometimes, God throws the dice where they can't be seen." —Stephen Hawking

PSALM 121

Submitted by Ruth Harris
The Ministers' Wives and Ministers' Widows Alliance of Petersburg and Vicinity
Petersburg, Virginia

I will lift up my eyes to the hills from whence come my help?
My help comes from the Lord, who made the heaven and earth.
He will not allow your foot to be moved; He who keeps you will not slumber.
Behold, He who keeps Israel shall neither slumber nor sleep.
The Lord is your keeper; the Lord is your shade at your right hand.
The sun shall not strike you by day, nor the moon by night.
The Lord shall preserve you from all evil; He shall preserve your soul.
The Lord shall preserve your going out and your coming in from this time forth,
and even for evermore.

~ ~ ~ ~ ~

God is my refuge and strength and He is my ever present help in trouble.

THERE'S STILL HOPE
Scripture: Romans 12: 9-21

Dr. Wilson E. B. Shannon

from *The Flagship Chronicle*
First Baptist Church (Centraila)
Chester, Virginia

Since September 11, our world will never be the same; however, according to God's word, it can be better. Throughout the scriptures, we are taught not to be overcome with evil, but to overcome evil with good. If the people of God would promote and hold on to the principles of love taught in the Bible, then the world we live in can be better.

The threat of terrorism has caused us to make many adjustments, but God's power will never diminish. His grace and mercy will see us through.

I am appalled at anyone associating what happened at the World Trade Centers with the will of God. Certainly, I consider it a form of blasphemy. However, I believe that any problem we have, God can fix.

As I look back over years past, God managed just fine when it came to chastising his children. I am not suggesting that everything America has done is right, but I am saying we didn't deserve this terrorism. This present form of terror in the world is an accelerated form of satanism in the world.

This is no time to fear, but to have faith. This is no time to hate, but to show love. This is no time to point fingers, but to pray. Our God will hear us when we pray, and He will answer in His own way.

It is very courageous for people to raise the American flag at a time like this, but it is just as important for Christians to lift the cross of Calvary. Our sacred symbol, the cross, reminds the world that God loves everybody and that He wants everybody to love everybody.

While we are at war, we want to remember our sons and daughters who represent us on the battlefield. We also want to work hard for peace in the world. At First Baptist Centralia, we have a God-given opportunity to reexamine our resolve by reading the Holy Scriptures, praying earnestly, and promoting love. As a result, the message of the church can be understood through-out the world.

Remember God is watching us and He expects us to truly be the salt of the earth, the light of the world, and the city set on a hill.

Keep the faith, First Baptist, because God will never leave us or forsake us.

THE BEGINNING OF ALL THINGS NEW

George Tom May, Lay Minister and Former Missionary in South Africa
First Congregational Church of West Brattleboro Vermont
W. Brattleboro, Vermont

I watched in horror on September 11 as millions of Americans did. We saw together an event that should have never taken place. "No, no," I pleaded in tears.

Out of habit I pushed the record button on the VCR as the media prepared to show again, the tragedy I had just seen. I pleaded once again in tears, "No, this can not happen in the USA."

In disbelief I watched again the Twin Towers and Pentagon attacks, and in frustration I threw the remote against the wall. The screen on the TV went blank; then the picture returned. I saw the Pentagon slowly restored, no smoke, no fire. Slowly, it was the Pentagon of September 10. As I continued to watch, I saw the smoke and dust removed from the streets of New York to gather at the base of the Twin Towers. In my confusion, my eyes could not believe the resurrection of this work place for thousands of folk like me. Best of all, my heart soared when I saw the beast of deceit and terror disappear and return to its origin as referred to in the book of Revelation Chapter 13.

Then I realized what had happened. When I threw the remote against the wall, I had placed in reverse the events of 9/11. I had erased death, destruction, and anxiety. September 11, 2001 had not happened.

Days, weeks, months have passed and I, like you, as hard as we try, cannot erase from history the day of 9/11. It happened and thousands of families around our world will suffer this event for generations.

In my darkness and sorrow of 9/11, my life and joy once again come from the book of Revelation. The beast 666 has been destroyed by the wounds in Revelation 21: 1-7.

We must believe as hard as it might seem that September 11, 2001 is not the end; it is the beginning, the beginning of all things new.

God Bless America and God Bless all those Americans who have served and now serve to preserve the United States of America.

THE MANY FORMS GRIEF WILL TAKE IN RESPONSE TO THIS AMERICAN TRAGEDY

Carla Wills-Brandon, Ph.D.
Galveston, Texas

There are those of us who have been directly impacted. We have loved ones who were either killed, injured or involved in the tragedy. Fear for their well being, grief over loss, anger and in some cases, revengeful thoughts, rage, are all NORMAL responses. In these cases, we must seek out understanding supports who will allow us to feel the feelings for as long as we need to.

There are those who are feeling normal, human compassion for the country, survivors, those lost, the rescue workers. Sometimes there are strong emotions tied to a sense of violation. Our home has been invaded, our brother and sister Americans have been injured or killed, and we have strong emotions about this EVEN IF we didn't personally know any of the victims. These strong emotions are also NORMAL.

Many have recently lost loved ones and were in the process of grieving when the tragedy occurred. This tragedy WILL INTENSIFY your emotions. Your grief, anger, fear, hurt and loss will be compounded. Know this is to BE EXPECTED and that it too is NORMAL. Don't judge yourself or feel you have back slided in your grief work if you find yourself in this position.

There will be those who find they have extreme emotions, but will not understand where they are coming from. These emotions will go beyond normal grief, loss, violation and anger. This tragedy will "trigger" for those who have violations of physical, emotional or sexual abuse history in their past, those emotions related to those specific traumas. So, not only will these individuals be experiencing normal shock, loss, fear and anger which normally accompanies such a tragedy on such a massive scale, but on top of this, they will also be feeling feelings related to past violations. My office was full of people who were experiencing a "double barrel" of such emotion, just yesterday. If you find yourself in this category, it is ESSENTIAL that you seek out support from people who will validate your emotions and assist you in separating out which feelings are about the here and now and which emotions are tied to the past.

I must share that I have received NUMEROUS e-mails from well intended celebrities, authors, and spiritual leaders who are talking in terms of "forgiveness." Though their intentions are well meaning, I must state that forgiveness right now, at such a tender moment, is not healthy, nor is it a reality. Anger is necessary for reclaiming a sense of power, for taking action, for unity purposes and for healing. Knowing how to express anger is what is important.

I'm a Jew and I have a cousin who is a Muslim. Tolerance is essential in understanding how anger should be processed. Directing anger at the identified perpetrator, as opposed to certain minority groups is most necessary. Already there have been attacks on innocent Muslims and I have heard numerous comments about not only Israel, but other religious faiths. After a period of healthy, appropriate anger work, acceptance then becomes possible, but to shame those who are experiencing anger is not helping matters.

Finally, some people find it necessary to have anger toward their concept of God. This is a part of their healing process and it is not appropriate for any of us to tell such a person they are wrong. In my religious tradition it is acceptable to argue with God on a regular basis. This does not mean that we as a culture disrespect God. We just have a relationship with God which works for us, as it has for 1,000s of years. Those who need to have anger toward God, regarding this tragedy, must be allowed, without judgment, to do so.

As a last note, I must share that I have also been working with teens and children with regard to the horrific scenes seen on television. Children DO NOT have the emotional maturity to know how to process this information. Most adults are having a hard time with it. Young children often think the plane they see crashing into a building, is actually, at that moment, crashing into a building. Teens, who are questioning the universe, recognizing life is full of complications can find themselves most frighten and confused if they watch these scenes on television and then don't have a solid, grounded adult to sort these things out with. When my cousin, other family friends and several other relatives were initially unaccounted for in New York and Washington D.C., my husband and I were most upset. It was important for us to take these concerns and the emotions related to them, to OTHER understanding, supportive adults, not to our children. Yes, we told our children we were worried, but we took our intense emotions elsewhere. Our children need to be reassured that we as adults are grounded enough to be there for them, to offer them structure. We limit T.V. time at our house, turn off the radio and then if such T.V. scenes do make their way to our children, or if they do hear things at school, we take quiet time to talk.

Images of Faith and Freedom

Chapter 9

*Council for America's First Freedom
The Annual America's First Freedom Student Competition
Theme:
"Religious Freedom—Cornerstone of Democracy"*

Prior to 9 / 11, the youth of America awoke each new day in quest of adventure, as their inherent liberties offered another day of exploring, learning and opportunity. They lived and spoke with pride, yet reverence, regarding the treasured liberties of their homeland—liberties that offered a foundation of strength, unity and purpose. Key to the solidarity of that foundation was religious freedom.

High school senior, Peter Nguyen commented: "As I kneel in church, I glance over to my father…I glance…at his hands. They show signs of wear, old age, and hardship, telling a story about toil, adversity and efforts to escape Vietnam…. [He] fled from these scenes of despair to preserve principles…held dear…. The principles of letting [him] choose who to revere, what to worship, and what to believe…. I kneel in my pew…without worry, without fear…"

Governor's School for Government and International Studies, Richmond, Virginia
Second-Place, Oratory
America's First Freedom Student Competition, 2000-2001

And what, since the horrors of 9/11? America's youth continue to awake to each new day in quest of opportunity. High school senior, Joseph Vitola, wrote: "Our democracy, with religious freedom as the first and foremost right, has been nurtured and defended by the courage and sacrifice of our diverse people for over 200 years…. We must continue to show the world that our democracy has and will continue to thrive…."

Catholic High School, Virginia Beach, Virginia
First-Place, Essay
America's First Freedom Student Competition, 2001-2002

Today, America's youth persevere in hope and faith, now grounded in "heightened" understanding of and commitment to the blessings of their freedoms. In tragedy, America chose to magnify its strength, its goodness and its heritage, as "the land of the free, and the home of the brave." Following are artistic expressions of that heritage and commitment, through the insightful vision of America's youth.

Mr. Jefferson's Dream by Elizabeth Hanks
First Place
America's First Freedom Student Competition, 1998/1999
Jamestown High School
Williamsburg-James City County Schools, Virginia

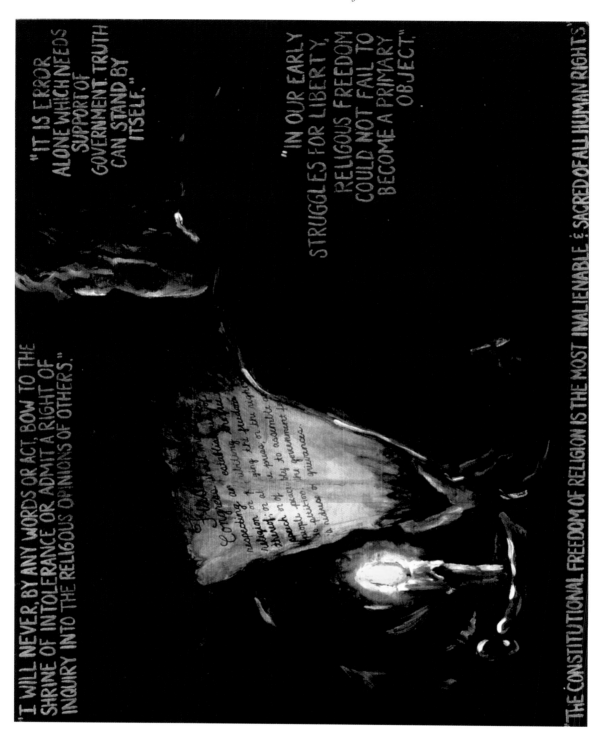

Erin Buckley
Citation for Excellence
America's First Freedom Student Competition 1999/2000
Mills E. Godwin High School
Henrico County Schools, Virginia

"Congress shall make no laws establishing articles of faith or a mode of worship, or prohibiting the free exercise of religion."

Final Senate version
Sept. 9, 1789

Religious Freedom—
Cornerstone of Democracy

Mary Copland
Second Place
America's First Freedom Student Competition, 2001/2002
West Point High School
West Point Public Schools, Virginia

Kellen Hancock
Citation for Excellence
America's First Freedom Student Competition, 1999/2000
Atlee High School
Hanover County Schools, Virginia

Melody Matheny
Second Place
America's First Freedom Student Competition, 1998/1999
Lafayette High School
Williamsburg-James City County Schools, Virginia

Nussi Abdullah
First Place
America's First Freedom Student Competition, 1995/1996
Mills E. Godwin High School
Henrico County Schools, Virginia

Melanie Oglesby
Second Place
America's First Freedom Student Competition, 1999/2000
Richmond Community High School
Richmond City Schools, Virginia

With Liberty and Justice for All by Amanda Reinke
First Place
America's First Freedom Student Competition, 1996/1997
Mills E. Godwin High School
Henrico County Schools, Virginia

William Old, III
Citation for Excellence
America's First Freedom Student Competition, 2001/2002
Cape Henry Collegiate
Virginia Beach, Virginia

"Give me your tired, your poor, Your huddled masses yearning to breathe free, The wretched refuse of your teeming shore. Send these, the homeless, tempest-tossed to me. I lift my lamp beside the golden door."

Courtney Barnette
Honorable Mention
America's First Freedom Student Competition, 2001/2002
Powell Valley High School
Wise County Schools, Virginia

John Taranovich, II
Citation for Excellence
America's First Freedom Student Competition, 2001/2002
Southampton High School
Southampton County Schools, Virginia

James Abraham
Citation for Excellence
America's First Freedom Student Competition, 2000/2001
Hermitage High School
Henrico County Schools, Virginia

David Byers
Citation for Excellence
America's First Freedom Student Competition, 2000/2001
Henrico High School
Henrico County Schools, Virginia

And the Light of Religious Freedom Shall Burn Forever by Stefani Little
First Place
America's First Freedom Student Competition, 2001/2002
Grafton High School
York County Schools, Virginia

April Hill
Citation for Excellence
America's First Freedom Student Competition, 2000/2001
Powell Valley High School
Wise County Schools, Virginia

Homer Ailstock, Jr.
First Place
America's First Freedom Student Competition, 1999/2000
Wakefield High School
Arlington County Schools, Virginia

Because He Lives

"God Still Leadeth Me"
Because He Lives
Unusual Thanks
Wait for One Another: Manners at the Lord's Table
Love, For the Best in Living
How Worship Can Change Life

Chapter

10

God Still Leadeth Me

Lord, Thou hast been our dwelling place, In all generations, Before the mountains were brought forth, Or Thou hadst formed the earth and world; And even from everlasting To everlasting Thou art God.

He leadest me, He leadest me,
He leadest me, My God still leadest me.

Thou turnest man to destruction, And bidst men's sons return; A thousand years in thy sight Are but as yesterday when past; And as a watch in the night Thou bearest them away like a flood.

He leadest me, He leadest me,
He leadest me, My God still leadest me.

Our sins are set before Thee, Our wrongs with in Thy light; For all our days passed in wrath, We spend our years as tales are told. Our years number three-score and ten, And by strength may reach forescore years.

He leadest me, He leadest me,
He leadest me, My God still leadest me.

Chas. D. Douglass, D. D.   *B. W. Ferguson*

BECAUSE HE LIVES!
Scripture: John 20:24-29

Dr. David G. Berry
First Presbyterian Church
Fort Lauderdale, Florida

September 16, 2001

Around 9:00 in the morning on Tuesday, September 11, the world as we know it changed drastically. Four commercial airliners were hijacked by fundamentalist terrorists and transformed into weapons of mass destruction. Two of the airplanes plowed into the World Trade Towers in New York City, causing an explosion of jet fuel that ultimately brought down the towers and wiped out thousands of innocent lives. One airplane crashed into the Pentagon— the Pentagon!—taking hundreds of lives. And one plane crashed to the ground after an apparent rescue attempt by some of the passengers on board. In the course of an hour and a half, so many lives were lost and so much innocence—our children's, our nation's, even our own—was taken away forever.

The emotions generated by this act of cowardly terrorism have run the gamut. Most of us were shocked and horrified, then angry—very, very angry. I sat with the staff watching the first news reports and could only pray. I began to hear the stories of people calling from the planes or the buildings and telling their families that they loved them and I couldn't hold back the tears. How did you feel in those first few moments after the tragedy? Were you angry? Did you want revenge? Were you ready for war? Is that how you feel? I freely confess my own anger. Somebody has to pay. America has got to respond. But I listened as Christians across the country were interviewed. I heard lots of anger, lots of calls for righteous retribution. But how many of those Christians expressed compassion and concern for the men who committed this act? How many of us really felt then or feel today any compassion for Osama Bin Ladin and his accomplices? Have you heard any prayers for their hearts and their souls? Are there any voices of reason and calm that will stand up for Arabs in this country who are scared to death about some general retaliation from their fellow Americans? I'm hearing people say, "Get rid of them. Kill them! They deserve it." But I have to wonder what Jesus is saying.

It's not been easy preparing for this sermon. I have to sort out my own emotions. I love my country. I love my children. I hate evil. And I have to reach out to others who are grieving. I have to pastor people who are hurting and angry and afraid. At our worship service on Tuesday night, which was a beautiful and powerful gathering of hurting people coming before the throne of God to receive his tender mercies, I offered three affirmations of faith that I still believe in. God is still there. God is still in control. God is still good. And I believe that with all my heart. God is not responsible for this tragedy. Rather, he's working to give strength and grace and to bring some good out of this horrific mess. I believe that. And so this morning I want to take a different tack. I want to address not only the tragedy of these terrorist attacks, but also our perspective as followers of Jesus Christ. What is it about our faith that will ultimately make the difference in the way we feel and the way we respond? One minister I respect said that Christians don't really know how to respond to a tragedy like this, they don't know how to respond to their anger and fear, they don't know how to respond to the evil in the world today because they don't really know Jesus Christ. I think she's right. She told about being invited to preach in a friend's church recently. His instructions to her were, "Don't preach more than ten minutes and keep it light." He called her three times to remind her not to preach more than ten minutes and to keep it light. That Sunday she waited for her turn to preach and the pastor of the church called the children forward for a children's sermon. He then proceeded to read the story of Benjamin Bunny. He read the whole book. It went on and on. No mention of Jesus. Nothing about the Bible. Nothing about faith. Just Benjamin Bunny. He went on for fourteen minutes about Benjamin Bunny and then gave her ten minutes to talk about Jesus Christ, as long as she kept it light, of course! And that's not an isolated incident in the church today! Her point was that we've forgotten the foundation of our faith, we've forgotten about Jesus Christ and, as a result, we don't have any idea what it means to speak and live and respond as a faithful follower of Jesus in the world today, especially when we're confronted by such evil and heartache. Too many pastors don't pray. Too many elders don't read the Bible. Too many church members don't really believe in the resurrection because, if they did, if they really believed that Jesus is alive today, it would totally transform the way they live, the way they do business, the kind of spouse or parent or friend they are, and the way they respond to evil and tragedy in the world.

Fifteen years ago a small group of radical Biblical scholars gathered in Indiana to form what they call the "Jesus Seminar." The purpose of the Jesus Seminar, which is still meeting today, is to discuss the sayings and teachings and miracles of Jesus and to decide which of them are authentic and which are not. They use a colored ball system of voting. For example, only about twenty percent of them decided that Jesus really spoke the Beatitudes and the teachings in the Sermon on the Mount. After fifteen years of work, less than fifteen percent of the life and teachings of Jesus have been declared authentic. They hope to come out with a Bible called the Jesus Bible where the sayings will be printed in appropriate colors. Red stands for a "yes" vote on authenticity. Pink is for "May be authentic," gray for "Probably not," and black for— you guessed it—"No, not authentic at all." Of course, maybe that's not so radical after all. Maybe some of us already have a Bible like that. Maybe after the attacks this week we can put "an eye for an eye" in red. We like that. We can understand that. But verses like "Father, forgive them," and "pray for your enemies," and "repay no one evil for evil" will probably become pink or gray or maybe even black.

Not long ago the Jesus Seminar voted on the resurrection. The result? The resurrection will be in black. Only ten percent of the scholars believe the resurrection actually happened! I find that absolutely amazing. The foundation of the early church was the resurrection of Jesus Christ. The New Testament writers go out of their way to scandalize us with the reality of the resurrected Christ. He appeared to the women and to the disciples, not once but several times. He ate with them and fished with them and they touched his hands and his sides and his feet. Those disciples who were cowards on Saturday after the crucifixion suddenly became courageous and fearless when they saw the resurrected Jesus alive and walking and talking just like he had been before. The resurrected Christ was at the center of the early church's faith and must be the center of our faith today if it is going to have any meaning and any power in our lives and in this world. You see, the response which the resurrection calls forth is never a true-false response, as if we could vote on its authenticity. The resurrection always requires a yes-no response. The question the resurrection poses is, will you follow Jesus? Will you be his disciple? And the answer to that kind of question is never true-false; it's always yes or no.

John Calvin's seal was the picture of an open hand reaching up to God. In the hand is a heart with a flame coming out of the top of the heart. And the caption under the picture is this: "My heart I give to thee, O Lord, eagerly and sincerely." In other words, the resurrected Jesus calls us to be on fire for him. Too often we're more like a damp squib. Do you know what a damp squib is? In Scotland they set off fireworks in celebration of Guy Fawks Day in November. The only problem is that it's always raining in Scotland in November. By the time you set off a firecracker in November, it's so damp that instead of a bang you get a little "pop." That's called a damp squib. There are too many Christians today who are like damp squibs in the world when we should be on fire for the Kingdom. Those early disciples were on fire, they could face anything—persecution, suffering, death—they could face it all because they had experienced the reality and the power of the resurrected Jesus in their lives.

Now, here's the point. Without this resurrection power in our lives we end up in a fog of religiosity and piety and false faith that will not sustain us in the real world today. We end up with a cultural faith where our church membership is about the same as our membership at the club and it will not sustain us in the real world today. It will not sustain us in a world where airplanes crash into buildings killing thousands of innocent people and stealing our sense of safety and security. It will not sustain us in a world where jobs are lost and families fall apart and loved ones get sick and die. There is evil and pain and heartache in our world and pious convictions and Sunday morning faith can not stand up against it. We need a real faith to sustain us in the real world! We need a living Lord to stand beside us in a world filled with death so that we can experience the real power of life that is abundant and eternal! The message of the resurrection is that death and evil and heartache do not have the final word on today. Jesus Christ has the final word on today. The words of our last hymn say it so well:

> *Because He lives, I can face tomorrow;*
> *Because He lives, all fear is gone;*
> *Because I know He holds the future,*
> *And life is worth the living just because He lives.*

Dr. Tom Gillespie, the President of Princeton Theological Seminary, tells the story of the first funeral he ever performed for a small child. The child was only five years old when he was killed in a tragic accident. He was the son of some of Tom's very closest friends. He said it was one of the most difficult things he ever had to do in the ministry. After the funeral Tom walked with the young mother and father from the cemetery to the car. They got in the car together and the mother looked out the window as they lowered her son's casket into the ground. Then she turned to Tom, put her hand on his leg, and said to him, "Tom, I've got to know. Do you really believe what you just said?" It was the moment of truth for a young pastor confronted for the first time with such tragedy. And he looked her in the eye and said with all sincerity, "Yes, Ann, I believe it." Do you? Do you believe it?

Thomas wasn't so sure, was he? He, like the rest of us, knew what happens to corpses. He, like the families who have lost loved ones this week and like the mothers and fathers in this church whose children are afraid to go to sleep alone now and like so many others, knew how strong the power of death and evil are in the world. He's just like us. He wanted to experience it for himself. He wanted to *know*. He wanted to see and touch and feel the reality and the power of the resurrection. It was never really a true-false issue for Thomas. It was always a yes or no for him. If I'm going to follow this Jesus, if it's really going to make a difference in my life, I've got to experience it for myself. And when he experienced it he fell on his knees and confessed *"My Lord and my God!"* And Jesus says to us, *"Blessed are those who have not seen and yet believe."*

Do you believe? I confess to you that I am just like Thomas. I need more than words. I need to experience it for myself. Reciting the creeds, as true as they are, doesn't move me to faith. But praying with a family around the deathbed of a loved one does. Reading the theology of John Calvin, as powerful as it is, does not move me to faith. But watching a teenager grow and blossom in this church does. Helping a friend work through a time of depression does. Working with a family through a miscarriage does. Praying a simple prayer or singing a simple song with my children does. It is in my life, in the routine and the upheaval, the boredom and the excitement, the good and the evil that I experience the power of the risen Lord Jesus Christ and it is in these places that I am moved to faith. In the lives of the people I encounter every day I am able to press my fingers into the nail marks and to experience the presence of Jesus.

Roberta Hestenes is a marvelous Presbyterian minister whom I admire a lot. A while back I heard her tell the story of her trip to China a few years ago after the 100 year flood that devastated the lives of hundreds of thousands of Chinese peasants. When she arrived in China she was pulled aside by the Chinese authorities who instructed her not to speak at all about her Christian faith while she was there helping the peasants. If she did, she would be sent home immediately. They took her into parts of China where no American had been for more than forty years and she witnessed unbelievable poverty and devastation from the floods. She rode around in the back of a jeep for more than two weeks, bouncing up and down on their roads and doing her best to help. One Sunday they took her farther into the country than ever before. After bouncing around in the jeep for several hours, she began to reflect on her situation. Here she was, surrounded by communist authorities in a foreign country, wearing her cross, and longing for some good Christian fellowship. Her heart was heavy and tired and she was getting worn down from the pain and poverty she was witnessing. "Lord, if only you would bring me the fellowship of some Christian person," she prayed, "I know it would lift my spirits." When they got to the village the communist leader came to her and said, "We seem to have an extra hour in our itinerary." Drawing on all his stereotypes of American women, he asked, "Would you like to go shopping?" And Roberta said, "What I would really like to do is go back down the road to that church I saw." The leader said, "There are no churches here!" Roberta said, "But I know I saw a cross off in the distance back down the road." The communist leader was not happy about it, but he got back in the jeep and drove her back the way they had come. Before long, Roberta shouted, "Stop!" and she jumped out and ran across rice patties and streams and fields until she came to a very small village with a cross on top of one of the buildings. An old woman came up to her and said to her through an interpreter, "Please come and see our church. Would you like to meet our pastor?" And Roberta discovered that there was a little medical clinic there in the church where they cared for the medical needs of people. She walked in and saw a woman lying on a table in the full throws of acupuncture.

There were needles everywhere. The old woman pointed to her and said, "I'd like you to meet our pastor." Roberta discovered that between 700 and 800 Chinese peasants crowded into that little church every Sunday to worship the risen Christ. And all the people in the little church that Sunday took hands and prayed together. Roberta said tears were running down her face but she couldn't wipe them away because people were holding so tightly to her hands. She looked at the pastor who also had tears covering her face. And then the pastor said to her, "Before you go, you must know that for more than thirty years we have prayed that some Christian person from the outside would come and share their faith with us so we would know that we are not alone. You are the answer to that prayer. We will see you in heaven."

Do you believe that Christ is risen? Do you believe that Jesus is alive? If you don't, then there is no answer to the tragedy of this past week or the pain and heartache that fills our lives because there is no hope for life now and in the future. But if you do, then Jesus will be with you every moment of every day and will give you the peace and the strength and the hope you will need to follow him.

Because He lives, I can face tomorrow;
Because He lives, all fear is gone;
Because I know He holds the future,
And life is worth the living just because He lives.

UNUSUAL THANKS

Clyde Johnson, Sr.
with Ronney King, Clifton Sparks, Jude Boykins, Marvin Jennings, Stephen Cheeks
Deerfield Correctional Center
Capron, Virginia

Special Thanksgiving Service

November 2001

Never before in the history of our nation have we celebrated Thanksgiving under these conditions. So lonely, so fearful.

September 11, 2001, has changed our nation in ways which will shape our behavior for years to come, if not forever. The after affects of the terrorists have left us feeling vulnerable, susceptible to attack. Our security has been threatened, shaken and unsettled; our fears hightened; our freedom highjacked; our economy left in shambles.

The skyline of New York will never be the same any more. The Twin Towers, once a beacon to the city, destroyed at the hands of saboteurs, unlike the Pheonix, will they rise again? Five thousand plus lives were lost on that fatal day. Men and women of many nations incinerated in a few moments all because of man's inhumanity to man. Widows and widowers weep; children left fatherless and motherless weep and a nation mourns...A nation at war, in search of the culprits...What Now?

Paul said in everything give thanks, for this is the will of God in Christ Jesus concerning you. To that end, we have invited some unusual guests to speak to us this Thanksgiving.

Salt: We are the salt of the earth—the salt that seasons. We are to season the earth with God's praise, glory, happiness, hope, goodness, and compassion. We are the salt of the earth—the salt that preserves. We are to preserve the love, mercy and grace that is Christ on earth. We are the salt of the earth—the salt that heals. Christ is our healing. As we lead others to Christ, the earth begins to heal. Christ not only heals our sickness and disease, but our spiritual, emotional, mental, and moral sickness. We are the salt of the earth—the salt that revives. We are to stir up stagnation. We are to bring back the fallen. We are the salt of the earth—the salt that strengthens. We are to strengthen and encourage one another into good works. We are the salt of the earth. Thanks be unto God for the salt.

Sin: In giving thanks for unusual things, how can we give thanks for sin? I give you King David who had been anointed by God at a very young age. It was quite obvious that God was blessing David. But David sinned, but it was this sin in David that humbled him. We thank God then for this sin. Sin caused David to write Psalm 51. It was this sin that caused David to repent, turn away from sin, and turn to God for help. It was God looking down through time and seeing this sin that put into effect the great plan of redemption. I can truly thank God for sin that causes us to realize that we need a Savior that can take all of sin away and make us presentable to stand before a Holy God.

Light: On September 11, 2001, our light was for a moment snuffed out. We were at a loss to understand the events of the day. We wondered if the end had come for the nation and ourselves. There was confusion and uncertainty marked by fear that our nation was under attack by an unseen enemy. Our light had gone out. For a time, we were left in the dark with nowhere to turn. Then out of the darkness, the light of God showed forth. He said he was the light of the world and refers to us as children of light. I thank God on this unusual Thanksgiving that we have the light in Christ Jesus and we are called to be lights in the world. Thank God for the light.

Blood: On September 11, 2001, the blood of the innocent was shed. They did not know why or by whom their death had come. Two thousand years ago, another innocent person died. His blood was offered as a sacrifice for the sins of man. Evil demanded Jesus' blood, as evil demanded the blood of the 5,000 on September 11, 2001. One was for naught and the other was for the sins of all mankind. Thanks be unto God for the blood of His only son. By it, we are forgiven; by it, we are cleansed; by it, we are the righteousness of God.

Thorn: A thorn is a source of constant trouble, irritation, or suffering. And I am to thank God for thorns. The Bible tells me that Paul had a thorn in his flesh, though it is not described. Whatever the thorn, it caused him constant problems and was at times a hinderance to his ministry. My thorns are a reminder of how I need God. My thorns keep me humble. My thorns keep me close to God. If not for the thorns, I would not know grace, mercy, and goodness of my God. The Bible tells us in Romans 5:3-5, "Not only so, but we also rejoice in our sufferings because we know that suffering produces perseverance; perseverance, character; and character, hope. And hope does not disappoint us because God has poured out His love into our hearts by the Holy Spirit whom he has given us." Thank God for the thorns.

Thank God for salt, sin, light, blood, and thorns.

WAIT FOR ONE ANOTHER:
MANNERS AT THE LORD'S TABLE
Scripture: The First Epistle of Paul to the Corinthians 11: 33

Dr. Harry S. Wright, Pastor
Cornerstone Baptist Church
Brooklyn, New York

-Excerpts-
September 16, 2001

This is a tough Sunday to say a word to the Lord's people. There is a dust in the nostrils of every boy and girl and every man and woman who love America. So on this dusty, bloody Sunday, I am privileged to look into your faces and say a word for the Lord.

I found inspiration in this marvelous letter from the Apostle Paul to the church he loved so much at Corinth. Paul gave us the earliest New Testament account we have of this oral tradition of the Lord's Supper. I think that most of us know that the earliest gospel is the gospel of Mark, but some ten years earlier, Paul picks up his pen and writes to the church at Corinth of what happened that night when Jesus was betrayed.

Paul now in Ephesus has heard embarrassing and strange things coming out of the church at Corinth. Paul has heard (and he had founded this church on his second missionary journey) that there is misbehavior on the Lord's Day when they gather around the table. Paul is disturbed by the embarrassing rumors going out from that church and is now triggered by this embarrassment to write this matchless letter to the church at Corinth with suggested tips.

Here's what was happening. There were some well-to-do members of the church on that day—on the Lord's Day. They brought their regular meals with them. And they sat down and ate their meal and drank their wine without concern whatsoever for the other members of the fellowship. There were some hungry persons there, but these well-to-doers ate well and in a gluttonous manner and their drinking was unchecked. Paul said some drank until they became drunk at the fellowship meal.

So they had combined their love feast—their fellowship meal with the Lord's Supper and they had become embarrassing in terms of selfishness—in terms of greed, and, most importantly, a terrible example being set by a church in a pagan city. So Paul sits down and writes this matchless letter which laid forth manners that ought to govern their behavior around the Lord's table.

Last Sunday, we were reminded that we ought to be preoccupied with Christianity. Paul said not with Cephas, not with Apollos, not with Paul, but with Christ. And I have decided, said Paul coming down from Athens where he had been chewed up for trying to compare Jesus with the philosophical ideologists on Mars Hill, that it is Christ Only! Christ Only as a kind of traveling affirmation of faith—all weather—lifelong—to undergird your lives—Christ Only!

Every American living anywhere on the face of the globe has dust in his nostrils. But Paul has a word for us today—a tip for the table, an invitation to etiquette to my brothers and sisters around the Lord's table. I have received of the Lord what I have handed on to you that

117

on the night in which our Lord and Savior Jesus Christ was betrayed he took bread and broke it and blessed it and, in like manner, he took the cup and blessed it again, passed it among the disciples and said this is my blood of the New Covenant shed for you.

Listen to Paul. Now this is a tough response to an embarrassing situation. If you are hungry, eat at home. Don't bring your full course meal to the church. Leave your wine at home. Drink at home. Eat at home.

Now as I stand at the Lord's table made ready, let me offer three words as tips for the Lord's table as we stand with dust in our nostrils today. Paul reminds us as we gather that we are here to proclaim the Lord's death until He comes. I need to say this in New York today standing around the Lord's table. I don't know anywhere I'd rather be—first of all in the church—than here at the Lord's table.

Paul reminds us that as we eat and drink we proclaim His death until he comes; this is a meal of memories—this is a memorial meal. But it is more than memory; it is also a commemoration—a celebration. Not only did Jesus live and die, but He is present. He is here with us today as we stand with dust on our lips, dust in our nostrils, dust and debris in our city and blood over our nations. Christ is here at the table that reminds us beyond memory. He walks with us. He talks with us. He tells us we are his own. But beyond that, Paul makes it clear that he is coming back.

So here is our word of hope today. Not only memory, but also a presence, and a futuristic confirmation that He is coming again.

LOVE, FOR THE BEST IN LIVING

Bertie Jeffress Powell
The Ministers' Wives and Ministers' Widows Alliance of Petersburg and Vicinity
Petersburg, Virginia

September 2001

Reflections for Troubled Hearts

Sometimes in my quiet moments I reflect
On the meaning of life, our purpose for being here
In this beautiful and ugly world,
With such good and evil people,
With so many difficult and pleasurable times.

I think about the "ifs": if the earth would not
Emit its tornadoes, hurricanes, and earthquakes;
If people would not emit their hate, callousness,
And ignorance; if the human body would not
Emit its diseases, pain, and decay—
We could know endless joy.

In these supposes I see an image of our existence:
It says that all living creatures are subject
To the unavoidable vicissitudes of life, nothing
Can be done; it says that all human beings are capable
Of preventing and changing those hardships
Which they themselves create; something can be done.
But what stands out predominantly in this view of us
In our world is that all of the controllable ills
Will surely be dealt with by people who love—
Love God, Love life, and Love their fellow men.

From Encounter *by Bertie J. Powell*

HOW WORSHIP CAN CHANGE LIFE
Scripture: Psalm 100: 1-5

Dr. J. Jey Deifell Jr.
First Church of Christ
Wethersfield, Connecticut

September 16, 2001

Scripture Reading

Psalm 100: 1-5: Make a joyful noise to the Lord, all the earth. Worship the Lord with gladness; come into his presence with singing. Know that the Lord is God. It is he that made us, and we are his; we are his people, and the sheep of his pasture. Enter his gates with thanksgiving, and his courts with praise. Give thanks to him, bless his name. For the Lord is good; his steadfast love endures forever, and his faithfulness to all generations.

Let us pray: Lord God, I am out of breath. We all are out of breath. Send Your Spirit that we may, indeed have the breath of Your Spirit in our midst, that we may receive from You the grace, love and life of Jesus. We pray in His Name. Amen.

On any normal week in these United States of America the statisticians tell us that about 35-40% of our population is in a place of worship, in a church like ours, a cathedral, a synagogue or a mosque. I have a feeling that this past week and this weekend the percentage is much, much higher. We all are seeking help for ourselves, for others, for the rescue workers, for the families and friends of the victims, for our leaders. We have come with deep feelings of shock, anger, sorrow and fear. Our questions, tears and concerns are overflowing and over-whelming to the point that we have been staggering all week. This is not a time for celebration, for entertainment, for "business as usual." Rather it is a time for reflection, for mourning, for coming together, for prayer and for worship.

A wise person once said, "When we worship, we recognize who we are and who God is." In worship today, we recognize that we, along with others, are hurting, needy and anxious people who are seeking God's comfort. In worship today we come with our minds seared with those pictures of destruction in New York City, Washington, D.C., and in Pennsylvania. The photographs of those missing and of the terrorists are also embedded in our minds. So we come asking God WHY? What do You want us to do, God? In worship today we come with feelings and apocalyptic concerns that we do not know how to handle. We don't know how to deal with them so we come with mustard-seed-sized faith seeking God.

Jesus said to a woman who was seeking "...the hour is coming, and is now here, when the true worshipers will worship the Father in spirit and in truth, for the Father seeks such as these to worship Him" (John 4:23). Do we come seeking God in spirit and in truth? I am really helped by the Prophet Isaiah when he says, "Seek the Lord while He may be found, call upon Him while He is near; let the wicked forsake their way, and the unrighteous their thoughts; let them return to the Lord, that He may have mercy on them, and to our God, for He will abundantly pardon. For my thoughts are not your thoughts, nor are your ways my ways, says the Lord. For as the heavens are higher than the earth, so are My ways higher than your ways and My thoughts than your thoughts" (Isaiah 55:6-9). Even though we cannot see or fully comprehend God or His thoughts, He is here now. He is here to be "our refuge and our strength, a very present help in times of trouble. Therefore we do not fear, though the earth should change…" He declares boldly, "Be still and know that I am God! I am exalted among the nations, I am exalted in the earth" (see Psalm 46:1-2, 10).

Another Psalmist has said, "For great is the Lord, and greatly to be praised; He is to be revered above all gods. For all the gods of the peoples are idols…" (Psalm 96:4-5a). I find it interesting that the Bible acknowledges that there are other gods and that there are people who are prone to worship other gods, in attitude and actions if not in words.

What is a god? How would you define god? I believe a god is any thing, person, thought or ideology that our heart clings to and we spend time and resources serving. Do we worship gods? Just look at how and why we do what we do. What is precious to us? What do we cherish and adore? What do we strive for? What is so important to us that we rearrange our agenda? It may be in personal or family life. It may be in our public or professional life. It may be in our leisure or retirement life. These are not necessarily bad things. They are quite normal for us. The trouble occurs when any of them upstage or displace the one true God. It then becomes an idol. Only the God of the Bible—Father, Son and Holy Spirit—is the One true God, worthy of our utmost worship. We come to adore Him and Him alone. "Worship the Lord with gladness; come into His presence with singing," says the Psalmist (Psalm 100:2).

Does God need our worship? No! He doesn't need anything. However He is pleased when we worship Him. Why? Because He knows that we need to worship Him. There are two major reasons: one is that we become like the gods we worship. If we adore and worship someone or some thing, they really affect us. If our god is power or control, we become persons who always have to have things their own way. We might become little dictators in our homes, our businesses, our communities. If our god is success or popularity, we become arrogant and vain persons. If our god is wealth or security, we become greedy, selfish and maybe even paranoid. If our god is health or beauty, we become hypochondriacs or prideful egomaniacs. If our god is our agenda or our cause, we become manipulators, militant aggressors or maybe even terrorists. The Bible's God says it very clearly in the first Commandment: "You shall have no other gods before me" (Exodus 20:3). God wants us to worship only Him that we may become more and more like Him, not like the other gods. So, the Psalmist says, "The Lord is good" (Psalm 100:5). When we worship God, who is good, we become, more and more, good people. The Bible says, "God is love" (I John 4:8b). When we worship God we become more loving. The Bible says, "…Truth came through Jesus Christ" (John 1:17). When we worship God we become more truthful. God is merciful. We become more merciful. God is grace. We become more gracious. God is faithful. We become more faithful.

The second major reason God wants us to worship Him is that he knows He can make changes when our hearts, minds, bodies and souls are open to Him. He can move into that opening, however small, and transform. He can remove the garbage. He can lift our burdens. He can encourage, strengthen, cleanse and mold us. When we focus our worship in the spirit and truth of God alone, other gods cannot change us to be like them. When we worship God alone, He has a strategic opportunity to bless us.

A good example of that occurs when teachers in their classrooms have strategic opportunities to bless their students. This happens when the student gives attention, respect and honor to the teacher. Then the student can receive more from the teacher and be blessed more. It is the same with God and us. If we honor, adore and worship God, we will be blessed more abundantly. He is a God of blessings. He wants to bless us.

If you are here and empty, God wants to feed and fill you. If you are here and you are tired, God wants to give you rest. If you are here worried, God wants to give you peace. If you are here hurting, God wants to heal and comfort you. If you are here concerned about what to do, God wants to give you wisdom. If you are here and need help, He is here to give you power and perfect love. The Psalmist says, "For the Lord is good: His steadfast love endures forever, and his faithfulness to all generations" (Psalm 100:5). God is good. He did not cause the evil this past week. Humans did! They chose to do evil. The Bible says, "…perfect love casts out fear" (I John 4:18). That is the way of God, the way of the Cross. I was reminded this week that perfect hate also casts out fear. That is the way of Osama bin Laden, the way of the terrorists, the way of Hitler, the way of the Ku Klux Klan. They worship a different god.

Which god do we seek to worship today? I hope we are worshiping the God who is seeking us, so as to love us perfectly that we will do justice, love kindness and walk humbly with Him (see Micah 6:8). What does it mean "to do justice?" Doing justice is not acting with hatred, seeking revenge. The Bible makes it very clear: "Beloved, never avenge yourselves, but leave room for the wrath of God…'Vengeance is mine. I will repay' says the Lord" (Romans 12:19). Doing justice is holding people accountable for their evil deeds. Doing justice is stopping and removing the forces of evil from doing further harm. I pray that in the months ahead, as we deal with the demoniac, we will not become demoniacal. There is a difference between justice and vengeance.

What does "to love kindness" mean? In the same passage about vengeance, it says, "If your enemies are hungry, feed them; if they are thirsty, give them something to drink" (Romans 12:20). Our Lord Jesus said in the Sermon on the Mount, "Love your enemies and pray for those who persecute you" (Matthew 5:44). That is too much and yet that is what He says.

Nancy Andersen, one of our staff members, wrote a letter to her friends. She says this, "How can we pray for those who caused so much death and destruction? We can pray that the Lord takes away their spirit of hatred…We need to pray and ask the Lord Jesus to work through us to cast out the evil from our nation. We need to pray for wisdom in our response to this crisis…Most of us are unaware of the horrors happening around the world on a regular basis. We only become alarmed when it is on our doorstep—when it is affecting our own lives…As children of God, we need to unite in prayer for our nation and our world. We need to connect again with our fellow human beings and care for one another. We need to acknowledge the Source of our light and goodness. We need to proclaim the Name of the Lord. We need to show forth His love and walk in His Light as he commanded us. We need to give up our self-interest and do our part to illuminate the shadow and the darkness. These terrorists have acted with intense passion. We, too, must act with passion as we carry out the mission given to us by our Lord."

The God we worship loves us so much that He wants us to do justice, to love kindness and to walk humbly with Him. How do we walk humbly with Him? the Prophet Isaiah says it clearly, "Let the wicked forsake their way, and the unrighteous their thoughts; let them return to the Lord, that He may have mercy on them, and to our God, for He will abundantly pardon" (Isaiah 55:7). If we are to walk humbly with God, we have to humble ourselves before Him. How shall we do that? We need to be honest about ourselves before Him. We need to confess how we have been worshiping other gods. We need to repent. We need to turn away from our idolatry and turn toward our merciful God. Then we can fulfill this passage from the Old Testament, "If my people who are called by My Name humble themselves, pray, seek My face, and turn from their wicked ways, then I will hear from heaven, and will forgive their sins and heal their land" (II Chronicles 7:14). Notice that it says "the people who are called by My Name," not other people, but us…that is, you and me! We need to humble ourselves, pray, seek His face and turn from our wicked ways. Then he will hear, forgive and heal.

In my heart of hearts I believe this is a wake-up call for America. I believe this is a turning point in the history of our country and maybe even for the world. I see a solidarity taking place in communities, in this nation and in the world community that I have never known or even read about before. It is happening now! God bless America! God bless this world!

Could it also be a turning point or a changing point in our personal lives…in the life of this congregation? Could it be that we are at a place now where we are to cast aside all other gods and to worship only the one true loving God—the Father, the Son and the Holy Spirit—so that He can, indeed, transform and change us to be more like Him? Let's face it. We have been playing games with God for a long time. Some of us are in the big league. Some of us are in the minor league. We've all been doing it. Maybe this is the turning point. Maybe this is the spiritual and moral awakening that we have been praying for.

Turn to the Call to Worship in the Bulletin. These words not only called us to worship today, they are calling us into a new future. I appeal to you therefore, brothers and sisters, by the mercies of God, to present your bodies as a living sacrifice, holy and acceptable to God, which is your spiritual worship. Do not be conformed to this world, but be transformed by the renewing of your minds, so that you may discern what is the will of God—what is good and acceptable and perfect. O come, let us worship and bow down, let us kneel before the Lord, our Maker! For he is our God, and we are the people of his pasture, and the sheep of his hand. (Romans 12:1-2; Psalm 95:6-7).

Let us pray:
O God, bless and keep loving Your world. O God, bless and shed Your Grace upon America. O God, bless and change each of us to become more like You.
In Christ's Name. Amen.

The Lord's Song in Our Own Land

"Amazing Grace, How Sweet the Sound"
The Lord's Song In Our Own Land
The Light That Never Goes Out
A Time for Prayer
Within This Cell: My Message of Hope
Faith Testimony: God Is Still Good

Chapter

11

Amazing Grace, How Sweet the Sound

Amazing grace! How sweet the sound That
saved a wretch like me! I once was lost, but
now am found, Was blind, but now I see.

'Twas grace that taught my heart to fear, And
grace my fears relieved; How precious did that
grace appear The hour I first believed.

Through many dangers, toils and snares, I
Have already come; 'Tis grace hath brought me
safe thus far, And grace will lead me home.

When we've been there ten thousand years, Bright
shining as the sun, We've no less days to
sing God's praise Than when we first begun.

Amen

John Newton   *Dr. A. M. Townsend*

THE LORD'S SONG IN OUR OWN LAND
Scripture: Psalm 137

Brant S. Copeland, Pastor
First Presbyterian Church
Tallahassee, Florida

24th Sunday in Ordinary Time
September 16, 2001

I chose this Sunday to depart from the lectionary and to select instead passages of scriptures that have spoken loudly to me in this past week. I am aware that there are young children among us this morning, and I will not be explicit in describing what happened last Tuesday. Most of us, whatever our ages, have already been exposed to more horror than we can take in. I do want to be explicit, however, in inviting you to hear God's word, which, in the words of an old prayer for illumination, "lifts us out of darkness and distress into the light and peace of God's presence."

God's people have traveled this way before. I know of no clearer guide to the journey than Psalm 137.

1 By the rivers of Babylon—there we sat down and there we wept
when we remembered Zion.
2 On the willows there we hung up our harps.

The landscape has changed. The skyline is not the same. The psalmist looks out the window and sees not the familiar towers of Jerusalem, the holy city, but the unfamiliar canals of Babylon, the city of the enemy, the city of exile. Gone are the landmarks of the psalmist's faith—the walls of Jerusalem, which were meant to repel every enemy and keep God's people safe, the temple which had become the guarantee of God's sure presence, the markets with their world trade, symbols of unending prosperity.

All of that is gone now—gone and far away. God's covenant people had learned to put their faith in those symbols, and amidst those familiar landmarks they had raised their songs of praise to the Lord. Now the landscape has changed, and they have lost their voice for singing.

3 For there our captors asked us for songs, and our tormentors asked for mirth,
saying, "Sing us one of the songs of Zion!"
4 How could we sing the Lord's song in a foreign land?

How, indeed? The songs of Zion proclaim God's power and might. They sing of God's sovereignty over all the lesser gods. Babylon, the enemy, who has shown the whole world how vulnerable God's people are, now mocks and struts and rejoices in their humiliation.

"Sing us one of the songs of Zion."

How can they sing when the landscape has changed so much, and they can't get they bearings? How can they sing when they don't know the way home?

God's people have traveled this road before. We have this song of lament to remind us and to show us the way.

We should never have placed our confidence in walls and towers and markets. They had no power to keep us safe. They were not proof of God's special blessings on us after all.

Now those symbols, as much idols as icons, lie in ruins, and we, like those who have gone ahead of us, are called to sing the songs of Zion. What shall we sing?

Shall we sing of rebuilding our former confidence, or shall we sing of something older still? Shall we try as best we can to reconstruct our former faith on those ruined symbols, or shall we invite God's Spirit to build our faith on something better, something everlasting?

The world has changed since last Tuesday, but God hasn't. The skyline of our self-confidence has been altered forever, but God's love for the world hasn't been altered. God's power to overcome evil hasn't lessened. God's compassion for the suffering hasn't been withdrawn. If anything, we can see God more clearly now than we could a week ago.

The songs of Zion mean something different now. No longer are they songs of our superiority over others, our pride in being number one, our moral supremacy, our goodness over the enemy's evil. Now the songs of Zion proclaim our utter dependence upon God, our constant need of grace and mercy, our longing for justice not just for ourselves, but for all who suffer.

We are still called to sing the songs of Zion, but to a new tune. Adversity, grief, and compassion have altered the melody. Now we sing with less pride in ourselves and more humility before God.

That, at least, is one path we could choose. There are others. We could put the songs of Zion to other tunes.

We could sing of revenge. We could sing of mass destruction. We could sing of hate for outsiders and expulsion of aliens among us. Psalm 137 itself provides the words to put to those tunes:

> 7 Remember, O LORD, against the Edomites the day of Jerusalem's fall, how they said, "Tear it down! Tear it down! Down to its foundations!"

> 8 O…Babylon, you devastator! Happy shall they be who pay you back what you have done to us!

> 9 Happy shall they be who take your little ones and dash them against the rock!

We already have the words. They are part of our sacred writings. Before last Tuesday we could not have imagined the feelings that would prompt such words, and we were embarrassed to have them in our Bible.

But not now. Now we know how so many other people in the world feel. We know what it's like to live in dread, to feel utterly powerless, to be consumed by anger.

We have tasted the fear of a Palestinian who lives in Israeli-occupied territory and of an Israeli who lives in a settlement surrounded by Palestinians. We have tasted the pain of a Christian in Sudan and a Muslim in India. We know what it's like now to feel so violated that we can imagine ourselves committing the very atrocities that have been inflicted upon us.

Thank God for these closing words of Psalm 137. Thank God that they are among the songs of Zion. God invites us to sing these words so that we can offer them to God instead of putting them into practice. We can feel them and sing them and give them to God. Thereby we purge our souls of poison.

These words are sacred if we offer them to God. If we embody them in our response to last Tuesday, however, we blaspheme the God who is the Father of Jesus Christ.

. . . Happy shall they be who pay you back what you have done to us!

Happy shall they be who take your little ones and dash them against the rock!

As honest lament these words are sacred. As national policy they are the wrong road to follow. Set to one tune they become the music of faith. Set to another, they become the song of Babylon on our own lips.

The wounds of our nation are too tender now to call for forgiveness. There is such a thing as a rush to forgiveness as well as a rush to judgment. Forgiveness will take time and a generous outpouring of God's Spirit. For now, let Christians refrain from joining in the chorus of hate, retribution, and xenophobia.

Let us weep with those who weep. Let us mourn with those who mourn. Let us be agents of reconciliation. Let us stand with those who fear that they will become the targets of our nation's wrath, the next victims of terror.

Let us, in other words, be God's people in our own land. Let us be the church of Jesus Christ, the crucified One, the child who was dashed against the rock in God's name, the Son of God who was nailed to the tree.

We have been here before. We have the words and the songs to sing. We have Christ's example to follow. We have the saints to surround us and bear us up. We have bread and wine for the journey.

God will show us the way home. We will not dwell in Babylon forever.

THE LIGHT THAT NEVER GOES OUT
Scripture: St. John 8:12

Rev. John E. Tyree, Pastor, 1933-1974
Chief Cornerstone Baptist Church
Dillwyn, Virginia

(*with special foreword and postscript written by Pastor Tyree's granddaughter*)

Excerpts
September 2001

Foreword
There is a fire burning even now at Ground Zero. We are amazed even through our grief. We are reminded of the magnitude of the event even though we want to forget. Will it ever cease to burn so that there will be one less monument to pain and suffering? Yes, it will. Man will extinguish it, although the hot smoldering iron is buried deep within and throughout the awful debris. Man will extinguish it, and we will no longer have that reminder of our collective tragedy.

What man will not—cannot—extinguish is our hope. It has shown like a red hot light all through this tragedy. It has made more and more dim the flames of destruction. It is our belief in THE LIGHT THAT NEVER GOES OUT that sustains us.

The Sermon
"I am the Light of the world. He that followeth me shall not walk in darkness, but shall have the Light of Life."

The word Jesus uses when He speaks of himself as "The Light of the World" signifies sunlight. The word He uses when he refers to John the Baptist as a burning and shining light signifies lamplight. In this bold affirmation, Jesus claims to be the true original, creative light, which is to the spiritual world what the sun is to the natural world.

He is a personal light. Truth is revealed by him because it dwells in Him. He gives light because He is light. His life is the light of men. Christianity is Christ. He is the "sun" of righteousness. In His light the world is to walk.

He is the universal light. Christ is the light of the world. The light which lightest every man that cometh into the world. Take away from this world the light of His presence, and the world would plunge into darkness and desolation.

He is an everlasting light. He is a light that never goes out. He continually shines in the midst of darkness of our earthly nights. Compared with Him, all other truth-bearers are temporary and transient lights—lights that burn for a little while and then are gone. Christ is unmistakably the light, for John the Baptist says, "I am not the light, but I come to bear witness of that light that all men may believe. I come to bear witness to that light that lightest every man that cometh into the world."

How ironic that sometimes during a storm, we turn off "the power" to our electric light so as not to draw lightening toward us, while in that very same storm we look to "the power" of Christ's light to guide us through the darkness—to protect us. In the storms of life, we look to the light of Jesus for his life-saving power.

The cry of the soul is for the light. Christ helps us to see the light of another day—a brighter day. He helps us to know that even as we move through shadowy days when our human view out of the window of life is dim, we can look out and still see His light and say, "The Lord is my light and my salvation; whom shall I fear?" We are continually renewed by His comforting words, "I am the Light of the world. He that followest me shall not walk in darkness, but shall have the Light of Life." Yes, Christ, the Eternal Light, is our hope.

(This message of hope was written by Rev. John E. Tyree forty-one years ago in March of 1960. He died in 1976. There is no time in Christ Jesus. Families, hold on. Christ will light your way.)

Granddaughter, Brenda A. Spencer

A TIME FOR PRAYER

Texts: Psalm 14:1-7; Jeremiah 4:19-28; 1 Timothy 1:12-17; John 14:25-27

Larry Bethune
University Baptist Church
Austin, Texas

The Fifteenth Sunday after Pentecost
September 16, 2001

What a glorious day we shared last Sunday! How our hearts were made glad by a capacity crowd from across our community insisting "God is love!" against the "God is hate" message of our promised protestors. And when we learned their flight from Dallas had been stopped by storms, some of us were elated while others regretted they had missed seeing that triumphant gathering.

But we cannot feel glorious today. We cannot feel elated. We cannot feel triumphant. On Tuesday an act of hatred took place which made last week's no-show pickets a silly cartoon by comparison. Suddenly words like "love" and "hate" took on a far greater significance, and "family" and "community," an even deeper meaning. We felt like Jeremiah when he saw the devastation the Babylonians brought to Judah:

My anguish, my anguish! I writhe in pain! Oh, the walls of my heart! My heart is beating wildly; I cannot keep silent; for I hear the sound of the trumpet, the alarm of war. Disaster overtakes disaster, the whole land is laid waste. Suddenly my tents are destroyed, my curtains in a moment. How long must I see the standard, and hear the sound of the trumpet?

Jeremiah even quotes the words Genesis uses to describe the chaos before creation:

I looked on the earth, and lo, it was void and without form; and to the heavens, and they had no light. I looked on the mountains, and lo, they were quaking, and all the hills moved to and fro. I looked, and lo, there was no one at all, and all the birds of the air had fled. I looked, and lo, the fruitful land was a desert, and all its cities were laid in ruins (Jeremiah 4:19-26).

Isn't that the way we feel today, as if something fundamental about our world has been altered, as if the creation itself were somehow undone in this crime of first order magnitude? There is no making sense of it. There is no going back to the way things were. Our nation is suffering and our sorrow will not cease. These attackers destroyed not just some buildings, not just a host of innocents and their rescuers, but our national sense of identity and well-being. Writes Robert Schrieter:

Suffering is the human struggle with and against pain. It is the experience of the breakdown of our systems of meaning and our stories about ourselves, and the struggle to restore those senses of safety and selfhood. Suffering in itself is neither noble nor redeeming. It is essentially an erosion of meaning. It is an interruption and destruction of those fundamental senses of safety and selfhood without which we cannot survive as individuals and as societies. Suffering only becomes redemptive or ennobling when we struggle against these corroding powers and rebuild ourselves in spite of the pain we are experiencing.

As individuals, and together as a people, we can, we will rebuild. This is the first day of a new week. Tomorrow we will get back to business. But our lives will never be the same again. We could not control or prevent what happened to our nation on Tuesday, but we can decide how we will respond. Billy Graham put it well in his message at the National Cathedral on Friday: "Yes, our nation has been attacked, buildings destroyed, lives lost. But now we have a choice: whether to implode and disintegrate emotionally and spiritually as a people and a nation; or whether we choose to become stronger through all this struggle, to rebuild on a solid foundation." We have entered a time of crisis, which is always a moment of both danger and opportunity.

It is not hard to see the danger. We are tempted to react to terrorists with rage and hate. We long for a commensurate violence which will make others suffer as we have. But we risk becoming terrorists ourselves in the process, wreaking vengeance on the innocent. Let us support the patience of our President and national leaders and pray they will withstand the political pressure for a quick violent reprisal providing emotional catharsis and pursue instead a strong but just and sustained response that will lead to peace.

And in these confusing days there is also the danger of misplaced blame and division, from stupid remarks to criminal action. Almost immediately this week I heard reporters insulting the people who handle security at airports, before we even knew how the hijackers got on the planes. One gaggle of pundits was blaming the intelligence community and another the people who had handcuffed the intelligence community with cutbacks in funding or laws protecting freedom and privacy. Mosques were attacked here in our own state, and Arab-Americans, or even Arab appearing American citizens had to fear for their children because of blind racist reprisals. This is not the time for blaming, for dividing us one against the other, for manipulating people for personal gain through their fears, for political exploitation, or for wasted, silly words. In this time of terrible woundedness, we should all remember the starting principle of the Hippocratic oath: "First, do no harm." Let us pray for such people, because they're wounded, too.

On the other hand, this is a time of opportunity. As Schrieter suggests, we are experiencing "the breakdown of our systems of meaning and our stories about ourselves, and the struggle to restore those senses of safety and selfhood." Thus it is a moment of essential spiritual formation. When our systems and stories break down, we may see where they were built poorly to begin with. Then we can rebuild them stronger than before. Therefore today I want to suggest three things about this painful but significant spiritual moment that might guide us as we move forward together as a people. I want to say today that this is the time for faith in the face of evil. This is the time for hope in the face of fear. And this is the time for love in the face of hatred.

First of all, this is the time for faith in the face of evil. Among all the messages of rage and retaliation this week, some of our wisest religious leaders have called for a spiritual reassessment and reawakening as a response to what happened Tuesday. Such evil should make us turn inward and reevaluate, literally re-value our reality before God. We must let go of the peripherals that pre-occupied us before and live out of our core values as a people. Jeremiah understood the devastation that came upon his land as the judgement of God against them. Up until this week, I always found it hard to understand why many leaders on both sides of the American Civil War spoke often of the suffering of the war as "the hand of God" upon the nation. But this week we saw the most violent day on American soil since the Civil War, and an evil so terrifying that we must pause to reassess. What have we done to create such hatred against us in the world? How have we participated in glorifying and spreading violence? How has our wealth in

131

relation to their poverty, our pride in relation to their vulnerability, our media in relation to their teachings poisoned their souls? Where have we let our casual speech turn to insult and animosity so that we added to the great sea of hostility in this world? And why should it take such a national tragedy to draw us together and treat one another with dignity and kindness and respect?

Please hear me clearly. I'm not saying anybody deserved what happened this week. I'm not saying anybody is to blame but the people who made this cowardly attack and those who helped them. I'm not offering any justification for their evil. I'm saying that such unspeakable evil should turn us inward to God, to purge ourselves of any hatred, to purify ourselves from any guile, to understand anew what really matters and what does not.

For instance, Gina was telling me about the CEO of some company interviewed on television this week. Almost all of his employees were killed in the collapse of the tower because their offices were above the floors where the plane struck. He had not come in that morning because his daughter was starting nursery school. He was crying and speaking with awe of the insistence of those few who remained that they go back to work on Monday. And then he said something too seldom heard in American business in recent days. He said, "From now on in our company, people will be more important than high profits, because people are what matter most. People, and not things." That's the kind of spiritual transformation we should all experience in the light of this experience of evil. We must re-value our reality, value freedom over comfort, unity over selfishness, and people over things.

I also believe, this is the time for hope in the face of fear. We are suddenly vulnerable where we once felt secure. But was that security well founded? Let us be honest about our limitations. We are all merely mortal. We cannot guarantee our next breath. We will all surely die. And there will be no security until all the world is secure and shares in the goodness of God's earth. Perhaps we have foolishly put our security in our military might. Maybe we let our great national wealth make us feel safe. Could we have put our trust too much in our leaders to protect us from all harm? There is no security in this life. There is no safe place. And there is no one worthy of trust, except our God. Jesus said, "Peace I leave with you; my peace I give to you. I do not give to you as the world gives. Do not let your hearts be troubled, and do not let them be afraid" (John 15:27). Only in Christ can we have an inner peace and sense of safety that will never fail us. Every other trust is misplaced, every other form of security an unreliable idol in the end.

Our hope is in almighty God, and God alone can make us secure. Christ has promised to those who trust a place prepared beyond this place and a life eternal beyond this life. In the meantime, and it can be inexpressibly mean, we overcome fear by hoping in God. God is faithful. God will not disappoint. God will be with us to bring us to new beginnings. How does the great old hymn go? "Fear not, I am with you, O be not dismayed, for I am your God, I will still give you aid. I'll strengthen you, help you, and cause you to stand upheld by my gracious, omnipotent hand." Our lives are not made meaningful by how much stuff we own. Our lives are not made meaningful by how much time we have. Our lives are not made meaningful by how famous we become. Our lives are made meaningful by our service to God. Our lives are made meaningful by the people who love us, by the people we love, by the love of God we spread through our love of others.

And so, this is also the time for love in the face of hatred. I spoke at length about love and hate last week, but now those words mean something at a deeper level and more powerful, more real and much more important than they did then. I have to tell you, as I watched the twin towers burning, and then as I watched them fall, I thought of my wife, I thought of my children, and I wished they were near. I thought of my friends who live in New York. I thought of you, and of all the dear people God has placed in my life. And I wanted to be with all of them at once, to tell them how much I love them, how important they are to me. It shouldn't take such a catastrophe to get us to love, but surely in the light of this last Tuesday, our mission to advance the love of God against hate in the world is all the more important and critical and essential. The perverters of Islam—and Judaism—and Christianity—must be denounced for their egomaniacal projection of personal animosity upon the Divine. In all of these historic faiths there is no justification to hate in the name of God. But we cannot win this war with words. We must win it with love in action. We must love the world—and by that I mean every person we encounter—with the love of God. We cannot merely repeat it in chorus, we must show the world that "God is love." In the final analysis, what else but the love of God in every human heart can prevent this age-old cycle of violence and horror from destroying us all?

Therefore, most of all, my beloved church, this is the time for prayer. Now you know I hesitate to quote Gerald Mann to you, but Gerald said something in a television interview this week I like very much. He said, "We need to pray, not until God hears us but until we hear God." And I think if we would listen to God today, a grieving, brokenhearted God would call us, in spite of the chaos about us, to faith, hope, and love.

This is the first day of a new week, and for Christians, the first day is always a celebration of the resurrection, of God's power to bring life out of death and a new creation out of the chaos of the old. Our world has been turned upside down this week by evil and violence and hate. Let us have no more to do with those killers. Rather, let us be about the things that make for life as we rebuild our systems of meaning and retell our stories of life. With Christ, by the help of Almighty God, let us be the architects of a new creation. For this is the time, if ever there was a time, for faith, hope, and love. And the greatest of these is love. Amen.

WITHIN THIS CELL: MY MESSAGE OF HOPE
September 14, 2001
Clinton Conyers
Riverside Regional Jail
Hopewell, Virginia

Excerpts
September 2001

Preface

I know you do not know me. You may be discouraged by my letter coming from jail. However, I have been blessed these last two months by being here. I have done a lot of reading, writing, praying, fasting, meditating, and exercising. Most importantly, I have been listening to God's people on many different spectrums. So don't concern yourself with the writer. Just listen to my message of hope.

WITHIN THIS CELL

Within this cell of my mind, I have allowed the freedom of God's will to be done. As my nature grappled, I was trying to relive every blessing as my eyes kept searching. Yes, He has acknowledged me, but He is not quite ready to relinquish me of my burdens. But everything will be all right. Offering someone like you support, even during the many times one can fall short, is like a blessing in disguise to allow your efforts to come forth. I mention this not as a plea but as a bond as we both strive to hold on to what is true inside. Though the paths ahead of us are unplotted and dotted with hot tears like rain, even this parched soil can bear growth. Soon we will see a morning dew. So don't hide your tears. Let them fall gently on the soil.

FAITH TESTIMONY: GOD IS STILL GOD

Inez G. Scott
Ministers' Wives and Ministers' Widows Alliance of Petersburg and Vicinity
and Tabernacle Baptist Church
Petersburg, Virginia

September 16, 2001

As we assembled for worship on the Sunday morning after September 11 in First Rock Baptist Church in Prospect, Virginia, I shared words of inspiration with the church family. I tried to help members understand that it does not matter how dark life may seem at the moment. The most important thing to remember is that God is still God and He knows what he is doing. I don't know why he allowed the tragedy of September 11, but we do know he could have stopped it if he had wanted to. He allowed it to happen for a reason. However, if we want to reign with Him, then we must suffer with Him and trust His decisions in situations beyond our control.

Many ask the question why? But as born again believers, we know that God is still all mighty, all knowing, and an omnipotent way maker. He is a burden bearer and helps us daily to carry our heavy load; however, we know He is also a God of wrath. Many things that are going on in our homes, on our jobs, in our schools and churches are displeasing to the Lord. We know that God is not pleased with our sinful activities of life; yet we have turned away from His ways and gone the way of the wicked. In many cases we are afraid to hurt someone's feeling, so we sugarcoat the solution rather than take a stand for the Master. Thus, He allows suffering to get our attention and this causes us to be humble and valuable to the kingdom of God. Further, suffering will cause many to escape eternal damnation by repenting and changing their wicked ways. God sees the big picture; He knows our value. This is only a test.

Yes, we are pressed on every side by trouble, but we are not crushed and broken. We are perplexed but we cannot give up and quit (II Corinthians 4-8). We must continue to tell His story as never before. He will renew our spirit everyday, for our troubles are small and will not last very long. In fact they produce for us an immeasurable glory that will last forever. So we don't look back at September 11, or the troubles we can see right now, rather we look forward to what we have not yet seen. For the troubles we now see will soon be over, but the joys to come will last forever.

God's Unfailing Love

"Love Divine, All Love Excelling"
God's Unfailing Love
After Tuesday 9-11
Security
Scars of Hope
A Prayer for the Church and Nation

Chapter

12

Love Divine, All Love Excelling

Love divine, all love excelling, Joy of heav'n, to earth come down;
Fix in us thy humble dwelling, All Thy faithful mercies crown.

Breathe, O breathe Thy loving Spirit Into ev'ry troubled breast;
Let us all in Thee inherit, Let us find the promised rest.

Finish then Thy new creation; Pure and spotless may we be;
Let us see our full salvation Perfectly secured by Thee.

Amen

C. Wesley   *Samuel W. Beazley, 1873*

GOD'S UNFAILING LOVE
Scripture: Romans 8: 38,39

Winfred Walton, Bible Instructor
Oak Hill Baptist Church
Buckingham, Virginia

September 2001

It is at times of tragedy such as *9/11/01* that we inevitably ask "why." This is true of the faithful and those of no faith. It seems that in all of us there is at least a suspicion that events don't just happen but rather there is a plan, a larger scheme of which our lives are just a small part. As an instructor and long time student of the Bible, I believe that to be the absolute truth.

From my understanding of the Bible, (God's revelation to mankind) God has revealed himself to be sovereign over all that exists and that nothing happens in the earth or in the entire universe without his knowledge or permission. (Psalms 135:6; 2) Evil has been allowed to enter and continue to exist in the earth over which a loving God is sovereign ruler. Although mankind may never know all that pertains to God (Romans 11:33-34; 3), we believe that even in the allowing of evil to exist until the time he has determined (Revelation 21:5: 22:3; 4), there is a divine purpose. Though we may not know all, it is possible to know that which He has revealed in His Word, the Bible.

From our knowledge of the Bible, we can be sure that first, God is not the one who causes death and destruction or any other calamity that comes upon the earth. Secondly, the force of evil that comes only to steal, kill and destroy can only do so to the extent that it is permitted. (John 10:10; Job 2) We are also taught in scripture that God is able to take these tragedies and use them for good (in the big picture and plan) and cause them to benefit those who trust Him. (Romans 8:28)

The question is often asked, "How can a loving God allow such tragedy to come upon innocent people, even children? I submit that the lives lost were not lost in vain. Rather they were part of a plan and through their sacrifice, (though not an act of God), we who survived may benefit. The end of their physical lives is not in any way an indication of limits on God's love for humanity.

Through the awful loss of innocent physical life, there can be positive results in the lives of us who remain. There can be a new vigilance concerning the enemies of our society at large. The country can be drawn together in unity against common enemies. Families can be brought to realize how fragile life really is. All can be brought to the realization that we can't take each other for granted, but we can draw close to each other and demonstrate and speak words of kindness and love while we yet have one another. It is the hope of this writer that many will be strengthened in their faith and others will be brought to faith in a God who loves unconditionally, a God from which nothing can separate us from His love. (Romans 8:35, 37-39)

AFTER TUESDAY 9/11

Reverend Andrew J. White Sr., Pastor
Zion Baptist Church
Petersburg, Virginia

September 2001

The date 9-11-01 will live in infamy and the dramatic, shocking and bizarre events, which occurred on that day, have drawn an indelible line in the American psyche. What took place may have seemed unthinkable and unbelievable, but it certainly split time forever into "BT," before Tuesday and "AT," after Tuesday. The brutal attack on the twin towers of the World Trade Center in New York and the Pentagon in Washington, D. C. along with the crashed plane in Pennsylvania, delivered a "wake-up-call" to this country reminding all of us that we can no longer find security in our economic and trade superiority nor realize real defense from our military establishment. Our real security and our sure defense are found only in the Lord.

Today, we are a changed nation, a different people who realize that we are one nation that must love, respect and appreciate all people. We also have been made aware that terror has been a part of the American way, even though we have not been willing to accept that fact. The Night Riders and raiders in their white sheets and with their torches have spread terror, fear, intimidation, and death throughout the Southland; a justice system which was everything but just controlled the courthouses and courtrooms of America; a dual education system in many states of this country really subjected many of its citizens to the educational terror of misinformation and ignorance.

Yes, we must seek out and destroy terror in all of its varied forms wherever it exists in this Nation or anywhere in the world. This is our challenge.

The writer of the 91st Psalm reminds us that even before or after 9-11—*"He that dwelleth in the secret place of the most High shall abide under the shadow of the Almighty. I will say of the Lord, He is my refuge and my fortress, my God in Him will I trust. He shall cover thee with his feathers and under his wings shall thou trust. Thou shall not be afraid of the Terror by night, nor the arrow that flieth by day. For He shall give His angels charge over thee to keep thee in all thy ways."*

"SECURITY"
Scripture: Psalm 46

Reverend Dr. Raymond Q. Lawing
Fork Union Baptist Church
Buckingham, Virginia

September 2001

Danger, trouble and weakness are the lot of humanity. Some dangers we see; many are unseen. Daily physical forces threaten the well being of the body. We have no knowledge of the many untoward conditions that could wreck our health and bring us down to the grave. The tragedy of September 11, 2001 comes to mind. Yet, there is nothing new under the sun, for in Luke 13:4 the tower in Siloani fell and killed eighteen people. Powers of evil are constantly working against the welfare of the soul and spirit. We spend our lives in the midst of dangers and troubles. Job said, "Man who is born of woman is of few days and full of trouble." So weak are we that we cannot cope effectively with the unfortunate conditions we meet. Therefore, humanly speaking, we have no freedom from danger. But, in God there is complete freedom from danger, fear and doubt. God is our refuge. He is a tower of strength into which we can run and be entirely safe. Whatever the danger, however terrible the trouble, we may flee to God and He will protect and shield us. In the midst of danger from without and danger from within, He has promised to preserve and deliver us and what He has promised, He will do without fail. God is not a man that He should lie; neither the son of man that He should repent; hath he said and shall he not do it? Or hath he spoken and shall he not make it good.

Finally, God is a help in trouble, a help always at hand, a help for any and every situation, even for the situation and circumstances of September 11, 2001 and for the ramifications that will follow. Therefore, let us stop crying out in complaints, let us stop crying out in despair, and let us stop crying out in sorrow. But let us cry like the heroes of faith— "In Him we live and move and we have our being."

...On the Sabbath After

SCARS OF HOPE

Scripture: John 20: 19-31 [RSV]

Allen E. Mosimaan

Trinity Presbyterian Church
A Center for Christian Spiritual Practice
Nashville, Tennessee

A Sermon Delivered September 16, 2001 at Trinity Presbyterian Church's Family Camp

On the evening of that day, the first day of the week, the doors being shut where the disciples were, for fear of the Jews, Jesus came and stood among them and said to them, "Peace be with you."

When he had said this, he showed them his hands and his side. Then the disciples were glad when they saw the Lord. Jesus said to them again, "Peace be with you. As the Father has sent me, even so I send you."

And when he had said this, he breathed on them, and said to them, "Receive the Holy Spirit. If you forgive the sins of any, they are forgiven; if you retain the sins of any, they are retained."

Now Thomas, one of the twelve, called the Twin, was not with them when Jesus came. So the other disciples told him, "We have seen the Lord." But he said to them, "Unless I see in his hands the print of the nails, and place my finger in the mark of the nails, and place my hand in his side, I will not believe."

Eight days later, his disciples were again in the house, and Thomas was with them. The doors were shut, but Jesus came and stood among them, and said, "Peace be with you."

Then he said to Thomas, "Put your finger here, and see my hands; and put out your hand, and place it in my side; do not be faithless, but believing. Thomas answered him, *"My Lord and my God!"*

Jesus said to him, "Have you believed because you have seen me? Blessed are those who have not seen and yet believe."

Now Jesus did many other signs in the presence of the disciples, which are not written in this book; but these are written that you may believe that Jesus is the Christ, the Son of God, and that believing you may have life in his name.

On a Sunday morning a congregation gathers for worship and a family gathers around the baptismal font. Their young daughter, Alisa, three months old, is being baptized. I step forward and ask of the parents three questions. These same three questions were asked of my parents when I was baptized, and asked of Marianne and me when our children were baptized. The first question has long caused me to stumble just a bit. It goes like this: "Trusting in the gracious mercy of God, do you turn from the ways of sin and renounce evil and its power in the world?" I stumble a bit because, unlike my forbearers in faith, I have never given serious consideration to "evil" as a power in the world akin to "sin." After this week, that is a notion that I will have to rethink.

Ronald Reagan, while he was President, tried to convince us of the "Evil Empire" embodied in that nation that no longer exists, the Soviet Union. I saw his words as political posturing and saber rattling. I was sure that no nation or empire is built wholly on a devotion to doing evil. I am willing to admit that I was wrong.

Lloyd Rediger wrote a book a few years ago entitled *Clergy Killers*. It wasn't a mystery novel but a psychological profile of the unique relationship that exists between a pastor and a congregation. Rediger warned of relational entanglements that can ruin ministers, ministries, and churches. Rediger makes an impassioned plea to folks like me to believe in evil and its power in the world. I learned much from the book, but I shrugged off the "forces of evil" diatribe. I have to re-think it now.

In this place, where we have spent time relaxing, enjoying the beauty of God's creation, and away from the mind-numbing news reports, it is so very easy to embrace the goodness that is present in the world. We embrace one another with a morning hug before breakfast and know the goodness and love of our relationships. We exchange a word of peace and know the goodness of our oneness in Jesus Christ. Here, for a couple of days, we have been shielded from evil and its power in the world. Thanks be to God for this respite.

When we leave here we will pull into the driveway and pick up Sunday's paper and glance at the front page before the garage door closes behind us. We hit the television remote control and the TV will pop on to the station we were watching before we left home, and CNN is once again in our living room with the very latest report from New York, Washington, and Pennsylvania. A talking head explains the options for retaliation.

"Trusting in the gracious mercy of God, do you turn from the ways of sin and renounce evil and its power in the world?" I certainly renounce evil as I prepare to live with its consequences. Perhaps none of us should have been caught off guard. Of course we were surprised by the attack itself, by the destruction, the careful planning that such an attack obviously entailed, and by the hatred of our nation that would cause people to go to such lengths. What should not catch us off guard is what caught me off guard: evil and its power in the world. We have known of it since Cain killed Abel; since Noah built the boat; since Pharaoh slaughtered the innocents; since Jesus hung on a cross.

As dark as this week has been, as Christians we confess that the ultimate human expression of evil was not flying a 767 into the World Trade Center; it was nailing God to a cross and waiting for God to die. On that Friday afternoon 2,000 years ago we proclaimed *"We need and want no God over us, for we are ourselves all gods. Crucify Him,"* we shouted, not for the innocent man, but for the omnipotent God. That was humanity's darkest hour to which September 11, 2001 is but a pale reminder. There is evil in the world and we are capable, each and every one of us, of serving as evil's accomplice.

God, however, is capable of overcoming evil. Sometimes nations go to war; every war is both fought against evil and participates in evil actions. Some wars drag out for years on end, but then comes a day of peace, grace, hope, and new life. There are people in the world who enslave themselves to evil, wreaking terrible consequences upon others. Yet most people, the world over, of every religious faith, and of no particular faith seek the good for themselves and others. Death looms for every one of us, not just those whose lives are senselessly snuffed out in a terrorist attack; but Easter's resurrection overpowers the darkness of death and promises that our God is a God of life. God's power to bring life, peace, hope, and grace is greater than evil's power to bring death, fear, despair, and hatred.

For Christians, every event in human history must be viewed through the lens of Easter. If there is truly a day in human history that changed life as we know it, that day is Easter, when at dawn women went and found that the tomb into which Jesus' body had been placed was now empty. Every event, including Tuesday's terrorist attacks, Christians must view through the lens of Easter.

On Easter day, the doors were closed for fear of those who had killed Jesus. The disciples gathered in an upper room. Jesus appeared among them and said, *"Peace be with you."* He showed them his hands and his side. The disciples were overcome with joy to see the Lord. But Thomas was not with them. When the others told him that they had seen the Lord, Thomas said, *"Unless I see the mark of the nails in his hands, and put my finger in his side, I will not believe."*

A week later the disciples were again in the house, and this time Thomas was with them. Again Jesus appeared to them and said, "Peace be with you." Then he showed Thomas his wounds. *"Put your finger here. Reach out your hand and place it in my side."* Thomas looked and said, *"My Lord and my God."*

Thomas recognized Jesus, not by his face, not his voice, not by the color of his eyes, but by his scars. Not only did he recognize Jesus by the scars but also he recognized Jesus as the Lord, the very representative of God.

Jesus in that room is wounded. Wounded as humans are wounded. Wounded by the cruelty of humans. But Jesus in that room is also wounded as God is wounded. A wounded God who knows what it means to be a wounded person. A wounded God who knows what it is to receive wounds from another person. A wounded God who willingly takes on wounds that no one deserves. This is who Thomas sees—a God who loves so much that God becomes wounded and vulnerable. The scars show a God who knows what it means to bear scars.

These are no easy scars that Jesus bears. Five high school girls nearing graduation make a pact to remain best friends, forever. To seal their pact they prick their fingers and mix their blood. It is a tiny scar, it barely hurt, and it was more a showing of commitment than a descent into hell. Jesus's scars are different.

Will Willimon, the Dean of the Chapel at Duke University, tells this story. In one of the churches he served before going to Duke, there was a woman who had been assaulted in her back yard at ten o'clock in the morning. With the aid of a good therapist, a supportive husband and family, she slowly began putting her life back into order. She called Willimon one day because her therapist said that she needed to tell her story to someone besides her family or her pastor. She said to Willimon, *"I think I will tell Joe Smith."*

Joe Smith was a member of the congregation who was a sometimes-recovering alcoholic who had lost a handful of jobs in the past few years. So he asked, "I thought you might want to tell your story to another woman. Why did you choose Joe?"

She said, *"Because he has been to hell and lived to tell about it."*

We can recognize people by their scars. We know God by the scars that God still bears from the cross.

The worst pastoral care situation I have ever faced was with the death of a child who was struck by a car that his father was driving. We gathered in the emergency room, the small body wrapped in a blanket, the mother lying with the child, the father and grandfather weeping. There I stood as some representative of God. I tried to be clear, at least in my own mind—which would hardly focus—on the character of God that I represented. I was not there representing the God who called this child home. I wasn't there representing a God who willed or caused this tragedy. I was there as a representative of a once-wounded and forever-scarred God who, too, lay on the bed weeping.

The scars our nation will now forever bear as a result of Tuesday's terrorist attacks are scars that God bears as well. The tears we shed for those whose lives were lost are mingled with the tears God sheds for those same people. The reality of evil that so disrupts our understanding of how the world works disrupts the world of God's goodness, too. Yet God, scarred at the cross, overcomes every evil with grace, love, forgiveness, and new life.

A PRAYER FOR THE CHURCH AND THE NATION

References: [2] Psalm 73:25-26; [3] Psalm 12:8; [4] Habakkuk 3:17-18; [5] Habakkuk 3:19

Copyright David Horner 2001
David Horner
Providence Baptist Church
Raleigh, North Carolina

September 16, 2001

Foreword

At the time of this writing, Pastor David Horner had been in India and was in Singapore waiting for air travel to resume to the U.S. following the attack upon New York City and the Pentagon. Although he had hoped to be home on Sunday, September 16, he asked his wife Cathy to read his prayer at Providence's weekend worship services on his behalf.

A PRAYER FOR THE CHURCH AND THE NATION

Almighty and Most Glorious Lord,

With grateful hearts we bow before you,
proclaiming your matchless strength,
taking comfort in your sovereign dominion, and
confessing our complete dependence upon You.
We come to You and join together with all who love your name
to declare that You alone are the Lord.

While all around us, people lose heart and hope,
we find our future anchored in Christ and our peace resting upon Christ
who alone upholds all things by the power of His might.
Whom have we in heaven but You?
And besides You, we desire nothing more on earth.
One by one, we cry out, "My flesh and my heart may fail,
But God is the strength of my heart and my portion forever."

In a fallen world, You have told us that
"When vileness is exalted among the sons of men,
the wicked strut about on every side."
But you have drawn us near,
held us close, called us Your own and
sheltered us beneath the shadow of Your wings.
What can man do to us when our lives are in You?
May the devastating losses of these days of terror
never be wasted on futile thoughts of revenge, but

144

may we take captive every thought born of the tragedy.
May each of those thoughts serve us well and act
as a sober testimony to the frailty of human existence, and
as a grim reminder of the unlimited wickedness of total depravity.

For those who mourn,
for those whose sorrows weigh heavily
upon hearts crushed with grief,
O God, be their comfort and their peace.
For the brokenhearted, be merciful and bring
a touch of healing,
a sense of Your presence, and
a promise of hope.

In days past, we have enjoyed Your great favor,
consumed Your gracious bounty, and
scarcely even said, "Thank You, Lord!"
On this day, our hearts cry out to You with gratitude for the way
the lines of our lives have fallen to us in pleasant places,
the beauty of our heritage has marked us as a blessed people, and
the fullness of our joy has been limited only by our own short-sightedness
and ingratitude.

Now as the dark clouds surround us, we still give thanks, for you are the Lord.
Now as the nations roar with indignation, we will give thanks, for you are
our Sovereign God.
Now as the foundations are shaken and the false sense of security has been exposed,
we come before the God of all creation, the Lord of heaven and earth,
and we give thanks!
"Though the fig tree should not blossom, and there be no fruit on the vines,
though the yield of the olive should fail, and the fields produce no food,
though the flock should be cut off from the fold, and there be no cattle in the stalls…"

Though the centers of trade and the towers of commerce should fall,
though the strongholds of warriors and the bastions of might should crumble,
though the comings and goings of the nations cease…

"…Yet I will exult in the Lord,
I will rejoice in the God of my salvation.
The Lord is my strength!"

May we know the perfect sufficiency of our Savior,
the blessed comfort of the Holy Spirit, and
the everlasting mercy of our Father,

as we enter into uncharted waters together.
Father, we ask that You give
comfort to our troubled minds,
peace to our anxious hearts and
rest to our weary souls.
In the difficult days ahead, our desire would be for You
to bring the greatest glory and highest praise
to Your Son, our Savior, the Lord Jesus Christ!
Our hope and our trust are in You, O God our Father;
Guard our hearts as we persevere in your peace.
This we pray in the powerful name of Jesus, Amen.

The Spreading Flame

"Great King of Nations"
The Spreading Flame
Letter to Friends in America
The Evil Eye
A Prayer on September 12
You're Not Alone: One Sorrow, One Hope

Chapter

13

Great King of Nations

Great King of nations, hear our prayer, While at Thy feet we fall;
And humbly with united cry, to Thee for mercy call.

When dangers, like a stormy sea, Beset our country round,
To Thee we looked, to Thee we cried, And help in Thee was found.

With one consent we meekly bow Beneath Thy chas-t'ning hand,
And pouring forth confession meet, Mourn with our mourning land.

With pitying eye behold our need, As thus we lift our prayer;
Correct us with Thy judgements, Lord, Then let thy mercy spare.

Amen

John H. Gurney, 1851   *Rev. John B. Dykes, 1800-1876*

THE SPREADING FLAME #1

Scripture: Acts 8:4-13; 26-40

Pastor William R. White
The Bethel Pulpit, Bethel Lutheran Church
Madison, Wisconsin

September 16, 2001 — The 15th Sunday after Pentecost

This has been a week when each of us has rediscovered our ground zero. When we heard that terrorists had attacked New York by striking the World Trade Center, few of us called our banks to inquire about the balance in our checking accounts. Nearly all of us began to pray or we picked up the phone and called the people we love—God and family, our true ground zero. Not for a moment did I think terrorists were headed to Lawrence, Kansas, where son Scott lives, or Atlanta where daughter Sara is working, or Windsor, Wisconsin where Sally labors, but we all called each other just to hear the voices of the people we love. Only after I hung up did I want to hear more news from New York.

Brother Norman is a pastor on Long Island, which is a bit removed from south Manhattan. When I asked him how he was, he told me he was fine but that his city, New Hyde Park, was in turmoil. "There are traffic jams everywhere," he said, "and people are driving in reckless abandon. One man counted four cars running the same red light," which is a bit much even for New Yorkers.

"How do you account for this behavior?" I asked.

"That is the same question I asked a man who had driven through this jumbled mess and who reported the erratic driving," my brother recalled. "This is what he said, 'These are people that have nothing to hang onto.'"

In difficult times we always look for something to hang onto. The book we know as "The Acts of the Apostles" is the story of a people who knew what to hang onto.

Acts records the amazing growth of a people who simply outlived, out-loved and out-served all of their religious and pagan neighbors. In a time of scarcity they not only fed their own families, but all who were poor. They not only prayed for their own members, they prayed for all who lived near them, even their enemies. The presence of God was alive and electric in their gatherings. One day as I was reading Acts, I was listening to Paul Simon's *Graceland,* CD. I heard him sing, "These are the days of miracles and wonders," and thought—exactly. The story of Acts is the story of miracles and wonders.

Over 5,000 men were converted in a single day during an experience filled with incredible energy, light and fire on the Festival of Pentecost. These converts returned to their home countries and immediately established mission stations that welcomed the traveling apostles who not only taught, but fed the poor, healed the sick, helped the lame walk, and assisted people with the deep addiction of their lives. They were so successful that their opposition screamed, "These people are turning the world upside down," and so they were, in a peaceful manner. When someone struck them on the cheek, they offered the other. When they were thrown in jail they prayed for their jailors, and often converted them. Theirs was a non-violent revolution. They lived this way because they had something to hang onto, the words, and presence of the God who died forgiving those who nailed him on a cross.

In chapter eight we are told that Philip, one of the disciples of Jesus, went to Samaria, about a day's journey by foot from Jerusalem. There he dealt with severe cases of mental illness, and healed people who were lame or paralyzed.

Simon, a man who practiced sleight of hand magic was one of those who was baptized. He watched Philip and saw genuine acts of healing, real magic. In the message of Jesus Christ, Simon and others found something to hang onto. They became believers.

These were also the days of visions and dreams. God spoke to Philip in this way and told him to go to Gaza where he would find an Ethiopian, a court official of the queen of Ethiopia. The Ethiopian was wealthy enough to be traveling by chariot, which is akin to taking a limo ride alone from Madison to St. Louis. Philip did what God asked him, and when he met up with the Ethiopian he found him reading from the prophet, Isaiah. Not just any passage mind you, but the section about the one known as "the suffering servant."

The passage he was reading, one of the Servant songs, is unique in the literature of religion. The key to understanding God, the passage says, is to understand that God is one who suffers. We think of God in terms of power, but this changes the picture. *Surely he has borne our griefs and carried our sorrows. He was wounded for our transgressions, he was bruised for our iniquities.* God's primary way of working in this world is through suffering love. This means that we know God best as a crucified man who hung on a tree, and we follow him most faithfully when we live in peace and compassion. We may sing "Immortal, Invisible, God only Wise," but that must be followed with, "O Sacred Head Now Wounded," to get it all straight. It is not primarily in power and majesty that we will understand God, it is in service and suffering.

When Philip met the Ethiopian official he was reading these words: *Like a sheep he was led to the slaughter, and like a lamb silent before its shearer, so he does not open his mouth. In his humiliation, justice was denied him.*

He asked, "About whom does the prophet say this, about himself or someone else?" It was then that Philip told him the story of faith. Our primary way of speaking of God has, from the very beginning, been in response to the questions asked by hungry people, inquiring people. The Ethiopian official was looking for something to hang onto, and Philip provided it. He gave him someone—a person. In this case baptism was immediate.

Are you looking for something to hang onto? 20,000 people gathered in the Library Mall at the University, 10,000 at the Capitol. Just under 1,000 were here at two services on Friday. For us, those were two of the six services that were conducted this week. It is not that we can't pray at home, it is that it is good to pray with others. When we prayed we gathered around those ancient words from the Psalms, often words that were uttered in pain, or a sense of loss. The laments are a part of the resources we have for moments like this.

Though we need to execute justice in the land, we will be defined more by our capacity to suffer, than our capacity to inflict suffering. We are deeply suspicious of war; too many innocent people get hurt, but the world will know our resolve for justice.

There were moments in our history when the flame of Christianity spread by the sword, but those were not our best moments. Our best moments, our most effective moments, have taken place when we have offered up the crucified God as the one to hold onto. *For not with swords loud clashing, nor roll of stirring drum, but deeds of love and mercy, the heavenly kingdom comes.*

In the first chapter of Acts Jesus says to his disciples: *You will receive power when the Holy Spirit has come upon you: and you will be my witnesses in Jerusalem, in all Judea and Samaria, and to the ends of the world.* The flame that was lit on Pentecost, began to spread from Jerusalem to Samaria…to Gaza…to Turkey, to Greece…and it keeps on spreading.

Though Madison is not quite the end of the world, the torch has been passed to us. We too are his witnesses, and we recognize the many opportunities we have to tell his story. We recognize that there are thousands of people who have no community. In 2002 we will pass the torch to a new Spanish speaking community here at Bethel. Like our ancestors who gathered in downtown Madison and spoke no English for the first seventy years of Bethel's existence, these people will worship God in a foreign tongue. But they are our brothers and sisters. They will soon lift up their voices in this very room, though at a different hour. We welcome them because they too need someone to hang onto.

Some have declared that it really doesn't make any difference what you believe, just so that you believe something. Some have declared that faith is neutral. Others have said that the real test is the sincerity of the believer. But this week we have discovered that to be utterly false. As long as people are shaped by their gods, as long as people take their orders from their belief system, it does make a difference. In Boston and New York men and women, ready to die, took part in a jihad, an unholy war that claimed over 5,000 lives of innocent people. Do not say that these people were cowards. They were brave, though misguided. There is no religion that approves of the killing of innocent people.

We are bearers of a story, the story of a suffering savior. The story of one who bore the sins of the world, who offered an alternative to hatred when he forgave his enemies. Jesus stopped the cycle of violence by forgiving his enemies. He did not tell his followers. "Go get the bums." Rather, he said, "Father Forgive them, they don't know what they are doing." We are the possessors of the one story that can save individuals and can save a nation. This is a story about a God who brings down the terrorists, without bringing down the innocent at the same time. Ours is the story of a God who provides us with hope, when things seem bleak.

The story of our God needs to be shared in our homes, in our neighborhoods, and across the world. The flame must continue to spread, for the health of us and the nations.

LETTER TO FRIENDS IN AMERICA
FROM MEETING FOR SUFFERINGS

Europe
September 13, 2001

Foreword

Britain Yearly Meeting: *The Quaker body which represents the interests of the thirty thousand Quakers in the Yearly Meeting of the Religious Society of Friends in Britain (England, Scotland, Wales, the Channel Isles and the Isle of Man).*

Meeting For Sufferings: *This is the standing representative body entrusted with the care of the business of the Britain Yearly Meeting through the year. The meeting first met in 1675. Its original purposes included obtaining redress from both houses of parliament in cases of individual suffering and seeking to liberalise the laws relating to religious toleration.*

13 September 2001

TO FRIENDS AND MEETINGS IN THE USA

Dear Friends

On behalf of Britain YM we write to express to you our deep sense of shock at the terrible events in New York, Washington and Pennsylvania last Tuesday. We hold you all in the Light of Christ at this tragic time.

With this letter comes our love and concern for those killed, injured or bereaved as the result of this horrific act of inhumanity. We pray for them as those who survive come to terms with the impact of this tragedy, and we pray for national leaders, especially those of the United States of America, that they may respond with wisdom and in ways that will heal the hurts of the world.

George Fox spoke of having a sense of all conditions. We can begin to have a sense of the condition of the hurt, the frightened, the shocked, the bereaved, but it is more difficult to enter into the mind of those responsible for this outrage. Whoever they are, they too are children of God and we pray that we may better understand their hurt and anger and that they may turn away from the hatred and fear which drives them to such acts of wickedness. God is with us and weeps with us.

In Loving Friendship,

Helen Rowlands
Clerk, Yearly Meeting

Roger Sturge
Clerk, Meeting for Sufferings

THE EVIL EYE
Scripture: Matthew 6: 22,23

Rudolph Dunbar, D.D., Pastor
First Baptist Church of City Point
Hopewell, Virginia

Sunday Morning Worship Sermon

September 16, 2001

Nelson's new illustrated Bible dictionary defines "evil eye" as a symbolic phrase that refers to the sinful will of an envious, selfish person. "Evil" is also defined by the same source as a force that opposes God and his work of righteousness in the world. So, the acts of terrorism on America Tuesday past can be identified by a nation founded on the principles of "in God we trust," as evil. The attacks are the results of a perpetrator—the evil eye, who did it to Americans with America's own mode of transportation, made guided missiles.

In the law of the debts, Deuteronomy 15:9 submits, "Beware lest there be a wicked thought in your heart, saying, the seventh year, the year of release, is at hand, and your eye be evil against your poor brother and you give him nothing, and he cry out to the Lord against you, and it becomes sin among you." Loans made in the 6th or 7th years would not be repaid, but Moses insisted that the same kind of generosity be shown to everyone at all times. Justice and righteousness must always be combined with compassion. That would work fine, but on the other side of the coin, problems arose when those who abided by the law had to be associated and/or negotiated with those who did not abide by the law.

In such instances, the good would release the debt, but his debt would not be released by the evil eye. For instance, I always want favor from you, yet, I never give favor to you. Everything must be in my favor, but nothing in your favor, and vice versa. The word insisted that the same kind of generosity be shown to everyone at all times. We must remember that the same things we do to others can be done to us.

There is an account in Matthew 20:1-16 in which Jesus tells the parable of the laborers—workers who were paid equally. The last on the job, working less hours than the first, was paid the same as the first who worked more hours than the last. Seeing this, the ones working the most hours murmured against the goodman of the household who hired them saying, "You have made the last who have worked only one hour equal to us who have borne the burden in the heat of the day." But listen to what the goodman said: "I do thee no wrong. Did not thou agree with me for a penny?

"Take that which is thine and go thy way. I will give unto the last, even as unto thee." And in that verse 15, he says: "Is it not lawful for me to do what I wish with my own? Is thine eye evil, because I am good?"

Whoever is responsible for the attack on the U.S. doesn't feel that America can do as it wishes with its own. And since America doesn't appear to be doing as they think it should, their eyes became evil. But I want us to look at this today as it relates to salvation. This is about God's generosity, God's grace. How dare we begrudge those who turn to God in the last moments. In all reality, no one deserves eternal life. Many people we don't expect to see in the kingdom will be there, and by the same token, many we expect to see in the kingdom will not be there.

The thief who repented as he was dying on the cross will be there along with people who have believed and served God for many years. Oh, there are many today who resent God's gracious acceptance of the despised, the outcast, and the sinners who have turned to him for forgiveness. There are many today who are jealous of what God has allowed another person to have. Rather than be jealous, rather than be envious, rather than be selfish, we should focus on God's gracious benefits to us and be thankful for what we have.

Matthew 6:22,23 submits, "The light of the body is the eye: If therefore thine eye be single, thy whole body shall be full of light. but if thine eye be evil, thy whole body shall be full of darkness. If therefore the light that is in thee be darkness, how great is that darkness." Here, the light and the eye stand for our intentions and choices. The person with a good eye focuses on God alone and is totally loyal to His kingdom. His life is full of God's light. The person with a bad eye makes other things the goal of his life. Because he has purposefully turned from God, his darkness is great.

Spiritual vision is our capacity to see clearly what God wants us to do and to see the world from his point of view. But this spiritual insight can easily be clouded. How so? With self-serving desires, interests, and goals. They block the spiritual vision of God. The best and only way to restore it is through serving God. A single eye is an eye that is fixed and stayed on God. I want us to know today that each one of us is a typical America, vulnerable to attack.

The Bible shows that Jeremiah was a victim of the evil eye attack, simply because he prophesized in the name of the Lord. He was placed in stocks and cast into a cistern. Daniel was a victim of the evil eye attack because he prayed to his God three times a day, and refused to yield to other gods under King Darius. John the Baptist was a victim of the evil eye attack because he made known the wrong of King Herod having his brother's wife. He was beheaded upon the request of Herodius, made through her daughter to King Herod.

Even Jesus himself was a victim of the evil eye attack, because he went about doing good, turning the world upside down, proclaiming righteousness unto the Kingdom of God to promise salvation to all believers. Judas, following the Last Supper, went out and sold your Lord and my Lord to Roman authorities for thirty pieces of silver. But what he didn't know was that this would make it possible for the redemption of man's soul. Jesus would have to die before man could inherit eternal life.

He was placed on an old rugged cross where he died. But he was also taken down from the cross and buried in a virgin tomb, after which he became alive, rose from the dead, and lives forevermore. And my Christian friends, if Jesus was a victim of the evil eye, what about you and me? He reminded us that, "If the world hates you, remember that it hated me first." The world hated Jesus, and the world hates us for loving Jesus today. The word was alive then, and the word is alive today as well. Beware of the evil eye because we are living in evil days. Amen.

A PRAYER ON SEPTEMBER 12
Scripture: Lamentations 1:1, 4

The Rev. James C. Peck, Jr., Minister
First Congregational Church, United Church of Christ
Austin, Minnesota

September 12, 2001

Almighty God, we have much to bring before you on this morning after. With mouths gaping and hearts breaking and tears flowing, we see something our minds cannot imagine. In the deepest part of our being, we know this attack is an attack on each of us, not only those who most immediately suffer.

But our hearts turn first to them. We ask for your mercy, strength, and comfort for all those who are awaiting word about loved ones. We cry with the children, parents, grandparents, and friends. We weep for those who can weep no more, whose eyes are dry, and whose hearts are heavy. Surround those who have been shaken by this horror with a sense of your present love. Though they are lost in grief, may they find you and be comforted.

We give thanks for the dedication and work of firefighters, police officers, medical professionals, members of the military, and all others who have placed their lives in danger to rescue and protect others. We also ask for your care for those who are investigating these events. Their nerves and bodies are strained. Give them strength and courage as they continue their duties. Let us never take them for granted.

We pray for the leaders of governments throughout the world, those whose words and actions affect the lives of others. We especially pray for our leaders as they make decisions about our nation's response to this attack. In your wisdom, guide them to seek justice, not vengeance, in all the actions they consider and decisions they make.

We pray now for those who foster violence, for those who do not forgive others. By your Spirit, change their hearts. By your Spirit, protect us from becoming like them.

We are tempted today, and will be tempted in the days to come, to lose hope and to feel our efforts at peace are futile. Keep present in our hearts and minds the image of your resurrection, our only source of comfort and hope. Through Jesus Christ, who was dead, but now lives, and reigns with you now and forever. Amen.

YOU'RE NOT ALONE—ONE SORROW, ONE HOPE

Adapted from: *The Informant*: Serving Buckingham, Cumberland, Prince Edward,
and Charlotte, Virginia, October 2001 Issue
Mr. Charles W. White, Founder, Owner, Editor-in-chief

~~Whites~~
~~Blacks~~
~~Arabs~~
~~Jews~~
~~Christians~~
~~Protestants~~
~~Catholics~~
~~Muslims~~
~~Native Americans~~
~~Asians~~
~~Latinos~~
~~Southerners~~
~~Northerners~~
~~Westerners~~
~~Republicans~~
~~Democrats~~

We The People

A Service of Healing and Witness

"MI SHEBEIRACH"
(The Prayer For Healing)
A Service of Healing and Witness

Chapter

14

MI SHEBEIRACH
(THE PRAYER FOR HEALING)

Mi she-bei-rach a-vo-tei-nu
M'-kor ha-bra-cha l'-i-mo-tei-nu
May the source of strength
Who blessed the ones before us
Help us find the courage
To make our lives a blessing
And let us say, Amen.

Mi she-bei-rach i-mo-tei-nu
M'-kor ha-bra-cha l'-a-vo-tei-nu
Bless those in need of healing
With r'-fu a sh'-lei-ma
The renewal of body
The renewal of spirit
And let us say, Amen.

May the One who blessed our fathers, the source of blessings for our mothers;
May the One who blessed our mothers, the source of blessings for our fathers;
and "r'-fu-a sh'-lei-ma" means complete healing.

(The text is from the traditional prayer for healing that is said during the Torah service on Saturday mornings. Names of those who are in need of healing are mentioned aloud by the Rabbi and any congregants before the prayer is chanted.)

A SERVICE OF HEALING AND WITNESS

Rev. Joan Gelbein and Rev. Michael A. McGee
Unitarian Universalist Church of Arlington
Arlington, Virginia

Remembrance Sunday, September 17, 2001

CHALICE LIGHTING

May those
whose lives are gripped in the palm of suffering
open
even now
to the Wonder of Life.
May they let go of the hurt
and Meet the True Self beyond pain,
the Uncarved Block
that is our joyous Unity with Holiness.
May they discover through pain and torment
the strength to live with grace and humor.
May they discover through doubt and anguish
the strength to live with dignity and holiness.
May they discover through suffering and fear
the strength to move toward healing.

—*Rabbi Rami M. Shapiro*

Call to Worship—Rev. Michael A. McGee

It's been a long, long, painful week for all of us. It's hard to believe that the terrorist's attacks in New York and Washington took place only five days ago. It seems like years. It's impossible to put into words the depth of grief and despair we have all felt during this week. The shock of losing so many people and the terror of how they died has brought a torrent of tears and a flood of anguish for each and every one of us.

No words can express the pain, the grief, the fear, the anger that we have felt. Nothing can be said to erase the images of jetliners crashing into the World Trade Center, the towers collapsing with thousands of people inside, and the fiery gash in the Pentagon. And no words can adequately heal and make us whole again.

But this morning, in this religious community of caring people we will use our words, our love and our compassionate commitment to do what we can to heal each other and to bear witness to what has happened.

I would like to share this statement with you from the new president of the Unitarian Universalist Association, Rev. William Sinkford. Bill read this statement here in our church at the vigil on Wednesday night.

Dear Friends,

The events of this week have shattered our sense of safety. Many of us are in shock. Many of us are afraid. Many of us long to know what to tell our children. Some of us grieve the loss of friends or loved ones. All of us search for our response as people of faith.

The images of destruction will not allow us to escape. The collapse of buildings mirrors a collapse of confidence, rocking the fragile foundations of our lives. Our world will never be the same.

Our work to heal ourselves and to heal the world seems puny in comparison with the destruction we see.

How shall we respond?

First, let us hold in our hearts and in our prayers the families of those who were killed and wounded in New York, Washington, D.C., and Pennsylvania.

Let us stand with those who grieve and those who wait the long hours for news of loved ones.

Let us know our fear, but not allow it to overwhelm us. For most of us, life normally seems safe and secure. But people in many parts of the world, and many people in our part of the world, know violence and potential violence in their daily lives.

The terrorist attacks are being likened to the bombing of Pearl Harbor, a day that "will live in infamy." Pearl Harbor did galvanize this nation into action, and my hope is that this tragedy, too, will impel us to address the brokenness of our world that makes violence an un-imaginable solution. Remember also that Pearl Harbor led to the impounding and imprison-ment of thousands of innocent Japanese Americans. There are Arab and Muslim communities in this country and around the world that grieve as we do, and fear as we do. I hope our congregations will reach out to those communities and stand with them.

We must seek justice and, as our President says, to punish those responsible. But retri-bution will not create safety, nor move us toward justice. This tragedy tests our faith. Where is God in this? Where is the Spirit of Life? May our congregations be centers of support where we can bring our questions and our fears, where we can find the presence of the holy in our coming together.

Yours in faith and hope,

William G. Sinkford

READINGS

JOAN
(from *Rabindranath Tagore*)

…I feel the age we live in is drawing to a close—
Upheavals threaten, gather the pace
Of a storm that nothing slows.
Hatred and envy swell to violent conflagration:

Panic spreads down from the skies,
From their growing devastation.

If nowhere in the sky is there left a place
For the gods to be seated, then, Indra,
Thunderer, may you place
At the end of this history your direst instruction:
A last full stop written in the fire
Of furious total destruction.
Hear the prayer of an earth that is stricken with pain:
In the green woods, O may the birds
Sing supreme again.

MICHAEL
(Reading from an Iroquois Prayer)

We wait in the darkness!
Come all ye who listen,
Help in our night journey:
Now no sun is shining;
Now no star is glowing;
Come show us the pathway:
The night is not friendly;
The moon has forgot us,
We wait in darkness!

JOAN
(Reading from A. Powell Davies)

When sorrow comes, let us accept it simply, as a part of life. Let the heart open to pain; let it be stretched by it. All the evidence we have says that this is the better way. An open heart never grows bitter. Or if it does, it cannot remain so. In the desolate hour, there is an outcry; a clenching of the hands upon emptiness; a burning pain of bereavement; a weary ache of loss. Anguish, like ecstasy, is not forever. There comes a gentleness, a returning quietness, a restoring stillness. This, too, is a door to life. Here, also, is a deepening of meaning —and it can lead to dedication; a going forward to the triumph of the soul, the conquering of the wilderness. And in the process will come a deepening inward knowledge that in the final reckoning, all is well.

MICHAEL AND JOAN
(Adapted from Walt Whitman's *"Song of Myself"*)

Michael: What do you think has become of the young and old men?
And what do you think has become of the women and children?

Joan: They are alive and well somewhere;
The smallest sprout shows there is really no death,
And if ever there was it led forward life, and does not wait
at the end to arrest it,
And ceased the moment life appeared.

Michael: All goes forward and outward…and nothing collapses,
And to die is different from what any one supposed, and luckier.

Joan: Agonies are one of my changes of garments;
I do not ask the wounded person how he feels…
I myself become the wounded person,
My hurt turns livid upon me as I lean on a cane and observe.

Michael: I am the mashed fireman with breastbone broken…
Tumbling walls buried me in their debris,
Heat and smoke I inspired…I heard the yelling shouts
of my comrades,
I heard the distant click of their picks and shovels;
They have cleared the beams away…they tenderly lift me forth.

JOAN
(Reading from Anne Frank)

In spite of everything, I still believe
that people are really good at heart.
I simply can't build up my hopes on a foundation
consisting of confusion, misery, and death.
I see the world gradually being turned into a wilderness,
I hear the ever-approaching thunder, which will destroy us, too,
I can feel the suffering of millions, and yet,
if I look up into the heavens,
I think that it will all come out right,
that this cruelty will end,
and that peace and tranquility will return again.
In the meantime, I must uphold my ideals,
for perhaps the time will come
when I shall be able to carry them out.

MICHAEL
(Reading from Anonymous—who was a woman)

Lead us from death to life,
from falsehood to truth.

Lead us from despair to hope,
from fear to trust.
Let peace fill our hearts,
our world, our universe.
Let us dream together,
pray together,
work together,
to build one world,
of peace and justice for all.

Homily – Rev. Joan Gelbein

My feelings are a jumble. It was such a vicious, brutal attack, the terrorist strikes in New York and Washington last Tuesday morning. The kind of hatred that motivated this complex plan to hijack airplanes and crash them into buildings filled with thousands of people takes my breath away.

I find this tragedy beyond understanding, beyond the capacity for ordinary feeling; I can't take in the overwhelming enormity of what has happened.

I see-saw, as I'm sure most of us are doing now, between grief, confusion, uncertainty, fear, anger.

I feel profound vulnerability, both as an individual, and as part of a nation that has seemed to be invulnerable; shielded by great ideals, great power, and righteousness.

I'm upset when I watch, on television, the response of some Palestinians to this devastating horror—they are dancing and celebrating in the street. I am frightened when I read in the newspaper that someone in Iraq is quoted as saying that the only people who could be responsible for such a complicated attack would be the Israelis, and they are saying, "Death to Israel!"

I have a sense of desolation over the horrendous loss of life. I shrink back from my own imagination of what it must have been like on one of those planes; on one of those high floors of the twin towers of the World Trade Center. Listening to the stories of survivors on television, and hearing the anguish of family members searching for victims, turns me into a weeping mess.

Most of my life has been spent as a New Yorker; that's my home town; I REALLY know those people. Living in the Northern Virginia-Washington area, and being a part of this church community for over twelve years, I have found another unique home town, full of amazing people I love. These two cities of my heart have been violated, cracked open, shocked, and tested.

Now, the whole nation is galvanized by this profound unthinkable violation; this incredible act of hatred. A veil has been lifted, a line crossed; we are all changed.

And our faith has been severely challenged as well, if not breeched. As Unitarian Universalists we hold a great faith in humanity and in its capacity for goodness.

Our faith is grounded in hope.

We may be skeptics and iconoclasts, but we are not cynics. And, we may be optimists, but we are not naïve fools. We know there is evil.

For every insane terrorist, there have been hundreds, thousands, of rescue workers in the smoking rubble, and just people, risking their lives in hi-jacked planes, and on the endless staircases of the World Trade Center. I am deeply touched by all the acts of heroism that I hear and read about.

We have always been a religion that sees the primacy of affirming respect for the dignity and worth of every human person. It is in this fundamental value of our faith, that we find, and will continue to find, the resource for hope and action.

Rabbi Michael Lerner, Editor of TIKKUN Magazine, just wrote that, "We in the spiritual world will see this as a global incapacity to recognize the spirit of God in each other—what we call the sanctity of each human being.…But we live in a world, increasingly interconnected with everyone, and the forces that lead people to feel outrage, anger and desperation eventually impact on our own lives.…[We need to]…return to the notion that every human life is sacred, that the 'bottom line' should be the creation of a world of love and caring, and that the best way to prevent these kinds of acts is not to turn ourselves into a police state, but turn ourselves into a society in which social justice, love, and compassion are so prevalent that violence becomes only a distant memory."

The world is not a safe place and no one ever said it was. But, we believe that humankind must maintain its circle around the campfire; the light and warmth of hope and compassion we build, and build again, and build, yet again, in the dark.

So we come to our faith community, to this familiar space, among these familiar people, to be comforted, to be close, to renew our spirits, and find some precious little bit of clarity and direction.

We all have some thoughts about what happened and why; we all have opinions about the perpetrators, and about the way our own country's policies or actions may or may not have contributed to this tragedy. Those things we can, and must, talk about later.

For now, we come in compassion and sorrow; in solidarity with the whole family of Americans mourning this incomprehensible loss. There is a place here for anger, but not enmity. Let our spirits bend toward sympathy, not revenge; healing, not retaliation. To make a difference in consequences and outcomes, we must be grounded in our faith.

Let us respect and stand together with all people of good faith and good will. In our church there has been a tangible outpouring of concern for Muslims in our midst. We can unite in this congregation, and hand-in-hand with other UU congregations in this area, to oppose any acts of revenge and bigotry targeted against any Muslims or anyone from the Middle East. We can offer sanctuary; we can offer a hand of friendship. We can practice our values.

We deplore violence. Hatred and retaliation inspired in bigotry is wrong and dead-ended. It is love and hope that will bring us together to find a path to a more peaceful world, as we seek and find comfort from our faith community in dealing with this national tragedy. If we would make peace, we will need to radiate peace. To do peace, we must be peace. Shalom, and amen!

Homily – Rev. Michael A. McGee

If you are like me, the shock of Tuesday has been melting into a terrible sadness. What was at first unbelievable and incomprehensible, is now turning into a horrifying reality as we see bodies removed from the rubble and people desperately searching for loved ones.

It's no longer just the horrifying numbers of people who have been killed and injured; now it is the names and stories of the individual human beings who will no longer be with us, stories that remind us that these were real people whose loss will be felt by so many, for so long.

We can't help but think that it could have been any one of us or a loved one who was on one of those planes or in the Trade Center or at the Pentagon on Tuesday. I was actually on my way to the airport in Cleveland on that morning. I had flown from National Airport to Cleveland the night before on my way to a denominational meeting in Chicago, spending the night with our daughter and son-in-law who drove me to the airport the next morning. But when we arrived, the airport was blocked off by police who informed us that a plane had just crashed into the World Trade Center. That was the first of many shocks.

We returned to our daughter's home to call family members and watch the horrifying events take place. We sat there together shocked, outraged and grief-stricken. I was fortunate to be with family members, but I desperately wanted to return here to Arlington to be with my wife, Terry, and all of you—especially when I heard that the Pentagon had been another target. Fortunately, our son, Brendan, was at Kent State University, not far from Cleveland, and he drove me home on Tuesday night.

On that six-hour journey Brendan and I listened to the news on the radio and talked with each other about the significance of the day. Brendan told me that he had heard people describe how they remembered exactly where they were when Pearl Harbor was bombed and John Kennedy and Martin Luther King, Jr. were assassinated. And now he will always remember where he was on September 11, 2001, and the pain of losing his innocence.

It was an eerie drive home. Few cars were on the road. We saw many flags at half-mast and no airplanes in the sky. We passed Pittsburgh, where one of the planes crashed nearby, and we passed the battlefields at Gettysburg and Antietam, the two bloodiest days in American history—until Tuesday. Signs along the toll-road warned drivers to stay out of New York City and Washington D.C.. When we finally arrived, I was glad to be home, to have Terry and our family to console each other and to be with all of you for the vigils this week.

This past week has been horrifying. And the future will be difficult as well. Buildings will be rebuilt, planes will resume flying, and we will go on with our lives. But always there will be a tear in the fabric of our national and personal lives where the darkness of this time will be ever-present, a darkness that will always remind us of the terror and grief of Tuesday.

This tragedy has made it clear that we are all inextricably connected to each other in the interdependent web of all existence. All of us have experienced the pain of losing these people, whether we knew them or not. Their loss has reverberated around the world.

And we also cannot help but be infused with the courage, compassion, and hope that holds us so tightly together now as a nation and a world. Though the differences are many, we are experiencing the oneness of human community—at least for this week—and that inspiration will hopefully help us to strive to create the Beloved Community as a reality in the future.

Now it is time to give witness to the interdependent web by doing everything we can to make it stronger. This is a time to commit ourselves to not only helping the victims of this tragedy, but for each of us to be a light of gentleness and compassion in the world.

Those who are responsible for these horrific acts will be brought to justice, but we need to be certain that the innocent are not harmed. This is a time to stand side by side with those of all religious traditions—including our Muslim brothers and sisters—in solidarity against hatred and terrorism.

This is also a time for all of us to look deeper into the causes of these acts and to find ways to respond with justice. Let us not simplify the struggle as a war between good and evil, but instead let us ask the hard questions about why there are those who hate our nation so fanatically. And let us also ask the hard questions about why it is that hatred, violence and prejudice are so deeply rooted in each and every one of us.

This is a painful and challenging time. It is a time when we are witnesses to injustice but we must bear witness for justice. This is a time when we are witnesses to hatred and violence but we must bear witness for love and compassion. This is a time when we are witnesses to death and destruction but we must bear witness for life and creation. This is a time when we are witnesses to despair and hopelessness but we must bear witness for hope and the triumph of the human spirit. —Amen.

Benediction

We affirm the unfailing renewal of life.

Rising from the earth, and reaching for the sun,

all living creatures shall fulfill themselves.

We affirm the steady growth of human companionship.

Rising from ancient cradles and reaching for the stars,

people the world over shall seek the ways of understanding.

We affirm a continuing hope that out of every tragedy

the spirits of individuals shall rise and build a better world.

    —Leonard Mason
    —Shalom, Salaam, Blessed be, Amen.

In the Face of Evil

"It Is Well With My Soul"
In the Face of Evil
And It All Happened Tuesday Morning
Ground Zero
Prayer of St. Francis of Assisi
Rector's Sermon

Chapter

15

It Is Well With My Soul

When peace, like a river, attendeth my way, When
sorrows, like sea billows, roll; Whatever my lot, Thou hast
taught me to say, It is well, it is well with my soul.

Though Satan should buffet, though trials should come, Let
this blest assurance control, That Christ hath regarded my
helpless estate, And Hath shed His own blood for my soul.

My sin—O the bliss of this glorious tho't!—My
sin—not in part but the whole, Is nailed to His cross, and I
bear it no more; Praise the Lord, praise the Lord, O my soul!

It is well with my soul,
It is well, it is well with my soul.

Amen

H. G. Spafford   *P. P. Bliss, 1838-1877*

IN THE FACE OF EVIL
Scripture: Genesis 3:1-7 Romans 8:31-37

Memorial Service for an American Tragedy

Rev. George A. Turner
St. Paul's Presbyterian Church
Peterborough, Ontario, Canada

© George A. Turner

16th September 2001

As I pondered the events of this past week in the United States, some words flashed into my mind—words spoken five years ago in the small Scottish town of Dunblane when sixteen young children and their teacher were callously gunned down. As school principal, Ron Taylor, struggled to understand that nightmare, he said quietly but powerfully, "Evil has visited us today."[1]

Without any doubt, last Tuesday morning, evil visited New York and Washington. As we watched the events unfold on television, it all seemed so unreal at first. The horror of planes slamming into buildings. The terrifying collapse of the twin towers. Panic-stricken people running for their lives amidst smoke and debris. The nuclear-winter-like conditions of the ruins. It all seemed straight out of a disaster film like *Volcano*,[2] or news footage from Chechnya, or film coverage of an earthquake in China.

But then we woke up to the realisation this was not a movie set, not news footage from a war zone, not a natural disaster. No, this was worse. Cold and calculating terrorists had used planes carrying innocent people to inflict death and suffering on other innocent people. And we could not conclude other than that a dark and sinister force was at work in these events. Evil had not only visited two American cities but had visited our world in a most momentous way.

This being so, how do Christians respond in the face of such evil? Is it right to support retaliation against the instigators of such terrorism and the countries that harbour them? One young man, calling a CBC radio phone-in programme, said that, for religious reasons, he believed any kind of military response was wrong; that other methods of containing terrorism should be found. Subsequent callers, though, argued that terrorists only understood one reality and that was force. If no armed retaliation took place, then it would almost be like declaring "open season" for terrorists to continue playing havoc with innocent people at this new level of violence—and even worse.

In sorting through these different arguments, let us not forget Christians have long held that those who break God's law in any way, and certainly those who do so in such horrendous fashion, must be held accountable for their evil actions—even if military force must be used to pursue this end, as in the war against Hitler.

But, to gain the support of Christian people, such military action would have to comply with the principles of a Just War. That it only be undertaken in terms of self-defence or to redress a wrong and that any force used must be in proportion to the injury incurred, and also not target innocent victims.[3] Further, resorting to arms should not merely perpetuate the cycle of violence and retribution leading to the creation of another generation of terrorists willing to continue their *Jihad*[4] against western society.

However, in the face of such evil as we have seen this past week, there are other, even deeper questions that vex us as Christians. Why, most importantly, would God allow evil to exist in this world he has created? Why would he countenance such evil things as happened to those innocent people in New York City and Washington? Unfortunately, the Bible does not answer the "why" question about evil. No matter how closely we read them, the Scriptures consistently cast evil as a mystery wrapped in an enigma, surrounded by a conundrum. The Book of Genesis simply says that evil was not always present in the world but entered through the archetypal act of disobedience by Adam and Eve in the Garden of Eden[5] and, as such, is potentially present in the hearts and minds of all people.

But, though there is no real clue regarding the origin of evil, the Bible tells us with great certainty that, in the battle against evil, God is not dead, not in exile, not weak, not uncaring but—despite all indications to the contrary—still very much in control. Something we see very powerfully in God's Son, Jesus, as he confronts and conquers the evil forces arrayed against him leading to his death on Calvary and his subsequent resurrection. Something which is also stated powerfully in Paul's words when he tells us that nothing but nothing, not even principalities or powers, can separate us from God's love.[6]

If this be so, then why does evil still seem to have such free reign to wreak the havoc witnessed this week? Perhaps it's because we live "between the times," so to speak. Between that past time when the war against evil has been won and that future time when we will experience the full effects of that victory.

It's rather like living between D-Day and VE-Day at the end of the Second World War. Between the time the Allies invaded Normandy in 1944 and the final overthrow of the Nazi regime in 1945. During that in-between time, the final outcome of the war was never actually in doubt even though the evils of Nazism were still very real and had to be fought and overcome battle by battle. If we see Christ's death on the Cross as D-Day and his final return as VE day, then we get some idea of how evil has been conquered in essence but still has to be overcome in many of its particular manifestations.[7]

Yes, certainly, evil visited our world this week in a terrifyingly new brand of insane fanaticism. But let us equally be very certain that no matter how terrible its appearance or how terrifying its effects, such evil will not prevail. It may take some time to bring about its defeat. Much more than any earthly war that is waged, it may even take the return of our Lord in glory. But, in this greatest of all battles he "has sounded forth the trumpet that shall never call retreat"[8] and ultimately, he will be victorious in all, and over all, and for all times.

References
1. *The Scotsman*, 14 March 1996
2. *Volcano*, starring: Tommy Lee Jones, Anne Heche. Director: Mick Jackson. 20th Century Fox, 1997
3. The Just War, *www. xrefer.com* Cf. also Principles of the Just War…Additional Readings: Mark Edward DeForrest, Gonzaga University, www.mtholyoke.edu/acad/intrel/pol116/justwar.htm

4. Holy War
5. Genesis 3:1-7
6. Romans 8:31-39
7. Oscar Cullman, *Christ and Time*, Gordon Press Publications, August 1977
8. "Mine eyes have seen the glory," The Battle Hymn of the Republic, Julia Ward Howe, #225 *The Book of Praise*, The Presbyterian Church in Canada, Toronto, 1972

AND IT ALL HAPPENED TUESDAY MORNING

Gracie J. White
The Ministers' Wives and Ministers' Widows Alliance of Petersburg and Vicinity
Petersburg, Virginia

September 2001

And it all happened Tuesday Morning, September 11, 2001, right before our eyes. We were about the business at hand: eating breakfast, getting kids off to their first days at school, looking at the TV morning shows, walking from our parked cars to our workplace, getting off the subway; as the scene, as played in a movie, unfolded before us.

We witnessed the collapse of the symbol of our economic/financial center and the symbol of our government and military might. Smoke billowed and dust and debris covered the grounds near the sites of the World Trade Center, and the Pentagon. We saw people running from and jumping from buildings as they tried to save their lives. And rescue workers, firemen, and policemen were running frantically to the chaos equally bent on saving what was left of humanity.

Instantly, what we considered important changed. No more freting about shark attacks, or where Chandra Levy was. (Yes, this was tragic too.) But we found our nation flexing its muscles to fight a war against terrorism abroad!

So how did we cope; how did we handle all of this? On the Sabbath after, we flooded the places of worship for we needed solace, we needed answers to questions that we did not know how to ask, we needed to bond with others. We went with a seriousness of purpose; we went to gain succor for life.

Black, white, and brown hands reached across the spans to grasp each other as people prayed and gave broad affirmation to what we were about, for we are of all creeds, all colors, all religions, and all nationalities. We all gain insight and wisdom from a power that is above us that guides our destiny.

We have gained courage as we watch the undaunted efforts of those who rescued, and from this we feel that God has rescued us. Hopefully, we have gained love for each other, and we are closer to acknowledging the Fatherhood of God and the Brotherhood of man.

GROUND ZERO
Scripture: Jude 1:5-8; 12-25; Revelations 21: 1-3

Reverend Quinton Borders, Assistant Pastor
Brentwood AME Zion Church
North Brentwood, Maryland

-Excerpts-

Late October 2001

The world is changing. The world has changed. We are a living in a time that is so unfamiliar to us that it is scary. Something happened a month and a half ago that does not seem real. We saw the destruction of two buildings that some of us may have visited before, or just saw in pictures. We now know the name of Osama Bin Laden, but who is Osama Bin Laden? We know the word Taliban; we now should know where Afghanistan is. Nevertheless, where does it all begin for us? If you have continued to watch the news, two words tell us the beginning—Ground Zero. The title of the message today is just that—Ground Zero.

The pictures of New York that we see today of metal and rubble and smoke that was once The World Trade Centers is now called Ground Zero. We normally have associated these words with nuclear explosions. It is considered the point directly under the bomb. The planes that crashed that day were bombs because of the amount of fuel they carried. But that does not clearly define Ground Zero. What actually defines Ground Zero is the ensuing Chaos that took place and the Chaos that is taking place today. Not the kind of Chaos that depicts people running here and there, but the kind that takes place in our minds. The kind of Chaos that takes place in our hearts when we do not understand how so many lives could be lost. The kind of Chaos that has us afraid to live our lives. That kind of Chaos that tells us to say God Bless America while we drop bombs on people who are just as confused as we are. The kind of Chaos where laws are changed that put us back into slavery, and we go on as if nothing has changed. I thank God for Chaos, because there is Chaos and Ground Zero and there is Chaos and God.

Chaos/Ground Zero has been with us throughout all time. Genesis 1:1—In the Beginning God Created the heaven and the earth. There is a theory on the interpretation of the six days of creation called the gap view; it states "that Genesis 1:1 describes an original creation which was followed by the fall of Satan and great judgment." Genesis 1:2 says and the earth was without form, and void: and darkness was upon the face of the deep. The Spirit of God moved upon the face of the waters. The gap view states, "this verse describes the recreation or restoration that took place." I call it Chaos/Ground Zero. What about the story of Adam and Eve and the forbidden fruit? Chaos/Ground Zero. Then there was a man named Moses who led his people out of Egypt; who came down from the mountaintop with the Ten Commandments and saw those very same people worshipping a false God. Chaos/Ground Zero. Who could forget the day the world began to change at the birth of Jesus? Chaos/Ground Zero. We have already talked about how Chaos and man can be destructive, but what about the crucifixion of Jesus? Chaos/Ground Zero. There can be no death without a resurrection. Chaos/Ground Zero.

What is most amazing about all of these examples is how easily we forget the power of

God. We have become so dependent on the news media and man that we forget the one book that has foretold it all. Some have a King James version, some have the New King James version, some have the NIV, the NRSV; it doesn't matter the version you have as long as you use it. If you look at each one of the stories I just talked about, you will see how God's amazing grace was able to transform the Chaos; was able to transform Ground Zero and bring forth new life. I go back sometimes and look at the pictures of 9/11 and I see death and destruction; then God reminds me that he is still in control.

We all have received the e-mail about Nastrodamus and the twins being destroyed and how 9 has always been considered the number of mystery; it is said to embody the power of silence. Oh, we could not say anything that day because we did not know what was going on. What about 11? When combined they mean messenger. I was told one day that it really was about the number 5. Five is the number of humanity and symbolizes man in a two-fold aspect, for man stands at the apex of physical evolution, the forerunner and image of God. Man can reach up and take the hand of his Father in Heaven, and at the same time take his brother's hand and raise it as well. Do not get me wrong; nothing replaces scripture, not these numbers or anything, but why are we as a people afraid to explore something that is common to other parts of the world? I do not mean go out and play the numbers. That is not what I am talking about! But, 9/11 was no coincidence and neither was the ninth hour when the planes hit.

I am through. All I came to tell you was how even in the midst of the Chaos, when God's transforming power takes place in you and you become restored and recreated, a new heaven takes place. Revelation 21:1-3;[1] And I saw a new heaven and a new earth: for the first heaven and the first earth were passed away; and there was no more sea.[2] And I John saw the holy city, new Jerusalem, coming down from God out of heaven, prepared as a bride adorned for her husband.[3] And I heard a great voice out of heaven saying, Behold, the tabernacle of God is with men, and he will dwell with them, and they shall be his people, and God himself shall be with them, *and be* their God.

PRAYER OF ST. FRANCIS OF ASSISI

Submitted by
Reverend Lillian A. Shearin
Mt. Pleasant Baptist Church
Mechanicsville, Virginia

(*In memory of Claudette Washington Myers*)

Lord, make me an instrument of Your peace. Where there is hatred, let me sow love; where there is injury, pardon; where there is doubt, faith; where there is despair, hope; where there is darkness, light; where there is sadness, joy.

O, Divine Master, grant that I may not so much seek to be consoled as to console; to be understood as to understand; to be loved as to love; for it is in giving that we receive; it is in pardoning that we are pardoned; it is in dying that we are born again to eternal life.

RECTOR'S SERMON

The Rev. Edward S. Prevost, Rector
Christ Church, Episcopal
Winnetka, Illinois

September 16, 2001
15 Pentecost

Amid the chaos of last Tuesday morning, one man attempting to flee the collapse of the second World Trade Center tower was blinded by the ash and smoke. A boy then took him by the hand and led him into a church in lower Manhattan and to the Baptismal font which was filled with water, where he rinsed the ash and the soot from the man's eyes who could then see his savior.

Many of us this past week have found ourselves asking where we can see God in the terrible tragedy our nation has experienced. Where is God to be found in such violence, in such cataclysmic loss of life, in such profound suffering, and in the hatred which caused it? All of our illusions of security, of invincibility, are now surely that: illusions. We are a nation and a people of grief and profound sadness, and we are allowed to identify with Jesus in his darkest hour on the cross when he cried out in his humanity, "My God, my God, why hast thou forsaken me?"

And yet, almost immediately God could be found and will continue to be found. God is to be found in our instinct to pray. Not only at Christ Church but also at churches and houses of worship throughout the country, people have come together for prayer and mutual support which I believe is the spirit of God at work among us all. I think also that God can be found in the heroic efforts of emergency personnel, medical personnel, police and fire departments, steelworkers, thousands of volunteers trying to save lives even as their own might be risked. I believe God can be found in the outpouring of support throughout the world-huge throngs of people gathering in Sarajevo, Athens, India, Dublin, thousands of people and the Queen of England singing our National Anthem at a service at St. Paul's Cathedral, London, the image of the Pope at prayer for us, the image of candles everywhere, the image of Billy Graham, Bishop Dixon of Washington, the Roman Catholic Cardinal of Washington, Washington's Chief Rabbi, and the chief Muslim cleric together in prayer at the National Cathedral. I also believe that God can be found in Dean Baxter's prayer, "that as we act we not become the evil we deplore," of our being aware that there is a difference between justice and vengeance.

Bishop Persell would share this with us:

Our prayer and compassion give expression to our relationship with God. They also call us to a relationship with the whole world for which Christ died and rose again...We are interconnected with all nations and all peoples. This interconnection holds the possibility of shared knowledge, resources, and wealth. Sadly, it also holds the potential for spreading infectious rage, distrust, and violence. We must avoid the temptation to hold particular groups of people or religious groups responsible for the actions of a few. The Christian's best response to both the potential and the danger inherent in our world today is to pray and act that our interconnection may, through compassion, become unity.

A friend from New York e-mailed us yesterday:

After the candlelight Vigil tonight, we all processed outside onto the front steps of the Cathedral of St. John the Divine, bringing our lit candles into the evening, into the city. Edward and John each had a candle too. Their first time. They are twins, about six years old. As we faced the setting sun, we put our three candles together. "Hey! Now it is one light!" Then we each moved our single candles away. "Hey! Now there are three lights!" We did this many times. Then, Edward said, "Hey! Now I have some of your light and you have some of mine!" John said, "I want to be part of that and I want my candle to be by myself." So we played with this mystery of union and separateness over and over again. Time came to go home, we all made sure we each had enough of each other's flame, and that our separate candles stayed lit…

And I believe that God can be found here in the proclamation of God's word in our celebration of the sacrament of Christ's body and blood, and in our formation as Christians of every age. God can be found in our continuing prayers for the world for which the Good Shepherd laid down his life so that we could become one flock, with one shepherd.

St. Augustine once prayed:

God of our life, there are days when the burden we carry chafes our shoulders and weighs us down; when the road seems dreary and endless, the skies gray and threatening; when our lives have no music in them, and our hearts are lonely, and some have lost their courage. Flood the path with light, run our eyes to where the skies are full of promise; tune our hearts to brave music; give us the sense of comradeship with heroes and saints of every age; and so quicken our spirits that we may be able to encourage the souls of all who journey with us on the road of life; to your honor and glory.

Amen.

The Weakest Link

"How Firm a Foundation"
The Weakest Link
People of Prayer—Agents of God's Divine Plan
Surviving in a World of Pain
Psalm 55:22
Indivisible

Chapter

16

How Firm a Foundation

How firm a foundation, ye saints of the Lord, Is laid for your faith in His excellent word! What more can He say than to you He hath said, To you who for refuge to Jesus have fled? To you who for refuge to Jesus have fled?

Fear not; I am with thee; O be not dismayed! I am thy God, and will still give thee aid; I'll strengthen thee, help thee, and cause thee to stand, Upheld by My righteous, omnipotent hand, Upheld by My righteous, omnipotent hand!

When thro' the deep waters I call thee to go, The rivers of sorrow shall not overflow; For I will be with thee, thy troubles to bless, And sanctify to thee thy deepest distress, And sanctify to thee thy deepest distress.

The soul that on Jesus hath leaned for repose, I will not, I will not, desert to his foes; That soul, though all hell should endeavor to shake, I'll never, no never, no never forsake, I'll never, no never, no never forsake.
Amen

George Keith, 1787   *John Reading, 1690-1776*

THE WEAKEST LINK

The Reverend Dr. Thomas K. Tewell
Fifth Avenue Presbyterian Church
New York, New York

September 16, 2001

"These tragic events that we remember so clearly force us to redefine the words weakness and strength."

Will You Pray With Me? Gracious God, pour through me the gift of preaching, that these words might give us comfort, hope and perspective for the living of these tumultuous days. To that end, bless and anoint this message, that every one of us here today, might receive your strength. This we pray in the strong name of Jesus Christ. Amen.

John and Michael were on the phone Tuesday morning September 11th at 8:45 AM — John from Charlotte, North Carolina where he works for First Union Bank; Michael from the offices of Cantor Fitzgerald in the World Trade Center where he was a bond trader. They talked every morning. In fact they spoke by phone so frequently that there was a direct open line so that the two of them could speak whenever they wanted. In the midst of their conversation about derivatives and investments, Michael cried out, "John, there's been an explosion. There's fire and smoke all around. I can hardly see. John, could you turn on your television set?

"There's an explosion in the World Trade Center. Could you help me to know how to get out?" John was madly turning on the television trying to find out what he could about the explosion. And then he said, "Michael, what do you want me to do?" And Michael said, "John, here's my home phone number. Would you call my wife Erin and tell her I love her." And then a searing sound came across the line…and the phone went dead. Although Michael's body has not yet been found, it appears that he died on Tuesday, September the 11th, 2001.

Stories like that one are seared in our memory banks. Many of you have told us that you saw one of the airplanes hit the World Trade Center towers. Many of you were right in that area and watched from your office the horrific sight of people jumping out of the towers and then watched with disbelief as the towers imploded. Some of you were in the World Trade Center and you got out and ran up the streets away from the flying debris and fire. Others of you have told us that when you got to a place of safety, you realized that your blouse or shirt was covered with blood and you assumed it was your own. Then you realized that it was the blood of others that soaked your clothing! There are images in our minds of bold, courageous firefighters and police officers who ran into burning buildings to save people while office workers ran out. Maybe the most poignant image is of a chaplain who was giving last rights to a firefighter when he was killed by a piece of flying debris. These images are seared in our memory bank and they will be there forever.

These tragic events that we remember so clearly force us to redefine the words weakness and strength. As Rev. Randy Weber said so beautifully in his prayer, we're a nation who thinks that we're not vulnerable. We live under the illusion of invincibility. We think that things like this couldn't happen to a strong nation like America. But haven't we learned this week that life is a precious and a fragile gift? I mean, it could be taken away from any one of us at a second, in a moment in time. And so instead of being strong, we realize now that we are weak. And may I say as lovingly as I can that our weakness is really a blessing. When we realize our human weakness we can start to admit, "I'm scared, I need help. I need God." In the Sermon on the Mount, Jesus reminds us that admission of need is the first step in following Him. The Apostle Paul reminds us that God's strength is made perfect in our weakness.

But, our culture sends quite a different message. Television shows like "The Weakest Link" send a message that weakness is to be avoided. If you don't know the answer to the questions and if you don't know it quickly enough, you're weak and the other contestants vote you off the show! If you've never seen "The Weakest Link," don't. "The Weakest Link" is a show that promotes a concept of strength that isn't real. Anne Robinson, the British comedienne, MC s the show and if you don't know the answer quickly enough, she insults you. And, worst of all, when a contestant leaves, instead of saying, "Well, you're leaving with some money. We're glad to have known you," she just says glibly, "You are the weakest link. Goodbye." And she couldn't care less about you!

I mention this TV show with tongue in cheek in order to make the point that our society dislikes weakness, but in the Christian faith weakness becomes strength. Haven't we learned from Alcoholics Anonymous, that it's not until we can say, "I need help," that we can overcome alcohol? In our weakness we discover the strength of God. We learned this last Tuesday. When tragedy struck, we opened our doors on Fifth Avenue and put out a sign for a 1:00 PM prayer service. One hundred fifty "numb people" came off the streets, with prayer requests and horrific stories. We prayed, read scripture and sang, "Our God our help in ages past, our hope for years to come, our shelter from the stormy blast and our eternal home."

And then after the 1:00 PM service, so many people came into the sanctuary for prayer that we put out a sign for a 3:00 PM service. I was out on the streets of New York in my robe between services and five young men in their twenties came up to me with wide eyes and began to tell me what they had seen. And because I was dressed in my robe, they assumed that I was a Roman Catholic priest. They approached me and said, "May we pray with you father?" And I said, "Yes you may my sons!" And right there on Fifth Avenue we grabbed each other by the arms and the six of us began praying together!

So we did another service at 5:00 PM and another at 7:00 PM. All of our Pastors, (Rev. Amman, Dr. Cootsona, Dr. McCloud, Rev. Weber and I), were praying with people for most of the day. At 10 PM, I went home and had a conference call with Christian, Jewish and Muslim clergy from around the city about a service for Thursday night and got off the phone about 11:30 PM. The group wanted our congregation to host the service and asked me to plan it. Now I have to tell you that I had only seen the television for five minutes that day. I had heard people's stories, but I hadn't seen the pictures of the destruction.

So when I finally saw the destruction…I was numb. I felt overwhelmed. When I thought about all that was ahead, I said to my dear wife, Suzanne, "Honey, I am not strong enough for this." And she held me as she has done so many times and said, "You don't have to be strong. Accept the strength of God and others." And I did. And so yesterday afternoon when I prayed with several hundred families of the Cantor Fitzgerald Corporation over at the Plaza Hotel, they came up one by one and said, "Dr. Tewell, thank you for your strength." And I smiled and said, "I'm not strong. I'm simply receiving the strength from God, and so can you!"

We are a fellowship linked in weakness and vulnerability. And the link that holds us together in our weakness is Jesus Christ, who died so we might live; who was weak so we might be strong! He is "the weakest link," reminding us that in suffering, in the cross, is our strength.

So this morning, I want us to look at Jesus and think of him as The Savior. The points of the sermon today are in an outline, S A V I O R. Think of it as two, three-point sermons back to back. I can see the excitement in your eyes!

S is for sovereignty.

In our Reformed faith, when we say that God is sovereign, we don't mean that God causes everything to happen that happens. God's sovereignty means that God is in control. It means that out of the darkest evil God can bring good. It means God wasn't asleep at the switch last Tuesday morning at 8:45. It also means that God allows free will. People with evil intentions have the freedom to do terrible things. And, if we're honest, there is the potential for evil in all of us. If God is sovereign then out of people's evil intentions, God can bring good. The truth is that God's sovereignty is a mystery. We can't fully comprehend it. Doubt and mystery are a vital part of faith. This is why Dostoyevsky said, "My hosanna has come forth from a crucible of doubt." God is sovereign. Out of tragedy, God can bring triumph! I don't understand it, but I believe it.

The A is for anger and all the other emotions.

This is a time to feel and experience our emotions deeply and not to deny them. God created tear ducts. Tears are not a sign of weakness. Tears are a sign of genuine strength. It is not weakness to feel our God-given emotion; it is our strength. Anger is an emotion to be felt. The psalmist is angry. Read all 150 of the Psalms. The psalmist is often angry at the nation of Israel or at other nations or at an individual. Sometimes the psalmist is angry at God! This week…many of us are angry. We're not sure who is the focus of our anger, but we're angry. Anger can be dealt with in a healthy way, if we give our anger to God. If we articulate our anger to God and to other people and don't stop praying, anger can be healthy. The unhealthy anger comes out when we target certain religious groups or certain racial ethnic groups as the object of our anger! We often take out our anger at innocent people who are hurting as much as we are! And terrorist attacks do not represent the God they worship! I hope that all of us as individuals can represent Jesus Christ in the way we go forth from this place and the way we treat people from the Middle East and from all over the world. May we not become the evil we deplore. Our anger must be healthy and not unhealthy.

The V is for vicissitudes.

I dare say, not a person who got on those four airliners, nor a person who entered the World Trade Center nor anybody who went into the Pentagon, nor any of those courageous firefighters or police officials thought that they would die on September 11th. I dare say that none of them went to work that day thinking that this would be their last day on the earth. I dare say that people went about their work like they do every other day. The word vicissitudes means change… it particularly refers to harmful and swift change that is beyond our control. Amid these vicissitudes of life many are experiencing an emotion that can only be referred to as "survivor's guilt." I'm thinking of an executive of a firm at the World Trade Center, who at 8:25 AM, Tuesday morning went out to vote. Within an hour and a half, 70 of the 120 people that he had hired were gone.

I'm thinking of several young women in our congregation who told us that they were late to work for their jobs in the World Trade Center. There is a sense of "survivor's guilt" in saying, "I should have been there. I would have been there had I been on time." There's a man from Greensboro, North Carolina, who is here in New York to have cancer surgery at Sloan Kettering Hospital. And he feels guilty taking up a doctor's time because that doctor should be with somebody who "needs him more." What I'm suggesting is that if God is sovereign, (and I believe with all my heart that God is sovereign), then these vicissitudes of life are not for us to explain or figure out. Our job is to put our trust in God and know that God has a purpose for every one of us! Our job is not to feel guilty that we are alive but to claim the purpose for which God put us on the face of the earth right now!

The I is for instruments.

We are not on the face of the earth simply to make money, accumulate material possessions or acquire power. We are on the face of the earth to be instruments of God's love and grace. The great Biblical scholar William Barclay says, "There are two great days in a person's life. The day we are born and the day we discover why." Our pastoral staff has talked to so many people this week who have never cultivated faith in God but who are now asking: why am I on the face of the earth? We've been reminded this week that the symbols of power in Washington and symbols of wealth in New York are vulnerable. They are not invincible and neither are we! So we're not on the face of the earth simply to acquire power or make money or have a lot of things. We're on the face of the earth to be instruments of God's love, grace and redemption to others. I believe that all 3,500 of us in this packed sanctuary this morning are called by God to go forth to be instruments—on a street corner with a candle, in a shop to the people with whom we work, in our place of business or in our apartment building or on the subway, the bus or wherever we are.

I love the story of the little boy who was scared of the lightning and the thunder and cried out to his parents, "Mommy and daddy, I'm scared." And they went up to his room to be with him. And they said, "Honey, you don't need to be afraid. God is right in the room with you." He said, "OK, mommy and daddy, I know that God is with me." And they gave him a hug and a kiss and went downstairs. Soon the lightning clapped, the thunder rolled and the little boy screamed. So the parents went up to his room and they said, "Now honey we told you God's in the room with you." He said, "I know that God is here with me—but I need someone with skin on!" We all need someone with skin on! We are called to be God with skin on for one another. We are called to be instruments of God's love!

The O is for one.

We are one. I hope and pray that walls between people will come down out of this tragedy. I've been so pleased this week to see walls falling down between white collar and blue collar workers. As fire engines go down the street here in New York, people stop and applaud! As a fireman or a police officer is seen anywhere in our city, people pat them on the back, and say "Thank you, we love you, we're grateful for you." People who weren't one before are now one. Who would have ever thought that our city, with all of our diversity, would be one?

Last Sunday night I represented Fifth Avenue Presbyterian at a service of re-dedication of the sanctuary of our neighbor, Central Synagogue, that is just down 55th Street from us. On August 28, 1998, fire destroyed the building. Last Sunday night Central's Rabbi Peter Rubinstein and many clergy participated in a magnificent service of thanksgiving to God for the rebuilding. Mayor Giuliani was thanked for his work then, even as we are so grateful for his courageous and wise leadership in this crisis. The Mayor received applause last Sunday night, when he said, "This is a time for diverse people to come together." He found it interesting that two of the people who got to Central Synagogue's fire very quickly were Cardinal John O'Connor and himself! The Mayor said, "I was surprised to find Rabbi Rubinstein and Cardinal O'Connor praying together. And I was even more surprised that Mark Green and I were praying together!" (Mark Green is a Democratic candidate for mayor in New York City). Now is a time for people who don't usually pray together to pray together. Now is a time to be in partnership with people of other faiths around the city. We are one.

The R is for redeemer.

Redemption, reconciliation and resurrection are central to the Christian faith. In our desire for oneness with all the other faiths, (hear me carefully here), I pray that we do not lose our particularity. The world needs the gospel. The uniqueness of Christianity is that we offer a Redeemer who brought resurrection out of crucifixion. We offer hope in the midst of hopelessness. We have some things to learn from other religions but we also have something unique to offer to other religions. May we not lose sight of the redemption that Jesus Christ offers.

Our closing hymn "Joyful, Joyful We Adore Thee" may seem unusual but I carefully chose it for today. We're not singing this hymn because we're happy. We're not happy. Happiness comes from the root word "hap" meaning chance. If by chance our circumstances are good, we're happy. But "joy" comes from the Greek word, *makarios*, which means "a deep abiding inner joy that no circumstance could ever take away because God is with us." God's presence is the source of our joy. God weeps with us. In our weakness God is our strength. Nothing (not even the events of September 11th) can separate us from the love of God in Christ Jesus our Lord.

I believe with all my heart that our church building was placed on the corner of Fifth Avenue and 55th Street for such a time as this. Many of you may have wondered why you were brought to New York. I believe that we were all brought here for such a time as this. The world needs hope. The world needs comfort. We do not know what the future holds but we do know who holds the future: Our Savior, Jesus Christ. May we discover his presence in prayer, in scripture, in one another and may we receive from Him the strength to lead this city, this nation and this world into the greatest days of authentic unity, joy and peace that our world has ever known. By the power of God Almighty, revealed in Jesus the Christ, our strength. May it be so. And may all the people of God say, "Amen."

PEOPLE OF PRAYER - AGENTS OF GOD'S DIVINE PLAN

Scripture: Matthew 13:22, 23; I Peter 5:5—7; James 4:3, 5:13—16;
II Chronicles 7:14, Luke 22:42

Pastor Eva P. Ellis
Bethesda Baptist Church
Colonial Heights, Virginia

September 2001

Excerpts

Prayer is a wonderful privilege given to us by God to play a part in his divine plan for mankind. By promising to answer our prayers, God has made it possible for us to become agents of his will on the earth. He has given us the privilege of making supernatural changes in natural circumstances. We who are Christians and covered under the Blood of Jesus have this opportunity because we are born again believers in Christ. To us, prayer is an amazing opportunity, but to God, it is more than an opportunity. He also sees it as a responsibility, so it is important for us to know about prayer. More things have been wrought by prayer than the world ever dreamed of. When trouble comes, someone is desperate for an answer. We need to *know* the *best* kind of prayer to pray and the "best" kind of prayer is simply the prayer that *gets* an answer. So what kind is that? James 5:16 says it is the "effectual fervent" prayer that brings answers.

There are many types of prayer, but three steps are vital in order to transform us into dedicated disciples of prayer:

1. *Casting our cares*—allows us to take everything that is worrying us, tie it all up in a bundle, and give it to God. In addition. when God has forgiven us, we must be grateful, and one way we show that gratitude is by forgiving others.

2. *A consecrated lifestyle*—not my will, but thy will be done, Luke 22:42. *The Prayer of Consecration* may be one of the shortest prayers ever uttered, but it often requires the longest journey to the heart. In Gethsemane, Jesus prayed the Prayer of Consecration after praying, "Remove the cup from me." He yielded to God in prayer.

3. *A United Front*—is united prayer when believers come together collectively. They can experience a fullness of the Holy Spirit that cannot be obtained by any other kind of prayer. United prayer brings powerful results. Real united prayer can affect the entire church, city, state or even a nation. This kind of prayer doesn't work by how many people are gathered, rather by the unity of hearts. It's not one person lifting up his voice, but all of them lifting up one voice. "1 mind" answered prayer is not man's idea, "It's God's idea."

We as people of prayer, agents of God's divine plan, must humble ourselves, and pray without ceasing, and seek God's face, and repent of any wrong doing and he will forgive us, and draw us a little closer to him. We can pray in the morning, noon, evening and at night upon our beds, before meals, before harvest, during work, in worship, at all times, in all circumstances, and in all trouble. The main idea is let us pray, trust and wait on the Lord. He still hears and answers prayers.

Now unto the King Eternal, Immortal, Invisible, The Only Wise God, be Honor and Glory forever and ever. Amen.

SURVIVING IN A WORLD OF PAIN
Scripture: Psalm 27

Reverend Raymond C. Bell, M.Div., M. A., Pastor
Potomac Baptist Church
Hague, Virginia

Service Excerpts by Odessa J. Roane
September 16, 2001

Preface
I am Odessa—that ordinary American who was drawn to my place of worship to find comfort and to seek understanding. I went; I sang; I prayed; but most of all, I listened. Hear now my pastor's words.

On this day following an unbelievable tragedy—the terrorist attacks on the World Trade Center in New York, the Pentagon in Arlington, Virginia and the plane crash in rural Pennsylvania—Pastor Bell came to us with a consoling message entitled "Surviving in a World of Pain," taken from Psalm 27. His question to the congregation was what should be the response of the Christian when tragedy happens and why would God allow such a thing to happen"? He stated that America has now realized that our borders are penetrable and our skies are unsafe.

We were assured that we have no way of knowing whether or not the victims were good or evil, but they were going about their normal routine. However, we must realize that there is evil in the world and it is not God-ordained, and it often happens to good people. It is like the serpent, stealthy. In trying to bring some consolation to the congregation, he advised that we must be like David who realized that God was his light and that he need not fear anyone (even in the midst of a darkened situation). For when trouble comes we have a deliverer, God.

He also stated that God is sovereign and desires that His people trust Him in all matters. Above all, we are not to blame God when evil happens or try to take vengeance into our own hands for God has told us that "vengeance is mine; I will repay." God wants us to trust Him in all concerns and exhibit the "fruit of the Spirit" as detailed in Galatians 5: 22–23.

Two scriptures (John 16: 33 and Matthew 5: 45) among many were shared. Our service was a memorial to victims, to the rescuers, our Commander in Chief and the armed forces. Special prayers were prayed for each group, even the perpetrators. We then gathered at the altar and prayed for peace in the world. Later the choir sang all patriotic songs, e.g. "God Bless America" and "America the Beautiful."

PSALMS 55:22

Gregory Scott
Fort Lauderdale, Florida

September 2001

"Cast thy burden upon the Lord, and He shall sustain thee:

He shall never suffer the righteous to be moved."

INDIVISIBLE
Scripture: Romans 8:28-38

Reverend Rick Torrence, Interim Pastor
Mount Olive Baptist Church
Arlington, Virginia

September 2001

What does what has happened say about our faith and our future? What is the word from the Lord?

Romans 8:28 says, "And we know that all things work together for good to them that love God, to them who are the called according to his purpose." Note these verses in the chapter. (35) "Who shall separate us from the love of Christ? Shall tribulation, or distress, or persecution, or famine, or nakedness, or peril, or sword?" (37) "Nay, in all these things we are more than conquerors through him that loved us." (38) "For I am persuaded, that neither death, nor life, nor angels, nor principalities, nor powers, nor things present, nor things to come…."

The Pledge of Allegiance reads, "One nation, under God, indivisible." The Word from the Lord is, "Indivisible." America is under attack. Our way of life is under attack. Our faith is under attack. There is a reason our nation is under attack. It is the same reason the early church was under attack: our belief in "One nation, under God, *indivisible*, with liberty and justice for all."

Paul wrote that nothing takes place which does not fit with God's purpose for His children. Jesus confirmed this truth when He stated that even the sparrow does not fall to the ground without His Father's knowledge.

"All things," whatever they are, work together for the good of God's people. "All things" means "All things." All events, all conditions, whether good or bad, whatever is done in the world. Death, sickness, disappointment, discouragements, shattered dreams, family problems, ungrateful children, "all things." Paul says, "All things...for good." All the trials of life, all events of the present, and all events of the past, even what happened at the Pentagon, and in New York City.

What that means to you and me is that there is no experience in our lives that is incapable of being used by God for our good. We may not understand it, but God says, "all things work together for good." Everything is permitted or designed by God for His purposes. Even adverse experiences will eventually carry good.

It does not say, "All things are good." There are a lot of things that are evil, and evil can never be good. But what Paul did say was that God makes all things, even evil things, work together for good. The good Paul speaks of is not determined by our understanding. God knows what is best for us.

Paul was an example, when he was given a thorn in his flesh, to prevent his being exalted above measure. "But," God said, "My grace is sufficient." "But, What shall separate us from the love of God?" It does not say there is no tribulation. "But" is not concerned about the tribulation. "But" is concerned about the remedy! Paul said in Hebrew 7:25, "He is able to save

185

to the uttermost." At the end of the chapter in Romans 8, he said, "We are more than conquerors through Him that loved us." Why, because "All THINGS work together for good." "What shall we say to these THINGS? If God be for us, who can be against us?" "But," faith says, "Nay in all these THINGS, you are more than conquerors..." Even Hell can't separate us.

Paul says, "For I'm persuaded that neither death, nor life, nor angels, nor principalities, nor powers, nor THINGS present nor THINGS to come, nor height, nor depth, nor any other creature shall be able to separate us from the love of God...!" In all these things we are more than conquerors." However, we let tribulation upset us, being criticized upset us, being lied on, being accused, upset us.

Paul says we are more than conquerors. When the three Hebrew boys went into a fiery furnace, they were conquerors. But, when they walked out, they were MORE THAN CONQUERORS. When Daniel was in the lion's den, he was a conqueror. But when he walked out, he was *more than a conqueror.*

When Jesus went to the cross, He was a conqueror. When He went to the grave, with the sin of the world on His shoulders, He was a conqueror. But, when He rose from the dead he was *more than a conqueror.* This too will pass. Only what's done for God will last. We have to not only be indivisible from the love of God, which is in Christ Jesus, but we must be indivisible from the body of Christ.

You don't have to walk around afraid. Jesus said, "Upon this rock, I will build my church and the gates of hell shall not prevail against it." (Matthew 16:18)

Life is Tough, God is Good

"O God, Our Help in Ages Past"
Life is Tough, God is Good
Where Was God on Tuesday?
Special Meeting of the Monday Evening Bible Class
Prayers

Chapter 17

O God, Our Help in Ages Past

O God our help in ages past,
Our hope for years to come,
Our shelter from the stormy blast,
And our eternal home,
And our eternal home.

Beneath the shadow of Thy throne
Thy saints have dwelt secure;
Sufficient in Thine arm alone,
And our defense is sure,
And our defense is sure.

Eternity, with all its years,
Stands present in Thy view;
To Thee there's nothing old appears;
Great God there's nothing new,
Great God there's nothing new.

Our lives thro' various scenes are drawn,
And vexed with trifling cares;
While Thine eternal tho't moves on
Thine undisturbed affairs,
Thine undisturbed affairs.

Amen

Isaac Watts, 1719   *Dr. T. Hastings, 1784-1872*

LIFE IS TOUGH, GOD IS GOOD
Scripture: Romans 8:28-35

Mark Mitchell
Central Peninsula Church
Foster City, California

September 16, 2001

A few years ago a movie came out called *A River Runs Through It.* It was the story of the Maclean family who lived in Montana in the early 1900s. The father was a stern Presbyterian minister. The mother was more nurturing by nature. They had two sons; Norman, the oldest, and Paul. As the two boys grew up it was clear they were very different. Norman was cautious and studious. He went to college and became a writer. Paul was a reckless daredevil, a handsome and quick-witted ladies' man.

These are the main characters in the movie, but the real subject of the movie is the river that runs through their part of Montana. The river was the focal point for the family's life and the catalyst for everything significant that took place in their lives. It was the place the father forged a relationship with the two boys while on Sunday afternoons they waded in and fished its deep pools. It was to that river that the boys would run after their studies to nourish both sibling rivalry and brotherly affection. Even in times of pain and sorrow they would come to that river and walk its banks.

The Maclean family knew failure and success and laughter and heartache and even death, but the river was always there as a kind of symbolic center of their lives. In the movie, you get the sense that Montana would have just been a wilderness and their lives just chaos if the river were not running through it all.

I would like to suggest this morning that there is a river that runs through all of the tragic events of this past week and all of those individuals who put their trust in God. That river is God and His unchanging purpose for this world and for our lives. Scripture says, "And we know that God causes all things to work together for good to those who love God, to those who are called according to his purpose" (Romans 8:28). Scripture says that in the midst of what appears to be chaos, God is in control.

But let's face it, not everyone believes that. Some say that we create our own purpose. Collectively and individually we are in charge of our destiny. It is completely up to us to make the world safe and secure from this kind of evil. Others say that there is no purpose at all. Who's in charge? No one is in charge. We are simply victims of blind fate.

But Christians say, "No! God is in charge. We don't understand why things like this happen, but we believe God is still on his throne. He knows the answers. He is in control. Scripture says, "It is he who sits enthroned above the circle of the earth…It is he who stretches out the heavens like a canopy…It is he who reduces rulers to nothing…No sooner are they planted, no sooner are they sown, no sooner do they take root in the ground, than he blows on them and they wither, and a whirlwind sweeps them away like chaff" (Isaiah 40:22-24). That sounds to me like a God who is in control.

But this raises some questions of its own. If God is in control, why would He let this happen? How could God allow this and still be considered just and good and loving? How can we still trust Him when He doesn't even see fit to protect His own children from being victimized by tragedy and evil? How can it be that "God causes all things to work together for good…"?

II.   God's purpose in suffering and evil (Roman 8:28-30)

Don't misunderstand this. It does NOT say that God CAUSES all things. It says He causes all things to work together. God does not cause evil. He does not cause evil men to do evil things. He didn't cause the hatred in the hearts of those hijackers. He didn't cause those planes to fall on the World Trade Center and the Pentagon. He didn't cause the towers to fall. He didn't cause children to be left fatherless or motherless. This is not God's judgment on individuals or on America as some say.

You ask, "Well then, who does cause these things?" The fact is there are many forces at work, which cause these things. There is a fallen angel called Satan. Scripture says, "He prowls around like a roaring lion." There is also this fallen world we live in. Creation itself is not what it was meant to be, and so people die in earthquakes and floods and famines. There are also fallen people like you and me whose hearts are bent towards selfishness and greed, and to whom God gives the terrible freedom to let hatred and violence rule our lives. If nothing else, this tragedy should remind us of the reality of evil and the enormous capability WE have for it. Yes, God causes all things to work together for good, but He doesn't cause all things.

There is something else about this verse. It does NOT say that all things are good; it says "all things to work together for good." The idea is that God can somehow orchestrate all the dissonant notes of this world and create something, which is beautiful. But it is not the Christian position to wear a plastic smile and rejoice in tragedy. Jesus said, "Blessed are those who mourn," and this is a time to mourn. It is not the Christian position to deny the reality of evil and suffering, or to call it good. This is not a good thing; it is an evil thing.

Joseph's brothers betrayed him and sold him into slavery and thought they had written him off from their lives forever. But years later they met up with him again and he was in a position to write them off forever. They were afraid, but Joseph said, "Do not be afraid…You meant evil against me, but God meant it for good…" (Gen. 50:20). Joseph doesn't candy coat what they did; he calls it evil; he calls it what it is. All things are not good, but He causes all things to work together for good.

I want you to notice in this verse that we are NOT told why these things happen; we are not even given reasons. We may never know the answers to our "why" questions. Instead of reasons, Gods word speaks about a purpose. Reason hangs on to an event and insists on an explanation; purpose hangs on to God and trusts that in the bigger picture He will work through it all. We still might ask the question, how could something as awful as this serve a good purpose? Let me list a few things.

First, we come to understand anew the reality of human frailty. How could it be that you could wake up one morning, grab a cup of coffee, kiss your family good-bye, take the subway to work, walk into your office, and perish when a jetliner flies into your building? But that's the game we play; those are the rules we live by every day. It just takes something like this to remind us this is the way it is. And we have to ask ourselves the question: am I prepared? Last

Sunday we had about twenty people in our services who took a critical step in being prepared. They made the choice to trust in Christ as Savior. All week I've thought, what if one of them ended up on one of those planes this last Tuesday? I'm so glad they made that choice because they were prepared.

But that's not all. Second, suffering and tragedy make us more compassionate and humane people. More people said hi to me this week on the street. We've seen displays of selfless courage and generosity and sensitivity to others in the wake of all of this. Scripture says that when God comforts us in our suffering, we are then able to turn around and comfort others with that same comfort we got from Him. We become more compassionate and patient towards others who are suffering. That's a good thing.

Third, something like this helps us to see the evil and hatred in our own hearts. There is a lot of anger and rage that we feel towards those who did this. It's normal to feel that. There would be something wrong if we didn't feel that. It's right to want justice and one day justice will be served. But we've been learning in the Sermon on the Mount how Jesus tells us to love our enemies and pray for our persecutors. Some of us need to repent of our deep hatred. We also need to sort out who our enemies really are. Our enemies are not Arabs or even Muslims; they're terrorists. We have wonderful people from the Arab world in this church. They are not the enemy; they are brothers and sisters in Christ.

I could say so much more about what God's good purpose might be in all of this. I could make a long list. I could talk about the new opportunities we have to show the world in both word and deed that Jesus Christ really is alive and He really does care. I could talk about how this might force us to trust His protection despite the fear in our hearts. How can we ever learn He is a strong tower if we never have to run there? I could talk about how good it is when something like this makes us really long for heaven. There are so many things I could put on that list, and they might help you understand God's purpose.

III. God's presence in suffering and evil (Romans 8:35-39)

But when you're hurting, when your heart is wrung out like a sponge, a list of ten good things God might accomplish through this stings like salt in a wound. Don't give a list of answers to the little girl clutching her dad's picture and hoping beyond hope he's lost in some hospital. Don't give a list to the young wives of all those fireman who bravely climbed the stairs of the World Trade Center only to have the whole thing collapse. When you are bleeding, you don't need answers; you don't need a list. Answers are great for an exam, but they often only reach the head, not the heart.

You see, the real answer to the problem of evil and of suffering is not about someTHING, it's about someONE. When you are suffering, when you are asking why, you are asking someONE. You are asking God; a person. And the answer is not some kind of dry, academic, theoretical list of answers; it's a person. When a child in tears looks up into the face of her father and says, "Why, Daddy? Why did that have to happen to us?" That child doesn't need answers; she needs daddy to reach down and pick her up and press her to his chest and pat her on the back and say, "I'm here. Everything is going to be all right. I'm here."

That's what we really need, isn't it. Our heartfelt desire is for our Heavenly Father to reach down and say, "I'm here. Everything is not out of control. I'm here." You see, God as our Father doesn't give us a list of reasons or answers, He gives us himself, and that's what we really need. That's why if you look a few verses down in Romans 8, Paul says, "Who will separate us from the love of Christ? Will tribulation, or distress, or persecution, or famine, or nakedness, or peril, or sword…(No!) But in all these things we are more than conquerors through him who loved us. For I am convinced that neither death, nor life, nor angels, nor demons, (nor hijackers, nor terrorists, nor buildings crumbling, or war threatening) will ever be able to separate us from the love of God, which is in Christ Jesus our Lord" (Romans 8:35-39). You see, in the midst of all of this, He gives us himself. The promise is that we won't be separated from Him. We might not have all the answers, but we have Him.

That is why in Isaiah 54, God becomes the husband to the divorced woman. In Exodus 15, He becomes the healer to the sick. In John 6, He becomes the bread of life to the hungry. In John 4, He is living water to a woman thirsty for love. In Isaiah 9, He is the Wonderful Counselor to the confused. In Psalm 10, He is the father to the orphaned. In Isaiah 62, He is the bridegroom to the woman grieving she'll never marry. And in Zacheriah 2, He becomes the wall of fire to those who need protection. In each case, He gives not answers but himself.

And do you know how it is we really know that He is good and loving in spite of everything? We know He is good because, as Paul says in v. 39, His goodness and His love are seen in "Christ Jesus our Lord." God is good not because He explains why He allows these things to happen, but because He explained himself on the Cross. The spotless Son of God bore all the sins of the more than forty billion people that have ever lived. And not just the general sins of the general world in a general way, but your sins and my sins in one horrifying span of nine hours; sins like greed and lust and racism and even murder. As Peter Kreeft said, "Amazing love how can it be, that God should plunge a knife in his chest for me." God is not some cool and indifferent college professor writing answers on a blackboard; He is the God who suffered. He is, as the hymn goes, *"Man of sorrows, what a name, for the Son of God who came. Ruined sinners to reclaim! Hallelujah! What a Savior!"*

You see, God wrote the book on suffering, and He called it Jesus. That is why God is good. Because He gives himself.

CONCLUSION

John Stott said, "I could never believe in God if it weren't for the cross." In his short play, *The Long Silence*, he wrote:

At the end of time billions of people were scattered on a great plain before God's throne. Most shrank back but some near the front talked heatedly with belligerence.

"Can God judge us? How can he know about suffering?" snapped a pert young brunette. She ripped open a sleeve to reveal a tattooed number from a Nazi concentration camp. "We endured horror…beatings…torture…death."

In another group, a black boy lowered his collar. "What about this?" he demanded, showing an ugly rope burn, "lynched for no crime but being black!"

Far out across the plain there were hundreds of such groups. Each had a complaint against God for the evil and suffering he permitted in this world. How lucky God was to live in heaven where all was sweetness and light, where there was no weeping or fear, hunger or hatred. "What did God know of all that people had been forced to endure in this world? God leads a pretty sheltered life," they said.

So each of these groups sent forth their leader, chosen because he had suffered most. A

 Jew, an African-American, a person from Hiroshima, a horribly deformed child. In the center of the plain they consulted with each other. At last they were ready to present their case and it was rather clever.

Before God could qualify to be their judge he must endure what they endured. Their decision was that God would be sentenced to live on earth as a man.

"Let him be born a Jew. Let the legitimacy of his birth be doubted. Give him work to do that even his family will think he is out of his mind to try to do it. Let him be betrayed by his closest friends. Let him face false charges, be tried by a prejudiced jury, and convicted by a cowardly judge. Let him be tortured. At last, let him see what it means to be terribly alone. Then let him die. Let him die so that there can be no doubt that he died."

As each leader announced his portion of the sentence, loud murmurs of approval went up from the throng of people assembled. And when the last had finished pronouncing the sentence, there was a long silence. No one uttered another word. No one moved. Suddenly they all knew that God had served his sentence.

"Man of sorrows, what a name, for the Son of God who came, ruined sinners to reclaim. Hallelujah! What a Savior!

Bearing shame and scoffing rude, in my place condemned he stood, sealed my pardon with his blood. Hallelujah! What a Savior!"

Who can deny His goodness and His love? Psalm 46 says, "There is a river whose streams make glad the city of God." The river that runs through the water of our lives is God. In the midst of tragedy and confusion, He doesn't give a list of answers, He gives himself.

WHERE WAS GOD ON TUESDAY?
Scripture: Romans 8: 18-39; Luke 24: 13-32

Reverend Sherry Parker
Dundee United Methodist Church
Dundee, Michigan

September 16, 2001
15th Sunday after Pentecost

We have heard a lot of words over these last six days. Word came first to most of us on Tuesday morning, September 11. "There's been a terrible accident. No, wait. This is no accident. Our nation has been attacked. And the devastation, the loss of life is incomprehensible." Since that shocking morning we have hungered for words. At first, again and again, to see the images carried on television, to confirm the awful truth. Then we needed to hear the words of our loved ones. It didn't matter whether they were in physical danger or not; we wanted their voices; we wanted to feel our connection to them. Many of us made phones calls, local and over great distances, to share words of shock, sorrow and love. Then we settled in to let the words of the news broadcasters, our leaders, the rescuers and the mourners wash over us. We have talked with people we know and we have shared words with strangers in check out lines, at the gas pumps and at restaurant counters.

Now we've gathered here as God calls us, longing for words of comfort, words of hope and words that will help us to makes sense of this tragedy and its future consequences. And as we move from a collective state of shock and begin to reflect on this disaster, our words come in the form of questions: Why did this happen? Did those people, our nation deserve this? Where was God on Tuesday? And just as we long to know exactly what happened on those planes, who is responsible for this, how many lives have been lost, and when will things be right again, we want answers from God. Because if we can understand what has happened maybe we can get a sense of control back and not feel so helpless.

I humbly admit to you that I will not be able this morning, by my feeble words, to give any satisfying and definitive answers to why. The problem of pain and suffering, the sense that evil just may triumph over good, is as old as humankind. Our glimpses into the character of God as creator and covenant maker in the Old Testament and Savior and Sustainer in the New Testament, reveal to us that it is not God's intention that human beings suffer. The prophet Isaiah spoke for God in the midst of trial and suffering:

"Can a woman forget her nursing child, or show no compassion for the child of her womb? Even these may forget, yet I will not forget you. See, I have inscribed you on the palms of my hands; your walls are continually before me. Your builders outdo your destroyers, and those who laid you waste go away from you" (Isaiah 49:15-17).

God grieves the loss and the pain we feel. God grieves this week with all people and every week as senseless violence takes victims somewhere in this world. Because it is God's will that we choose between good and evil, faithfulness and separation from him; there will be those who choose to walk away from the commands of God. As we've seen, the consequences of their evil choices boil over in waves of pain, grief, destruction and despair that envelope both the guilty and the innocent.

Job, an innocent man, suffered greatly. When he asked God, "Why?" the answer he received would not satisfy us today in our pain. God responded, "Job, who are you to ask the Creator of all things why I do what I do?" Job said, "I know that you can do all things and that no purpose of yours can be thwarted" (Job 42:2). Job's decision was to believe and to know that full understanding of what happens in this world is for God alone.

Some of us have struggled with the question of the fairness of this tragedy. It is not fair that so many innocent people died. If we are a nation under God, where is the blessing? Did our nation, our people, deserve this? The author of Ecclesiastes writes that for everything there is a season, and a time for every matter under heaven, for birth and death, for love and hate, for war and peace (Eccl. 3:1-8). In our comfortable worlds we have come to accept that as good people we will be blessed by an absence of tragedy. We will by our goodness, even our faith, earn some type of automatic exemption from fear and pain, loss and despair in this world. By that understanding we hear that those who escaped death this week were blessed. We sing, "God Bless America," assuming that this is a prayer that good things will happen to our nation. And yet, good people have died, nations suffer. Has God removed blessing from them? Those of you who have faced tragedy and death, know that there are no exemptions to who will suffer, who will have trials in this world. And faith questions must move from "Why me? Why us? Where is our blessing?" to "God, help us to understand what true blessing is."

Blessing is not a temporary comfort or security. It is not a sense of dominance and pride in the world. Blessing is the promise of God in all circumstances. Ultimately, it is the promise of Christ's return and God's reign acknowledged by all creation. That blessing is available to all.

Finally we are left with the question, "Where was God on Tuesday?" For the answer, I invite you to turn with me to Luke 24. Two men were walking along the road to the town of Emmaus. Their footfalls were heavy with grief. Their world has been changed forever. Where there was once hope, there is now only sorrow. Where there had been a promise of healing, there was now only the memory of a horrible death. As they talked, they may have asked themselves, "Where was God on Friday?"

Read Luke 24:13-32 . Before these men knew of God's presence, God knew them. As their feet came down, in the crunch of stone, in the churning of dust on the path, Jesus stepped with them. In their hearing, as memories of the words "Crucify him! Crucify him!" and "Father, forgive them," still echoed, Jesus opened the incorruptible promises of God. In their hearts made cold by the cruelty of this life, Jesus brought a spirit of fire. They couldn't let this man walk on. They said, "Come, eat with us." At the table, in the breaking of the bread, they knew that Jesus had been with them all along.

Where was God on Friday? God was about the business of salvation and forgiveness through Jesus Christ. God was on a cross. Where was God on Sunday? God was alive through Jesus Christ and offering hope to weeping women at a tomb, frightened men hidden away, and friends who walked together in sorrow. Where was God on Tuesday? God was with airline passengers on four planes. God was with office workers who had just come in for the day's labor. God was with fire fighters racing up stories of staircases. God was with those who ran in terror, those who could not and those who could only wait by the phone clutching pictures of loved ones.

Where was God on Tuesday? God was in the praying, the volunteering and each dust-caked hand that reached out to take another. God was in the midst of the fire, the thunder and the rubble. God was with his beloved creation, and God wept.

Where is God today? In all of this, God in Jesus Christ lives and walks beside us all, in times that we know it and in the most devastating of times when we have our doubts. Jesus' words are our guide for lives of peace making and embodying the love of God. As we share Christ's communion later in this service we will break bread together in acknowledgment and praise of his presence. He is the only thing that lasts, our steadfast hope and our ultimate peace.

A SPECIAL MEETING OF THE MONDAY EVENING BIBLE CLASS OF FIRST BAPTIST CHURCH HARRISON STREET, PETERSBURG, VIRGINIA

Pansy J. Jackson
Petersburg, Virginia

Monday Evening, September 24, 2001

If my people, which are called by my name, shall humble themselves, and pray, and seek my face, and turn from their wicked ways; then I will hear from heaven, and will forgive their sin, and will heal their land. 11 (Chronicles. 7:14)

THE OPENING HYMN: "O God, Our Help in Ages Past" Watts
THE SCRIPTURE: Psalm 46 Students
THE PRAYERS: Students
THE HYMN: "How Firm a Foundation"

THE TEACHING OF GOD'S WORD
FACT: "East and West: A Dilemma of Different Doctrines, Directions, Drives and Destinies"
FEELINGS: Shock, Anger, Guilt, Fear, Confusion, Sadness, Helplessness
FUTURE: The "Unfolding" of Our Personal Lives, Our Nation's Government, and the World's Existence
FINALITY: To Be Or Not To Be Ready? That Is the Question

THE BATTLE HYMN: "On the Battlefield" Bell and Banks
THE REAFFIRMATION: "Still, But Only" —Pan Sye

I am STILL alive, BUT ONLY by the Grace of God.
I am STILL saved, BUT ONLY by the blood of Jesus Christ.
I am STILL led, BUT ONLY by the guidance of the Holy Spirit.
Therefore, I STILL have something to give to someone.
by Pansy J. Jackson, 2001

THE TEACHER'S PRAYER: (At the cross with all students)
THE COMFORT HYMN: "It is Well With My Soul"

THE BENEDICTION

PRAYERS
THE ARCHBISHOPS OF CANTERBURY AND YORK

Dr. George Leonard Carey and
The Most Reverend and Right Honourable Dr. David Hope, KCVO

The Church of England

Anglican Communion News Service

(These prayers have been commended for use by churches, congregations and individuals at this time. The text of these prayers may be freely copied and reproduced, and can also be found on the Archbishop's website, www.archbishopofcanterbury.org.*)*

A PRAYER FOR THOSE IN MOURNING
Almighty God, you have led your children from darkness into light, and have promised to your faithful people comfort in time of sorrow. Grant to the dead, peace; to the bereaved, comfort; to the injured, healing; and to those who despair, hope; that in our time of trial we may know the consolation of your love. Through Jesus Christ our Lord. Amen.

A PRAYER FOR THE EMERGENCY SERVICES
Almighty God, whose son Jesus Christ healed the sick and brought comfort to the weary; give strength and courage to the men and women of the emergency services in America. Grant to them your love and presence in the heart of danger, sorrow, pain and anguish, that they may continue to find life and hope in the midst of destruction. This we pray in Jesus' name. Amen.

A PRAYER FOR THE WIDER COMMUNITY
Heavenly Father, your son Jesus Christ taught us to have trust in you; we pray that, out of this darkness the light of Christ may shine; that out of this pain may come healing; and out of this destruction may come new life and hope. Deliver us, we pray from hatred and malice, from fear and mistrust. Bless President Bush, his advisers and the people of America, united in grief and undivided in their sorrow, that the darkness of this present time may be turned into the dawn of new life, through our saviour, Jesus Christ. Amen.

A PRAYER FOR THE LEADERS OF THE NATIONS
O God our heavenly Father, whose love sets no boundaries and whose strength is in service; grant to the leaders of the nations wisdom, courage and insight at this time of darkness and fear. Give to all who exercise authority a determination to defend the principles of freedom, love and tolerance, strength to protect and safeguard the innocent and clarity of vision to guide the world into the paths of justice and peace. This we ask through our Lord Jesus Christ. Amen.

TWO PRAYERS FOR PEACE
Almighty Father, whose will is to restore all things in your beloved Son, the king of all: govern the hearts and minds of those in authority, and bring the families of the nations, divided and

torn apart by the ravages of sin, to be subject to his just and gentle rule; who is alive and reigns with you, in the unity of the Holy Spirit, one God, now and for ever. Amen.

O God, who would fold both heaven and earth in a single peace: Let the design of thy great love lighten upon the waste of our wraths and sorrows; and give peace to thy Church, peace among nations, peace in our dwellings, and peace in our hearts; through thy Son our Saviour Jesus Christ. Amen.

A SIMPLE PRAYER IN TROUBLED TIMES
God of love, turn our hearts to your ways; and give us peace. Amen.

A CHILD'S PRAYER
Lord in heaven, please listen to all those who are praying to you now. Those who are sad and crying, those who have lost friends and family, those who are alone and frightened. Help them to remember that you are there and you are listening. In Jesus' name, we pray. Amen.

A PRAYER FOR MERCY
Lord, remember Christ your son who is peace itself and who has washed away our hatred with his blood. Because you love all people, look with mercy on us. Banish the violence and evil within us, and in answer to our prayers restore tranquility and peace. Amen.

A PRAYER FOR REFUGEES
Almighty and merciful God, whose Son became a refugee and had no place to call his own; look with mercy on those who today are fleeing from danger, homeless and hungry. Bless those who work to bring them relief; inspire generosity and compassion in all our hearts; and guide the nations of the world towards that day when all will rejoice in your Kingdom of justice and of peace; through Jesus Christ our Lord. Amen.

A PRAYER FOR JUSTICE
Almighty God our heavenly Father, guide the nations of the world into the way of justice and truth, and establish among them that peace which is the fruit of righteousness, that they may become the kingdom of our Lord and Saviour Jesus Christ. Amen.

A PRAYER FOR RECONCILIATION
Gracious God, ruling the earth and its people not by terror but in love; we worship you. We confess that too often our words hurt others and our deeds are selfish; forgive us. In this time of uncertainty and fear, help us to love our enemies and do good to those who hate us, in the name of Jesus our Lord. Amen.

VERSES FROM THE PSALMS
Wait for the Lord; Be strong and he shall comfort your heart; Wait patiently for the Lord. *(Psalm 27.17)*
God is our refuge and strength, A very present help in trouble. *(Psalm 46.1)*
Be still, and know that I am God. *(Psalm 46.10)*

THE LORD'S PRAYER

Our Father, who art in heaven, hallowed be thy name; thy kingdom come; thy will be done; on earth as it is in heaven. Give us this day our daily bread. And forgive us our trespasses, as we forgive those who trespass against us. And lead us not into temptation; but deliver us from evil. For thine is the kingdom, the power and the glory, for ever and ever. Amen.

APPENDIX 1

Scriptures Accompanying Sermons and Prayers
(as received October 1, 2001 to January 31, 2002)

OLD TESTAMENT

NEW TESTAMENT

APPENDIX 2

SONGS PRECEDING MESSAGES

APPENDIX 3
Localities Represented
(as received October 1, 2001 to January 31, 2002)

Richmond, Virginia
Winston-Salem, North Carolina
Raleigh, North Carolina
Durham, North Carolina
Laurel, Maryland
Prospect, Virginia
Louisa, Virginia
Mineral, Virginia
United Kingdom
Austin, Minnesota
Galveston, Texas
Brooklyn, New York
Dillwyn, Virginia
Beaver Dam, Wisconsin
Loudon, Tennessee
Canton, Massachusetts
Austin, Texas
Tallahassee, Florida
Bethesda, Maryland
New York, New York
Colonial Heights, Virginia
Nashville, Tennessee
Wethersfield, Connecticut
Madison, Wisconsin
Europe *(Britain Yearly Meeting—Quakers)*
Paris, France
Peterborough, Ontario, Canada
Arlington, Virginia
Hopewell, Virginia
Richmond, Virginia
Hague, Virginia
Petersburg, Virginia
Westport, Connecticut
Fort Lauderdale, Florida
Foster City, California
Dundee, Michigan
Winnetka, Illinois
Cincinnati, Ohio

Buckingham, Virginia
Chester, Virginia
Pittsburgh, Pennsylvania
Greensburg, Pennsylvania
Capron, Virginia
Washington, D.C.
Cranston, Rhode Island
Mechanicsville, Virginia
Baltimore, Maryland
West Brattleboro, Vermont
North Brentwood, Maryland
Roanoke, Virginia

APPENDIX 4

Messages by Title and Contributor
(as received October 1, 2001 to January 31, 2002)

Submission	Contributor/Location
CHAPTER 1	
Faith Sees the Glory	Dr. Larry R. Kalajainen, The American Church in Paris & The Franco-American Community Center Paris, France
Why Do Bad Things Happen?	Reverend Rick McDaniel Glen Allen Community Church, Richmond, VA
Our Changed World	Pastor Carol Rogers Thornton The Mineral and Mount Pleasant United Methodist Churches, Mineral, Virginia
Faith in God	Dr. Bertie Jeffress Powell, Petersburg, Virginia
CHAPTER 2	
Where Was God on September 11?	Rabbi Martin P. Beifield, Jr., Congregation BethAhabah Richmond, Virginia
A Pastoral Newsletter	Pastor Nancy Ferree-Clark, Duke University Chapel, Durham, North Carolina
The One and Only Jesus: At the Crossroads of Good and Evil	Reverend Martin C. Singley, III, Tellico Village Community Church, Loudon, Tennessee
"Why Can't I"	Mr. Otho Neil Smith, WLSA Radio, Louisa, Virginia
"Humanity! Humanity! It's Love that Makes Us Great!"	Mrs. Pansy J. Jackson, Petersburg, Virginia
CHAPTER 3	
Rebirth of a Nation	Mrs. Sandra M. Poulsen, The Church of Jesus Christ of Latter-day Saints, Virginia's Greater Richmond and Tri-Cities Congregations, Richmond, Virginia

Where Was God on Tuesday?	Reverend Sherry Parker, Dundee United Methodist Church, Dundee, Michigan
Special Meeting of the Monday Evening Bible Class	Mrs. Pansy J. Jackson, Petersburg, Virginia
Prayers	Dr. George Leonard Carey and The Most Reverend and Right Honourable Dr. David Hope, KCVO, The Archbishops of Canterbury and York, The Church of England

APPENDIX 5

AD HOC COMMITTEE OF ORDINARY AMERICANS

Robert A. Almond	Richmond, Virginia	Educator
Arlene L. Anderson	Petersburg, Virginia	Educator
B. Friend Briggs	Chester, Virginia	Attorney
Reverend Shady Clark, Jr.	Richmond, Virginia	Pastor and Educator
Louise C. Fothergill	Colonial Heights, Virginia	Retired Educator
Lillian B. Freeman	Petersburg, Virginia	Educator
Julian L. Greene	Petersburg, Virginia	Senior Applications Analyst
Elva M. Hollins	Petersburg, Virginia	Educator, Retired
James W. Jay	Richmond, Virginia	Educator, Retired
M. Alice Johnson	Petersburg, Virginia	Educator
Clyde Johnson, Jr.	Norfolk, Virginia	Director, Multicultural Services
Natalie Harris Myers	Brooklyn, New York	Court Executive Officer
Alva E. Myrick	Petersburg, Virginia	Educator
JoAnne W. Norman	Richmond, Virginia	Executive Director, Business and Finance, Retired
Barbara A. Perry	Petersburg, Virginia	Service Representative, Social Security Administration
Sandra M. Poulsen	Chester, Virginia	Office Manager and Director: Student Competition Council for America's First Freedom
Bertie Jeffress Powell	Petersburg, Virginia	Professor Emeritus of Languages and Literature
Susan B. Rutkoski	Chester, Virginia	Homemaker
Beth D. Sattes	Charleston, West Virginia	Senior Educational Research and Development Specialist
Inez G. Scott	Petersburg, Virginia	Bank Customer Service Representative
Theodore S. Scott	Fort Lauderdale, Florida	Computer Programmer
Brenda A. Spencer	Chester, Virginia	Educator
Monroe D. Spencer, Jr.	Petersburg, Virginia	Benefits Specialist, Social Security Administration
Wanda F. Taliaferro	Petersburg, Virginia	Guidance Counselor
June S. Taylor	Ettrick, Virginia	Educator
Reverend Adrian P. Varner	Petersburg, Virginia	Assistant Pastor
Antrynette S. Walker	Petersburg, Virginia	Recreational Specialist and Co-Director
Gracie J. White	Petersburg, Virginia	Educator, Retired

APPENDIX 6

OPEN LETTER TO THE FAMILIES

September 11, 2002

B.A. Spencer
P.O. Box 2985
Chester, VA 23831

Dear Families:

We want to hear from you. We want to know if you found some small degree of solace or felt the outpouring of love from the contributors to this publication. It was compiled for you.

If you were in any way touched by...*ON THE SABBATH AFTER*, write us. Address your letter to B.A. Spencer, P.O. Box 2985, Chester, VA, 23831 or email us at *otsaproject@comcast.net*.

We may find that the collective responses are also "messages of hope" that would help bring comfort to other individuals who experience sudden sorrow. Please be aware that we may publish these letters and notes.

Sincerely,

Brenda A. Spencer

Brenda A. Spencer
Founder, OTSA Project